THE
KANTIAN PHILOSOPHY
OF SPACE

THE
KANTIAN PHILOSOPHY
OF SPACE

BY

CHRISTOPHER BROWNE GARNETT JR.

ASSOCIATE PROFESSOR OF PHILOSOPHY
THE GEORGE WASHINGTON UNIVERSITY

KENNIKAT PRESS, INC./PORT WASHINGTON, N. Y.

TO
NORMAN KEMP SMITH

PREFACE

THIS STUDY was begun in 1930. Its original purpose was to trace Kant's thinking in the crucial years of 1768–70, when he first formulated the theory that space is a pure intuition, and to discover what external influences, if any, led him to work out that doctrine. In 1932, Chapters VI, VII, and VIII were accepted by the Faculty of the University of Edinburgh as a thesis for the degree of Doctor of Philosophy. Even those three chapters have been considerably altered and expanded in the intervening years in the light of further investigations. A small section of Chapter VI was published in *The Philosophical Review,* July, 1937, under the title, "Kant's Theory of Intuitus Intellectualis in the Inaugural Dissertation of 1770." The editors are to be thanked for their kind permission to reprint it here.

My indebtedness to authors is so great that I cannot acknowledge it in detail. I should mention, however, the works of Vaihinger, Cassirer, Kemp Smith, Riehl, B. Erdmann, S. Alexander, Whitehead, Broad, and Paton. My thanks are due especially to Professor Warner Fite without whose encouragement and valuable criticisms the work would never have been completed. Professor Kemp Smith is also to be thanked for the kindly patience with which he guided my first steps into Kantian problems. The opportunity is also taken here to thank Professor J. H. Randall, Professor G. S. Brett, and the Committee on Publication of the American Philosophical Association for their interest in the book. Also the kindness of Dr. Herbert Putnam and others at the Library of Congress should be mentioned. Finally, Mr. William Bridgwater of the Editorial Department of the Columbia University Press is to be thanked for his careful aid.

I wish also to thank the following publishers for permission to quote passages: George Allen & Unwin Ltd., for Herbert James Paton, *Kant's Metaphysic of Experience;* the Macmillan Company, for A. N. Whitehead, *The Concept of Nature;* Harcourt, Brace and Company, Inc., for C. D. Broad, *Scientific Thought;* the Open Court Publishing Company, for Ernst Cassirer, *Substance and Function, and Einstein's Theory of Relativity,* and especially for John Handyside, translator, *Kant's Inaugural Dissertation and Early Writings on Space.*

CHRISTOPHER BROWNE GARNETT, JR.

Washington, D. C.
January, 1939

CONTENTS

THE
KANTIAN PHILOSOPHY
OF SPACE

CHAPTER I

INTRODUCTION

§ 1

"It is hardly more than a pardonable exaggeration," says Mr. Whitehead, "to say that the determination of the meaning of nature reduces itself principally to the discussion of the character of time and the character of space."[1] The purpose of our study is to contribute to that discussion by a critical examination of Kant's views of space as he developed them between 1747 and 1787. We propose to consider those views in relation to the theories of space of two of his main predecessors, Newton and Leibniz, and also in relation to the ideas of three important thinkers of the present day, namely, S. Alexander, Whitehead, and C. D. Broad. Our aim is to contribute to the determination of the meaning of nature, chiefly from the historical angle. We assume that an historical treatment of a philosophical problem has significance in its own right, and if critically worked out, is also valuable in a nonhistoric, systematic sense. Our choice of space rather than time indicates no bias against philosophies of change.

Some readers will doubtless wonder what the justification is for another treatment of Kant's philosophy of space. Why, they will ask, after the gigantic amount of Kantian scholarship towards the end of the last century, need the ground be ploughed again? It may have been justifiable sixty years ago, they will say, to sound the cry "back to Kant," but surely that cry did not go unanswered, and today the situation is very different. At the very outset, I should like to make clear precisely what our study does, and does not, try to do. In this way I hope to show in what way it differs from others in the same field and why there is a need even in 1939 for still another book on Kant.

[1] Whitehead, *The Concept of Nature*, p. 33.

In the first place, we do not attempt to trace all of the cross-currents in the philosophy of space from Newton to Kant. Cassirer[2] has already indicated many of the main tendencies. Our study will restrict itself to the views of space of Newton, Leibniz, and Kant, bringing in those of Samuel Clarke and Euler solely to the extent that they bear directly upon the ideas of these three men.

In the second place, although the views of Newton and Leibniz are dealt with at some length, as becomes the importance of those views, they are dealt with chiefly as leading up to, and fertilizing, Kant's philosophy. Consequently, the center of emphasis throughout the study is Kant.

In the third place, our study does not profess to deal systematically with Kant's general views. It is, of course, impossible to consider thoroughly his theories of space without bringing in his general position, or positions, at almost every turn. The consideration of his wider views is, however, subordinated throughout to the narrative of his development of his ideas of space. For this reason, our study must be considered as much more restricted in its purpose than the classical Kantian studies of such men as Erdmann, Vaihinger, Kemp Smith, Riehl, and Cassirer. When it overlaps with their work, it does so, I believe, from a fresh point of view and with new motives. The commentator on Kant's general philosophy is faced with so many different issues and problems that his account is apt to be inaccurate and incomplete in regard to special questions, even when his general approach is correct. All of the above-mentioned commentators have a good deal to say about Kant's theories of space. Their treatments of those theories are, however, without exception subordinated to their wider purpose of gaining a synoptic view of Kant's critical philosophy. Consequently, the theories of space have been considered solely as one sector of a wider front, and the conflict of interpretations of wider problems has obscured the issues in reference to space. For example, Vaihinger's treatments of Kant's theories of space are the most thorough and elaborate of all. Yet those treatments are colored throughout by the wider polemics that Vaihinger is carrying on against other commentators in regard to problems that have

[2] Cassirer, *Das Erkenntnisproblem*, II, 396–520.

little or nothing to do with space. Again, Vaihinger and Cassirer deal to some extent with the history of Kant's development of his views of space. Yet neither man does more than sketch some of Kant's earlier ideas in various widely separated years. No commentator has given an adequate account of Kant's changes in his views from one important year to the next. More specifically, no previous study of Kant has successfully explained his famous shift of views about 1769 by tracing it in detail. We shall try to sketch his views of space at that crucial time both by laying bare the details of his thinking, and by pointing out the external sources of his ideas. Without omitting relevant general issues and influences, the restriction of our study to space will, I believe, yield insight that has, of necessity, remained hidden to those commentators whose more general concern has necessitated the inclusion of problems irrelevant to the theories of space.

Fourthly, our study finds in Kant's theories of space in 1770 the explanation of his search in that year for certain intellectual intuitions as the forms of a nonsensuous real world. We shall try to account for the discrepancy between certain theories of space in the *Critique of Pure Reason* by showing that some of them had been worked out in 1770 on the assumption that two worlds are given immediately to the mind in intuition, while others were worked out later on the contrary assumption. In this way, we shall try to give an explanation of discrepancies which other commentators, notably Vaihinger, have pointed out, but left completely unaccounted for. In other words, our study agrees with such commentators as Vaihinger and Kemp Smith in holding that there are contradictions in Kant's views of space, in opposition to such men as Cohen and Paton who find them everywhere clear and consistent. But unlike other defenders of the composite nature of the *Critique,* we shall try to show, at least with reference to space, that there were certain clear motives back of each of the discrepant views. Unlike the studies of Vaihinger and Kemp Smith, our treatment of Kant's conflicting theories of space in the *Aesthetic* and the *Analytic* caps a unified account of the developments leading to that cleavage, and stresses, in particular, Kant's relation to Leonhard Euler.

In the fifth place, our study has as one of its specific purposes the consideration of the relation of space to perception in the philosophies of Newton, Leibniz, and Kant. This fact does not mean that our emphasis is primarily epistemological. The conflict in theory of knowledge between subjectivism of various shades and the various types of realism is a topic that would far outrun an analysis of space. Yet theories of knowledge are implied in every phase of the views of the three men, and our study to some extent follows up such implications. To do this, the fourth chapter has been devoted to Newton's and Leibniz's theories of perception; the clash between the two is traced as leading up to the consideration of Kant's views, particularly in the *Dissertation* (Chapter VI), the *Aesthetic* (Chapter VII) and the *Analytic* (Chapter VIII). While a study of this sort has no general thesis other than the story of the views of the three thinkers, one positive conclusion emerges: certain central portions of the Kantian philosophy of space, purged of some cases of special pleading and of some specialized Kantian terminology, form an admirable basis for a realistic theory of knowledge, providing answers to some of the problems of perception and clearing up certain difficulties regarding the relation of philosophy of space to mathematics and the special sciences. While there is some doubt as to the extent to which Kant accepted the implications of such realism, the distinction between his realistic foundation and his phenomenalistic and subjectivistic scaffoldings is sharp, and some of his reasons for erecting the latter are easily discernible.

Lastly, if the determination of the character of space is an important element in the determination of the character of nature, conflicting views of space imply conflicting conceptions of nature. Three important, conflicting views of space and of nature are held today by Mr. S. Alexander, Mr. Whitehead, and Mr. C. D. Broad. It is an important purpose of our study to determine the relation of the Kantian philosophy of space to the views of each of these men. Many leading Kantian commentators, while disagreeing on matters of detail, unite in ascribing to Kant's interest in mathematical physics the decisive role in his development of his theory of space as a pure intuition. In opposition, we hold that Kant developed his theory of space before he discovered the problem of synthetic *a priori* mathematical truth. Even after he made this important discovery, his views of space in 1770 and in the *Aesthetic* continued to involve a much wider concern with any and every object of human experience. Indeed, stripped of his narrow view of experience as coextensive with sense perception and of his doctrine of appearances, his theories of space in 1770 and in the *Aesthetic* are akin to the views of S. Alexander. The nature of space makes empirical metaphysics possible. On the other hand, in his later views of space in the *Analytic,* Kant shifted his attention to the problem of the relation of space to the procedures of mathematical physics. The nature of space becomes subordinated to, and determined by, the findings of the physicist in a way quite similar to the position of C. D. Broad. In this way, Kant's conflicting views of space assume contemporary importance in regard to the points of view of Alexander, Broad, and also Whitehead. It is our purpose to determine the relation of the Kantian philosophy of space to present-day theories.

In general, our study is not an historical treatment of all of the philosophies of space in the eighteenth century; it is not a general commentary on Kant; and it is not primarily a study of contemporary space theories. It traces a thread, however, that begins with the pre-Kantian thinking of the eighteenth century and leads through the ideas of Kant to problems of the present.

§ 2

IN CONSIDERING the possibility of a first philosophy, Aristotle said:

If there is something which is eternal and immovable and separable [from matter], clearly the knowledge of it belongs to a theoretical science,—not, however, to physics (for physics deals with certain movable things) nor to mathematics, but to a science prior to both. . . . If there is no substance other than those . . . formed by nature, natural science will be the first science; but if there is an immovable substance, the science of this must be prior and must be first philosophy. . . .[3]

Little as Aristotle had in mind the possibility of a philosophy of space as first philosophy, he has, nonetheless, defined here many

[3] *Metaphysica*, p. 1026ᵃ, ll. 10–13, 27–30.

of its leading issues. The issue between Newton and Leibniz, as well as, in a slightly different sense, between Alexander and Broad today, is precisely whether there is something "separable" from matter and immovable. Physics, according to Leibniz and Broad, deals with spaces bound up inextricably with matter—according to Leibniz, derivative from it as a type of relation; according to Broad, manifesting itself in various forms in various "fields." Both men repudiate the notion of an extra-material space, a container immovable and substantial. On the other hand, Newton and Alexander posit a type of immovable reality, different from, and more fundamental than, matter and its relations. According to Newton, this reality is space, as a sort of container separable from matter; according to Alexander, space-time, as the very *Urstuff* out of which matter is formed.

Physics, according to Newton, does not deal with space but assumes it. Like the subject of Aristotle's first philosophy it has divine ties and is immovable. According to Alexander, in metaphysics space-time is treated as empirically given; while in physics and mathematics abstractions are made from that more simply given space-time. Unlike Newton, Alexander works out a metaphysics—or, if you like, a first philosophy—with space (as an aspect of space-time) as its object. For him, as for Newton, space is in some sense related to deity. In a different, non-Aristotelian setting, perhaps Alexander has gone a long way towards the realization of the sort of first philosophy which Aristotle envisaged. Space-time, for Alexander, is not a "substance"; nor is it a container, "separable" from its contents. Yet, according to him, space-time, unlike things in it, is immovable. Most important of all, a metaphysics of space is in a very definite way prior to mathematics and physics.

Aristotle left the possibility open, however, that there is no substance immovable and separable from matter and, hence, no first philosophy other than natural science. To those who think of Leibniz in reference to his metaphysical theory of monads, it may sound strange to hear that, in his views rather than in Newton's, Aristotle's suggestion of the possibility of no first philosophy other than physics receives confirmation. Leibniz held, however, that mathematics and physics have the last word with reference to nature (in his sense, phenomena). According to him, nature is purely mechanical and space is an abstraction from it. Newton's bifurcation of nature into space and matter is sharply denied. While Newton opens the door to the possibility that space is the object of first philosophy, Leibniz definitely shuts it. Furthermore, Broad and (according to Cassirer) Einstein also reach conclusions which preclude any first philosophy other than physics. Like Leibniz, they eliminate completely Newton's bifurcation of space and matter. They reject such dualism even in such a modified form as Alexander's distinction between space-time as the ingredient of matter and matter itself. According to Broad, there are various nonhomaloidal space-times, denotatively many, in different physical "fields." Most important of all, beyond the physicist's account of nature there is no other.

By substances "formed by nature" Aristotle doubtless meant the substances dealt with in physics. Hence the first philosophy that he envisaged was probably concerned with immaterial substances not "formed by nature," possibly not unlike monads. On the other hand, Aristotle's distinctions raise the possibility of objects that are *in* nature yet different from, and more basic than, the objects of physics. Two conceptions of nature are possible. (1) Nature includes more than matter, in which case there is a first philosophy of nature, which deals with what is more basic in nature than matter, while matter itself is dealt with by physics. (2) Nature includes only matter, in which case physics is first philosophy. With these two possibilities left open by Aristotle, with the lines sharply drawn between Newton and Leibniz, and between Alexander and Broad, the student of nature today still faces the question: Is a metaphysics of nature, more fundamental than physics, possible? While the outcome of the disagreement today between Alexander and Broad is still in doubt, one rather persistent attempt to answer the question in the form that it took between Newton and Leibniz, was made in the eighteenth century by Immanuel Kant. Perhaps our study of Kant's attempt to solve the conflict in its earlier form may yield some suggestions concerning the later.

All genuine philosophy has as its goal such a metaphysics, the formulation of our most basic point of view with reference to what is most basic in nature. Such basic "standpointless" philosophy is assumed by some philosophers; these are dogmatists or uncritical rationalists. It is denied by others; these are skeptics. It is sought for by others; these are critical philosophers or epistemologists. Critical philosophers do not deny the possibility of metaphysics. They are merely more dissatisfied with *a* metaphysics, more patiently seeking for *the* metaphysics, more aware of the complexities involved in its possibility, more sure of their own initial lack of "standpointlessness" than others. A theory of knowledge which professes to have nothing to do with a final theory of reality, will, in the long run, turn out to be merely a theory of illusion. Consequently, all epistemology is pre-metaphysics or nothing at all. But the epistemologist is the first to disallow an untested theory of reality. He is the first to reduce it to its assumptions and to show that these assumptions express one point of view among others, one historical setting among others, one *Zeitgeist*. Consequently, the epistemologist seems to be on the side of relativism, to be continually suspicious of "standpointlessness," suspicious, in brief, of metaphysics. He takes this critical attitude not because he loves final truth less than others do, but more. As Warner Fite says in a different connection,[4] "A man may say that 'there is no God,' not at all because he is a 'fool,' but because, precisely in his 'heart,' he knows too certainly what he is seeking."

Our study turns to Kant's philosophy of space in an effort to discover whether physics is first philosophy. In tracing his attempt to reconcile the philosophy of nature of Leibniz, which reduced space to a minor role and gave physics the final word, and the philosophy of Newton, whose major premise was the existence of space as precisely the sort of object for metaphysics that Aristotle had suggested, we may hope to find some clues to a solution of the problem. In tracing Kant's views, as they grew out of a conflict that is still going on today in philosophy, perhaps we may find a way to the metaphysics that the critical philosopher is seeking. This study does not claim to have reached it but professes to point towards it as a goal. Until such a goal is reached or proofs of its nonexistence are found, Aristotle's question remains unanswered.

4 Fite, *Moral Philosophy*, p. 223.

CHAPTER II

NEWTON'S THEORY OF SPACE

§ 1

SIR ISAAC NEWTON had no considered philosophy of space. In various Scholia of the *Principles,* in certain sections of the *Optics,* and in Samuel Clarke's defense of Newton's teachings in his Controversy with Leibniz, some of the problems surrounding the conception were dealt with, but only in a fragmentary fashion. In spite of this fact, the theories of natural philosophy and mathematics of Newton were of greater influence upon Kant's philosophy of space than the more explicit philosophies of space of his other predecessors. The reason for this is not hard to find. In the first place, the use of mathematics in natural philosophy was a primary concern with Kant from the time of his first published writing, 1747, to the *Critique of Pure Reason,* 1781; in the second place, in the year when he formulated the main tenets of his philosophy of space, 1769, he was directly influenced by Leonhard Euler's exposition of the Newtonian theory of absolute space. It is, therefore, of highest importance to discover at the outset of this study the implications of Newton's physical and mathematical teachings for a philosophy of space.

At the end of his *Optics,* Newton defended the inductive method and described the nature of the truth which it yields.

As in Mathematicks, so in Natural Philosophy, the Investigation of difficult Things by the Method of Analysis, ought ever to precede the Method of Composition. This Analysis consists in making Experiments and Observations, and in drawing general Conclusions from them by Induction, and admitting of no Objections against the Conclusions, but such as are taken from Experiments, or other certain Truths.[1]

Did Newton mean here that there are truths other than those taken from experiments? Did he mean that there are axioms or hypotheses from which truths can be deduced, which can be

[1] Newton, *Optics,* p. 380.

used to correct the generalizations from experience? He nowhere answered this question satisfactorily, and, in the light of the absolute theory of space which he proceeded to develop, it would seem possible that he meant that there are truths of reason which may be used to correct the generalizations of natural philosophy. On the other hand, the weight of the evidence lies, in my opinion, in favor of the opposing view. Mathematics would seem, at first glance, to be one of the sciences which proceeds by the method of composition rather than by that of analysis and induction. Yet Newton stated specifically that natural philosophy was like mathematics in following the analytic method. In mathematics, he meant, there are observations and generalizations; and the wider principles of that science, which seem to be sources merely of deductions, are amenable to correction in terms of further observations. Far from being a source of deductive truth, a model for the truths of physics, and a possible source of "necessary" conclusions about such a conception as space, mathematics is like natural science in its dependence upon observation and inductive thinking. What then are the "other certain truths" to which Newton referred as the source of the corrections of inductive generalizations in mathematics and physics? Such certain truths would seem to be merely the results of other observations and experiments. Far from meaning that there are truths different in kind from inductive generalizations, he meant that for purposes of correcting one generalization, other generalizations may be considered to carry only the kind of validity involved in the experiments from which they are formed. But there is never in mathematics or natural philosophy any certainty surpassing that derived from particular observations and experiments, corrected by others.

Consequently, all hypotheses are out of place in natural philosophy. An hypothesis is formed, Newton held, by considering conditions beyond empirical data.[2] Such a procedure is unscientific since it involves considering data unrelated to observation.

[2] *Loc. cit.*: "For Hypotheses are not to be regarded in experimental Philosophy. And although the arguing from Experiments and Observations by Induction be no Demonstration of general Conclusions; yet it is the best way of arguing which the Nature of Things admits of, and may be looked upon as so much the stronger, by how much the Induction is more general." Cf. *Principles*, pp. 506–7.

Newton did not consider the possibility of true hypotheses being based in a particular case upon those very conditions which enable the mind to pass from one such case to others. He assumed that facts are hard and self-contained and yield a mere summation of characteristics, while hypotheses involve stepping beyond such characteristics. Generalization is always tentative, subject to alterations, and if a uniformity is found in nature, no conclusions must be drawn concerning the meaning of that uniformity: all that the inductive method allows is the establishment of the fact of that uniformity as widely as it has been observed. Such generality, he held, always falls short of genuine universality, but the student of nature must be content with this situation.

As satisfactory as this strict induction is with reference to the observations of nature, there are several difficulties in it. In the first place, is mathematics likewise merely based upon induction? Geometry may turn out in the end to involve mere generalizations concerning special cases, yet some explanation of this limitation would seem to be necessary. For geometry seems to be a science which proceeds by the method of composition. Even if, in the long run, the axiom concerning parallels should be found to be one possible hypothesis among others (and Newton's view would seem to leave this possibility open, at least from the point of view of the student of nature), there would seem to be, at the outset, a difference in kind between the particulars involved in geometrical figures and those involved in the data of nature. In describing his inductive method, Newton ignored the question of a possible difference between the inductive aspects of mathematical reasonings and those of natural philosophy. What sort of material is observed by the geometrician? Is it the same as that observed in perception? Does it perhaps contain the basis for a sort of generalization unlike those from the data of sense perception? The status of mathematical truth is left in a very unsatisfactory condition by Newton precisely because, from his own point of view, the question of its inductive nature or its strict demonstrative certainty could be ignored. This constitutes the first difficulty in his treatment of the inductive method.

An even greater difficulty is involved, however, in his account of the application of the inductive method to objects of perception in natural philosophy. In reference to nature, strict demonstration is impossible. Therefore, hypotheses are unwarranted and the truths in mechanics must be thought of as continually subject to further alteration and correction in terms of new experiments. Theologically speaking, the inductive generalizations now holding in the portions of the universe observed by us, may (by God's act of will) be supplanted in the future by others and may be at present supplemented in other unobserved portions of the universe by other different laws. As satisfactory as Newton's caution is in reference to perception and the laws of motion discovered inductively with the aid of perception, he was not correspondingly cautious in regard to other aspects of his theory. One of the factors in inductive generalization in reference to motion is the spatial nature of motion. Bodies move according to laws which are discoverable by observation and fall short of demonstrative certainty; but implicit in the nature of these motions lies, Newton held, a fixity in the nature of space in which these motions are performed. That motion occurs in a certain way he admitted to be established only on a factual basis. He did not in addition cautiously hold that the space in which they are performed is itself factually assumed and might at some later date become some other sort or might even, indeed, be supplemented at present in other parts of the universe by spaces of other sorts. He assumed that the nature of space is of a more universal sort, lying outside the scope of possible alterations in the laws of motion (by acts of God), and held that its nature involves a kind of necessity surpassing the inductively established nature of motions observed in it. He did not realize that he was leaping, by this assumption, beyond the very inductive conditions which he was urging students of nature not to transcend.

Unlike the laws of motion, the nature of space is, then, in Newton's view, independent of the data observed in experience. Those laws are relative, but space is absolute. What was the justification for his departure from his strict inductive method in his claim that the nature of space is fixed and independent of all possible variations of the laws of motion? An answer to this question can be merely conjectural, for Newton gave no argument in favor of absolute space.[3] He considered it to be a fact that space is three-dimensional, continuous, eternal, one, etc. He did not undertake to explain in what way space could be known to possess these qualities. He did not consider the possibility that we apprehend space (no less than bodies moving in it) by induction. Implicit in his assumption that space has an absolute nature lay the further assumption that, in opposition to the method of analysis or induc-tion which yields only generalizations from experience, there is one case in which the method of composition may be applied in-dependently of analysis. In the determination of the nature of motions the mind must proceed by induction; but in the deter-mination of the nature of space it may proceed directly by the method of composition. He did not consider whether the nature of space is determined by the laws of thought or in some other way. His assumption that space is an attribute of God is an ampli-fication of the theory that it is infinite, three-dimensional, con-tinuous, eternal, one, etc., but it is not an explanation of that theory. By assuming that space can be known to have an absolute (necessary) nature, in opposition to the nature of the laws of motion, he assumed that there must be some method of establish-ing such a nature different from the method of analysis or induc-tion, which he admitted to be incapable of yielding any necessary conclusions. It did not occur to him that the necessary nature of space might be considered (if it can be established) to give a greater certainty to the laws of motion than that yielded by the inductive method. It did not occur to him that the necessary nature of space, if incapable of leading to any necessary, unchang-ing laws of motion, might, nevertheless, restrict all possible laws of motion to certain kinds. It did not occur to him, for example, that the fact of a necessary three-dimensional space might be evi-dence that bodies in it must necessarily attract each other accord-ing to the inverse square of their distances. Nor did it occur to him, for example, that bodies might, in distant parts of space and time, attract each other, say, according to the inverse cube of the

[3] In this connection, Newton's experiment with the pail of water (*Principles*, pp. 80–82) should be considered primarily a defense of absolute motion rather than of absolute space.

distance, but that, because of the necessary nature of space, only certain kinds of laws cᶠ motion would be possible.

If, following his inductive or analytic method, Newton was unable to attribute any necessity to the laws of motion, was he justified in attributing a necessary nature to the space in which motions occur? If, on the other hand, he was justified in treating space as necessary, could not the motions occurring in it be found to be determined by necessary laws rather than by mere generalizations from experience? Immanuel Kant would seem to have considered both of these possibilities. If there is no criterion for determining the necessary nature of space, the conclusions which Newton reached regarding the relative nature of the laws of motion would have to be extended to include the nature of space in which those motions occur. Just as there may be other laws of motion now holding in distant portions of the universe as well as future changes in the laws of motion holding here, so it would follow that there may be other kinds of space than the three-dimensional, continuous, uniform one in which motions are observed to occur. Kant realized in 1747[4] that he would be driven to this conclusion unless he could work out some account of the necessary nature of space. Perhaps even his later theory of space as a pure intuition and a form of intuition fails to account for its necessary nature. In this case there is possibly no space having a necessary nature, and hence the laws of motion are possibly mere generalizations from experience. Believing in an absolute, eternal, unchanging space as an attribute of God, Newton held that the laws of motion are, nevertheless, relative; Kant, on the other hand, believed absolute laws of motion would flow from the necessary nature of space, if such a nature could be discovered.[5]

So far in considering Newton's views of space, I have assumed that his view of God had little influence upon them. I have done so partly because the spirit of his inductive method would seem to allow no arbitrary departure from observed materials. But we have found that his theory of an absolute space involves a departure from that method. It is tempting, at this point, to conclude,

[4] Cf. below, pp. 98–102.
[5] This view was implied in 1768, and worked out explicitly about 1769, cf. below, pp. 111, 118, 136–39.

as does Burtt,[6] that Newton's theological views exercised a decisive influence upon his theory of space. Considerable evidence can be brought forward to show that Newton formulated his absolute theory of space primarily to account for the theistic conception of the universe which he held.[7] Newton ascribed eternity to both space and God; in addition, he held that space is God's infinite omnipresence. It is undeniable that he found divine properties in space and held that space is a property of God. This theological aspect of space was elaborated by Samuel Clarke in his Controversy with Leibniz. It received confirmation in those few passages in the *Principles* and *Optics* in which Newton held that space is, in some way, the sensorium or place of perception of God.[8] These passages all support the view that, in Newton's opinion, space has a metaphysical reality, and they are of great importance in comparing his general views with those of Leibniz. But it seems to me that in accurately appraising Newton's views of space it is, nevertheless, a mistake to ascribe too great a role to these theological views.

In the first place, the famous Scholium at the end of the *Principles* in which his discussion of God is found was appended for the first time in the second edition of 1713. In the twenty-seven years intervening between the first edition and that edition, Newton's printed views of absolute space and absolute motion stood independently of such elaboration. In the *Optics* the doctrine of space as the sensorium of God appeared as early as 1704 but was incidental to a discussion of the nature of human perception.

In the second place, Newton seems to have departed from his inductive method chiefly in reference to mathematics; the theory of absolute space would seem to be not so much the outcome of his theological teaching as of the theory of the absolute nature of geometrical truths. Consequently, although it is doubtless true that later in life he found the closest connection between the nature of space and the nature of God, it is, nevertheless, unjustifiable to claim that his theological tenets were fundamental in his theory of space. The doctrine of absolute space is, admittedly, not proved by his theory of absolute motion; it is in opposi-

---

[6] Burtt, *Metaphysical Foundations of Physics*, pp. 256–63.
[7] Newton, *Principles*, pp. 504–5; *Optics*, p. 379.
[8] Newton, *Optics*, p. 345; *Principles*, p. 505.

tion to his inductive method; it is in harmony with his account of the nature of God; but it does not from these facts follow that Newton departed from the analytic method in order to square his account of space with his theory of the nature of God.

§ 2

IF NEWTON's view of space retains its chief significance without reference to his theory of the nature of God, precisely the opposite is the case in the elaboration of that view worked out by Samuel Clarke in his Controversy with Leibniz in 1715. It is impossible to say to what extent Newton himself was involved in that Controversy. It occurred in the two years following the second edition of the *Principles,* to which the famous Scholium on the nature of God was first appended, and was carried on through the mediation of the Princess of Wales. In Leibniz's first letter, he attacked Newton's views, and he may have expected a reply from Newton. Throughout the earlier stages, the debate involved chiefly the question of what Newton meant by his theory of a sensorium. As the debate expanded to include wider issues, Leibniz may have assumed that Newton was replying along with Clarke, for he said in reference to a specific passage in Clarke's reply: "Ces Messieurs soutiennent. . . ."[9]

The problem of the nature of space assumed a leading role in the Controversy because of the theological implications in the question of the divisibility of space. If space, as Clarke contended in elaboration of Newton's Scholium, is a property of God (His omnipresence) , would not the divisibility of space mean the divisibility of God? Leibniz would seem to have forced Clarke to consider this problem more deeply than either he or Newton had done before. Newton had found no difficulty in considering space divisible. In the *Principles,* he had held, "There are given successive parts in duration, [and] co-existent parts in space. . . ."[10] He had even defined place as the *part* of space that a body occupies. Although he did not emphasize the point, he held that space is divisible. He held that space has parts, and that their order is immu-

---

[9] Leibniz, Paper III, § 3.   [10] Newton, *Principles, loc. cit.*

table. They cannot be moved except by a contradiction, but they are genuine parts, not figurative parts, and hence space is divisible.[11]

Did Newton mean that space is infinitely divisible, or that it is divisible into indivisible parts or particles? In the *Principles,* he gave no direct answer to this question, but an indirect one: " . . . every particle of space is *always,* and every indivisible moment of duration is *every where. . . .*"[12] He did not say specifically that the parts of space are indivisible, but, in regard to time, which he treated in the same sentence as similar in its nature to space, he spoke of "indivisible" moments. He probably meant that space is divisible into parts or particles which are indivisible. This seems to be Newton's view of the "necessary" nature of space in the *Principles.* He nowhere held, as Clarke proceeded to hold, that space is only figuratively divisible. In the *Optics,* he stated a view which in part coincides with this view of the *Principles,* and in part contradicts it. He said: space is "divisible *in infinitum.*"[13] In accordance with the view of the *Principles,* he continued to hold that space (the whole of space) is divisible; but instead of claiming that it is divisible into indivisible parts or particles he held that there is no limit to the divisibility. There are no indivisible parts or particles, for division may proceed without end.

This contradiction in Newton's theory of the divisibility of space has important repercussions in regard to the question of the relation of space to God. In his earlier view, he implied that the difference between the whole of space and God lies in the divisibility of the former: God, like all immaterial substances, is indivisible. Yet in regard to the parts of space this difference would not seem to hold. It would seem that in the *Principles* Newton formulated his theory of the indivisibility of the parts of space without considering the likeness to God which was thereby implied. If the difference between space and God lies in the divisibility of the former, a thorough-going distinction between the two would involve the divisibility of the whole and also of the parts,

[11] Newton, *Principles,* p. 79: "As the order of the parts of time is immutable, so also is the order of the parts of space. Suppose those parts to be moved out of their places, and they will be moved (if the expression may be allowed) out of themselves."

[12] *Ibid.,* p. 505.   [13] Newton, *Optics,* p. 379.

as he held in the *Optics*. In neither view did he make clear the basis upon which characteristics belonging to space as a portion of God's nature could be distinguished from those belonging to it in its own right or even in such a way that they are not a part of God's nature. If space is an attribute of God, then each of its own qualities must be linked with the divine nature. The omnipresence of space cannot be arbitrarily considered to be God's omnipresence, yet its divisibility, not to be God's. Along such lines as these, Leibniz attacked the theory that space is divine omnipresence.[14]

Clarke could adopt either of two alternatives in his reply. He could retain Newton's theory of the divisibility of space and attempt to show that space is a different substance from God, or, contending that space is a property of God, he could try to show that no quality of space is not a divine quality. He chose the latter alternative. Space is not a substance, he held, but an attribute, a divine one. Space is not infinite and eternal; it is infinity and eternity. God is not infinity (immensity) and eternity; He is infinite (immense) and eternal.[15] Space is His infinity (immensity) and His eternity. Clarke did not face the question (not posed by Leibniz) whether, in this view, space would also be God's three-dimensionality, His uniformity, His continuity, etc. He faced, however, the question of whether space is divisible or indivisible. Believing that if space is an attribute of God and also divisible, then God would be divisible, and possibly realizing that, in spite of these considerations, Newton had made space divisible, Clarke went on to hold that space is indivisible—that is, strictly speaking, it is indivisibility, the indivisibility of God. Space is indivisible,

---

[14] Leibniz, Paper III, § 3: "Ces Messieurs soutiennent donc, que *l'Espace* est un *Etre réel absolu;* mais cela les mene à de grandes difficultés. Car il paroist que cet *Etre* doit être *eternel* & *infini.* C'est pourquoy il y en a qui ont crû que c'estoit *Dieu lui même,* ou bien son Attribut, son *Immensité.* Mais comme il a des *parties,* ce n'est pas une chose qui puisse convenir à Dieu."

[15] Clarke, Paper III, § 3: "Nor is there any Difficulty in what is here alledged about Space having *Parts.* For Infinite Space is *One,* absolutely and essentially *indivisible:* And to suppose it *parted,* is a contradiction in Terms; because there must be Space in the *Partition it self;* which is to suppose it *parted,* and yet *not parted* at the same time. The *Immensity* or *Omnipresence* of *God* is [not] a dividing of his Substance into *Parts.* . . . There is no difficulty here, but what arises from the *figurative* Abuse of the Word, *Parts.*"

but it may be figuratively treated as divisible. It has no parts, but it may be treated as if it had them. Consider a portion of space to be divided. Consider one of the parts to be outside, and beside, another part. Consider division as involving the movement of one of these parts so that it will remain outside the other but will be no longer beside it. In the case of material bodies, this process is possible. But the meaning of the separation of one part of anything from another part of the same thing is separation in space, that is, separation in such a way that space intervenes between the two separated parts. Hence in the case of space, no two parts can be considered to be separated without a third part of space thereby intervening between them, in which case space is both separated and not separated at the same time.

Clarke's argument here is an alteration of Newton's account of the immutability of space. Newton had held that space has genuine parts, but that the order of those parts is immutable: space is divisible, but the parts are not separable or movable from each other. Clarke confused mathematical and physical divisibility. Newton meant that space is divisible mathematically into actual parts, but none of these parts are physically separable from the others. On the basis of the physical inseparability of the parts, Clarke sought to establish the indivisibility of space, and hence the fictitiousness of the parts. Mathematical division is fictitious division; physical separation is actual division. Instead of concluding with Newton that physical immutability is compatible with actual divisibility, he held that physical inseparability is the same thing as indivisibility. In this way he formulated the theory of the indivisibility of space and the fictitiousness of the parts.

What is the nature of the "necessity" to which Newton appealed to establish the immutability of the order of the parts of space, and to which Clarke appealed to establish the indivisibility of the whole? It cannot be necessity which (a) flows from wider principles such as that of sufficient reason, for the characteristics of space are not deduced; or (b) flows from experience, which yields no necessity. Hence it must lie in the nature of the conception of space. Space cannot be otherwise, Newton held, than composed of parts in an immutable order. An alteration of the parts of space would mean moving them "out of themselves."[16] Space cannot be otherwise, Clarke held, than indivisible. To consider it to have separated parts is to assume those parts to be both separated and not separated at the same time. Certain necessary conclusions, both men held, must be drawn concerning space. These conclusions are neither deductions from wider, rational principles nor generalizations from experience.

Implicit in this theory of space is the idea that space is necessary for all change. Orders of bodies, Newton meant, can change, because they are all within the unchanging order of the parts of space. Bodies may be moved and divided, Clarke meant, because all such motion and division is within immovable and indivisible space. Their arguments point to the conclusion that the necessary nature of space makes the orderly changes of bodies possible. Space makes objective experience possible. The immutability of space is, according to Newton, the *sine qua non* of the mutability of everything in it. The indivisibility of space is, according to Clarke, the *sine qua non* of the divisibility of bodies in it. These arguments, when purged of the doctrine of the metaphysical reality of space as a property of God, are Kantian. The necessary nature of space flowing neither from wider, rational principles nor from experience, but lying at the basis of experience, was worked out more fully by Kant about 1769.

The portions of space, improperly called parts, are, Clarke held,[17] not partible without express contradiction in terms. Kant likewise came to the conclusion in 1770 that space is not composed of genuine parts but merely admits of limits.[18] His doctrines of space involve, in a sense, a different justification of Clarke's view of the indivisibility of space. Like Clarke, he held a contradiction to be involved in considering space divided, but he held that such a contradiction is not discovered by rational, conceptual analysis. He distinguished between two processes, *abstracting from* something, and *abstracting* something.[19] If we analyze a given particular conception "Peter" with reference to such a general conception

[16] Newton, *Principles*, p. 79.   [17] Clarke, Paper III, § 3.
[18] Kant, *Inaugural Dissertation*, § 15, Cn.   [19] *Ibid.*, § 6.

as "man," we can, by an appeal to the principle of contradiction, discover whether or not "Peter" is a "man." We do this by ignoring certain particular qualities of Peter and considering whether certain others are present or absent. This process is *abstracting from* the conception of Peter. On the other hand, in analyzing space, there is no general conception to which we can appeal. Nothing is given "save in the concrete,"[20] and nothing may be determined about space except by reference to what is given. The sole way to discover what qualities space possesses "in the concrete," is to attempt to detach spatial qualities from what is given. This process, Kant called *abstracting* rather than *abstracting from*. In abstracting, the mind does not have a foreknowledge of what qualities a conception must display if it is to fall logically *under* a general term. The mind merely accepts as intrinsic to the conception in question whatever qualities cannot be abstracted from the given material. Kant (like Clarke) held that it is contradictory to consider space divisible. If this contradiction is not determined by reference to a general conception, how is it arrived at? Even in Clarke's analysis, the appeal to establish the contradiction was not to a general conception. He did not claim that a specific space is not divisible because the general conception "space" lacks that quality and hence the specific space cannot possess it. Such an appeal would exhibit the contradiction by *abstracting from* the particular space. He held that any particular space can be found to be indivisible only by trying to consider it as parted. Kant came to the same conclusion by contending that space cannot be *abstracted*. Both men established the quality of its indivisibility by considering the nature of any particular space without reference to a general conception. Consequently, both men discovered a contradiction by a method different from the usual analytical procedure. It would seem, however, that only Kant was aware of the implications of this fact. Only he distinguished definitely between a contradiction discovered analytically and one discovered by reference to the concrete. But it is quite possible that Clarke suggested to him this important logical distinction.

[20] *Ibid.*

In contending for the indivisibility of space, Clarke also mentioned its infinitude. Infinite space, he held,[21] is partially apprehended by us, that is, it may be conceived in our imagination as
composed of parts. Apparently he meant that the partial nature
of our apprehension of infinite space is identical with our tendency
to consider it in our imagination as composed of parts. By implication, he equated the finitude of its parts with their fictitious nature. In fact, however, the problems of the infinity of space and
our apprehension of it as infinite are different from the problem
of the divisibility of space. Clarke's analysis must be viewed both
in terms of what he meant and also in terms of what his explanation of that meaning suggests, and what it possibly suggested to
Kant. What he meant is fairly clear: the partial apprehension of
infinite space is the conception in our imagination of space as composed of parts. He used this conclusion to re-enforce the view that
space is actually one and indivisible and held only incidentally
that it is infinite. What his view suggests is, however, something
very different. In the first place, if space has no actual parts, and
if we apprehend space, then do we apprehend the whole of space?
Again, if finite spaces are not actual spaces, but fictitious parts of
an infinite space, and if we apprehend not merely the fictitious
(by ourselves created) parts, then do we apprehend infinite space?
No intent reader of Clarke's words could avoid raising these questions. In the second place, is what Clarke called a partial apprehension of infinite space an apprehension of it *qua* space or *qua*
infinite? Clarke did not himself make this distinction, but it is
immediately suggested by his words. In what was for him an account of the indivisibility of space, he doubtless considered the
problem of how we apprehend space and also how we apprehend
its infinity. In the third place, although Clarke doubtless equated
a partial apprehension of space with a conception of it in the
imagination as composed of parts (that is, a conception of it *as if*

<hr>

[21] Clarke, Paper IV, §§ 11, 12: "*Parts,* in the *corporeal* Sense of the Word, are
separable, compounded, ununited, independent on, and *moveable from,* each *other:*
But infinite Space, though it may by Us be *partially apprehended,* that is, may in
our Imagination be conceived as composed of *Parts;* yet Those *Parts* (*improperly*
so called) being *essentially indiscerpible* and *immoveable* from each other, and
not *partable* without an express Contradiction in Terms . . . *Space* consequently is
in itself *essentially One,* and *absolutely indivisible.*"

it were composed of parts), the two processes are not necessarily identical. In fact, it might readily occur to the attentive reader that by the phrase "that is" Clarke was equating two essentially different teachings. Unless he meant that there are two different types of apprehension of space—namely, partial and total—and unless he meant that the former is apprehension of it *as if* it were composed of parts, it in no way would follow that a partial apprehension of space would involve a distortion of the object by the imagination. If a total apprehension of space is impossible, and if a partial apprehension means merely that the imagination distorts space by introducing the fictitious, finite parts, is there any apprehension of infinite, indivisible space as it is? If not, what is it that the mind treats as if it were divided? Only the results of such treatment, never the thing treated, would be given. Unless Clarke meant that there is some type of apprehension of space other than a partial apprehension of it as divided and finite, there would seem to be no way of establishing the contention that these apprehended qualities are fictitious rather than actual.

Clarke's account of the infinity of space left him in this difficult dilemma as long as he persisted in equating a partial apprehension of space with a distortion of space by the imagination. He equated these processes probably because he mentioned the infinity of space quite incidentally in his discussion of its indivisibility. As a result of this equation, he held that a partial apprehension is apprehension of a fictitious quality. The way out of the difficulty which even Kant failed to follow as he grappled with the problem of the infinity of space in the *Aesthetic,* lies directly in Clarke's words. If Clarke had held that infinite space may be apprehended, both as space and as infinite; that such apprehension is partial; but that the mind may, in addition, conceive of space as divided in the imagination into fictitious, finite, spaces, he would have at one stroke protected his view from the difficulties of a total apprehension of infinite space. He would have retained also his doctrine of the fictitious, finite parts resulting from distortion by the imagination of the partially given, infinite space. Kant was near this view in the first edition of the *Aesthetic*[22] when he held that space

[22] Cf. below, pp. 191–93.

is represented as an infinite, given whole. He held, like Clarke, that finite spaces or parts of space are not given to the mind; hence in some sense, infinite space is directly presented and so represented. But he failed to realize that this view did not mean that such a representation of space is necessarily total or complete. He failed to distinguish carefully between the object (space) and the act of apprehension (*Vorstellung*). The former is infinite and whole rather than finite and divisible into parts; the latter is, however, partial rather than total. Infinity and wholeness have nothing to do with the act of representation, which is partial rather than total. Incompleteness has nothing to do with the object represented (space) which is infinite and whole, rather than finite and divisible into parts. Failing to realize these distinctions, Kant concluded in his second edition of the *Aesthetic*,[23] that there is a total apprehension of the infinite whole of space only in the sense that an infinite number of particulars are *in* rather than *under* the general conception. Such a view means that the infinite whole of space is in no way directly or immediately apprehended and raises the same problem that Clarke had failed to solve, namely, if space has no genuine finite parts, and if it is not given directly to the mind in its infinite entirety, does the mind in any sense apprehend it directly as it is? Are the limits within space discovered there by the mind? No, for in that case they would enclose genuine parts. Hence those limits must enclose, as Clarke had held, fictitious parts, read by the apprehending mind into what is given. If such is the situation, what is it that the mind so distorts? It cannot be the whole of space, for that is not given to be distorted. It cannot be parts of space, for these are the results of the distorting process and not materials which are distorted. Hence Kant, no less than Clarke, failed to deal satisfactorily with the problem of the apprehension of the infinite whole of space. Both men would have avoided these difficulties, if they had distinguished carefully between the infinite whole of space and our partial apprehension of that infinite whole. In a word, they both failed to distinguish clearly between the objective conditions of existence and the subjective conditions of apprehension.

[23] Cf. below, pp. 195–97.

In dealing with the necessary indivisibility and infinity of space, Clarke nowhere attempted to establish that other important quality, its three-dimensionality. Yet it was this characteristic which first concerned Kant, long before he came to his own mature views of space. In 1747, in his *Estimation of Living Forces*, he was unable to refer the necessary three-dimensionality of space, in which he believed, to any more satisfactory source than the imagination.[24] Clarke held that space is indivisible, but that the imagination considers it to be divisible. Kant held that, so far as he could determine, the ground for the threefold dimensionality of space is still unknown. He spoke of things as "representable through the imagination in spatial terms,"[25] and held that the imagination is forced to represent space as three-dimensional. He admitted, however, that he had found no necessary basis for this quality and left open the possibility of other kinds of space. While Clarke held that the imagination distorts the nature of space and yields fictitious qualities, Kant held that space seems necessarily to have the nature which our imagination shows it to have, but he admitted in 1747 that he had not yet discovered the ground for such necessity.

§ 3

IN SUMMARIZING his views of space, Clarke assumed that space is a conception and that all conceptions are either nothing, ideas, relations, bodies, substances, or properties. He proceeded negatively to show that space must be a property because it is none of the other kinds of conceptions.[26] In the *Dissertation* of 1770 and in both the first and the second editions of the *Aesthetic*,[27] Kant adopted a similar procedure. He showed first that space must be a certain kind of representation and that for additional reasons it cannot be any other kind. It must be granted that what Kant showed space to be is something quite different from any of the alternatives treated by Clarke. Yet there are, as I hope to show,

[24] Cf. below, p. 98.

[25] Kant, *Inaugural Dissertation and Early Writings on Space*, translated by Handyside, p. 10. Cf. Clarke, Paper IV, §§ 11, 12.

[26] Clarke, Paper V, § 46 *n*.

[27] Kant, *Inaugural Dissertation*, § 15, D; *Kritik der reinen Vernunft*, A 23-4 = B 38-9.

clues in Clarke's arguments which may have suggested to Kant even some of his positive doctrines of space. In any case, there is a remarkable similarity between the negative portions of Kant's argument and the doctrines in Clarke's summary.

After showing why he believed that space is not nothing, Clarke held:

> That it is not a *mere Idea*, is . . . most manifest. For no *Idea* of Space, can possibly be framed larger than *Finite;* and yet Reason demonstrates that 'tis a Contradiction for *Space itself* not to be actually *Infinite.*[28]

This argument is of great significance in reference to Kant's views. We can best understand Clarke's meaning by referring again to his argument for the indivisibility of space. As we have found, he maintained that space cannot be literally divided, although the imagination treats it as divided. Actually it has no parts. We imagine it to be divided, but actually a contradiction is involved in this procedure, for between the assumed parts there would be the very thing that is supposed to be divided, namely, space. We have examined this view and mentioned the possibility of its having influenced Kant. It is even more important to analyze Clarke's treatment of the infinity of space in his contention that space is not a mere idea. We conceive space to be finite, he held, not because our imagination causes us to err, but because we are incapable of forming an idea of anything larger than the finite. We have ideas only of finite spaces, but we know that it is contradictory to consider space to be finite, and hence space cannot be a mere idea. This doctrine involves an important change in his thinking. No longer did he maintain that it is merely the imagination which gives us a false notion of space, which must be corrected by reference to space as it is. Our very faculty of forming ideas is so constituted that we incorrectly apprehend space to be finite. As in the case of the indivisibility of space, the mind is able to correct its error, but the error, he held, does not arise because of the imagination; it is involved in the very faculty of apprehension itself. Space cannot be a mere idea, for our idea of space is finite, which

[28] Clarke, *loc. cit.*

reason tells us space cannot be. Instead of raising merely the question of the validity of our acts of imagination, Clarke raised the deeper question of the possibility of the inaccuracy of our ideas.

Involved in this question are two issues, a narrower one, and a wider one. In the first place, narrowly speaking, what is the nature of space if it is different from our idea of it? Clarke believed that he had answered this question by his theory that space is a property, a property of God. But no unbiased student of the Controversy could fail to realize that, whatever are the errors of Leibniz's criticism of other portions of the theory of Newtonian or absolute space, his criticisms of the theory that space is an attribute of God are unanswerable.[29] Consequently, if, in addition to turning out not to be a property or a relation or a substance, space should turn out not to be an idea, the question remains: what is its logical status? Again, if it is by means of principles of reason that we clarify and correct ideas, is it also solely by means of such rational principles that we deal with conceptions which are not ideas? If such principles are criteria solely for dealing with ideas, what other type of criteria do we use in dealing with other kinds of conceptions? If space is not an idea, what is the source of its necessary nature, and what is its logical status in opposition to that of ideas? This narrower question concerns the nature of space.

Clarke's views lead, in addition, to a wider question. If the conception, space, is neither substance nor idea nor relation, and (contrary to Clarke's contention) also not a property, is there not a class of conceptions (of which space is only one example) which does not belong to any of these categories. If some conceptions are not ideas, and, if, for reasons Clarke went on to show, space is not a relation or a substance, and if, for reasons which Leibniz set forth, space is not a property, what is the logical status of certain conceptions (including space) different from ideas, substances, relations, and properties? Whereas the narrower problem involves the nature of space in opposition to substances, attributes, relations, and ideas, a wide logical problem is also suggested: Is there a new kind of conception of which space (as well as time) is only one example?

[29] Cf. below, pp. 39–42.

Clarke's views pointed to a solution of both of these problems. In the first place, just as he had discovered the contradiction in the notion of a finite space not by appealing to the general conception of space but by reference to any given space (in Kant's terms: to the concrete), so he similarly referred directly to space for evidence that it is infinite and hence not a mere idea. But whereas in his account of its indivisibility he clearly traced the special procedure of the mind by means of which the contradiction lying in the notion of its divisibility is revealed, in his account of the procedure by which space is shown not to be a mere idea, his references to the infinity of space are highly confusing. Far from claiming that the mind in some way partially apprehends the infinity of space, he held that *reason demonstrates* that it is a contradiction for space not to be infinite. If such a contradiction is established by reason, the implication is (at least according to analytical principles of reason) that various particular conceptions are examined and subsumed under a general one, their qualities conforming to those of the latter. According to this view, particular spaces would be found not to be finite, not because of the nature of space as immediately apprehended, but because, like any other general conception, space has a quality (infinitude) which its particulars cannot lack, just as the qualities of Peter cannot be the opposite of those of man (if Peter is a man).

But this account of the infinity of space is precisely what Clarke could not have meant, in spite of his words: "reason demonstrates." The infinity of space cannot mean that particular spaces (parts) share the quality (infinitude) of space in general, for the nature of space precludes the existence of several, particular, infinite spaces. Analytical reason can only demonstrate that particular conceptions do not contradict the *already known* nature of a general one. Unless it were already known that space is infinite, such reasoning could establish nothing about particular spaces, and if it were already known that space is infinite, such reasoning, far from showing that there are no actual particular spaces, would show that particular spaces must share the infinitude of general space. Consequently, Clarke's account of the infinity of space as demonstrated by reason is highly misleading, and we must dismiss this unhappy phrase, if we are to understand why he held that space is not a mere idea.

If we return to his other account of infinite space, his view that we have a partial apprehension of it—that is, a mistaken representation of it as having parts—we find keen insight in his account of the logical status of space, insight that may have influenced Kant. We apprehend infinite space. We are able, however, to frame ideas only of finite spaces. Hence we apprehend space in some way other than by framing ideas of it. Each idea of space yields a fictitious quality, namely, finitude. The fictitiousness of this quality is not demonstrated by reason by an appeal to the subsistence of the opposite quality in a general conception. Hence this quality is found to be fictitious in the same way that the quality "divisibility" is found to be fictitious, namely, by reference to space, apprehended directly as it is. But such apprehension cannot be by framing ideas, for the mind cannot begin to frame ideas until space has already been given. Unless space is already apprehended as it is, there is no object to be distorted by ideas. Therefore, in his account of the infinitude of space (as in his theory of its indivisibility) Clarke implied that there is one way in which space is apprehended as it is, and then, in contrast, another way in which it is apprehended as having fictitious, contradictory qualities. He set the stage for Kant to label the first process intuition and the second, conception. The second process Clarke himself called "framing ideas," and held that it yielded fictitious qualities. Because of his mistaken appeal to rational principles to establish the fictitious nature of these qualities, he failed to realize that there is another type of apprehension by which such fictitiousness *is* established. Yet such a process is definitely implied in his theory of a partial apprehension of the whole of space (detached from his mistaken equation of such apprehension with a distortion by the imagination). If this other type of process is admitted, the contradictory nature of finite and divisible spaces is established with reference to it and not by analytical reason. The apprehension of infinite space is different from framing ideas and involves an appeal to direct observation rather than to a rational principle. Space is governed by conditions other than those involved in the process of framing ideas, and hence space is not an idea. The truth or falsity of ideas is based upon their comparison with each other and their reference to a general idea according to the principle of contradiction; but the truth or falsity of analyses of space lies not in such a procedure, but in an appeal to direct observation by the mind.

It is impossible to say whether Kant followed such a line of thinking in shaping his view that space is neither an idea nor a substance nor a relation nor an attribute. His views in 1770 involve such a multiplicity of teachings different from, and in advance of, anything in the Clarke-Leibniz Controversy and his own earlier writings that it would be rash to assume that he studied the Controversy at any particular time. However, just prior to 1770, as I shall try to show, he worked out a theory of space, involving precisely the line of thinking which I have traced above. He distinguished between two kinds of representations (*Vorstellungen*) : those which are amenable to conceptual analysis, that is, conceptions (*Begriffe*) ; and others which are determined in a different way, that is, singular representations (*Einzelvorstellungen*) or intuitions (*Anschauungen*).[30] It is, furthermore, true that he discovered a difference in the way in which the individual examples of conceptions are related to them (Peter is *under* man) ,[31] and the way in which the individual examples of intuitions are related to them (this space is *in* space) . From this difference of relation he concluded that there is a difference in the kind of necessity involved in predications about them. It is, furthermore, true that he discovered evidence of the nature of these singular conceptions (or intuitions) to lie in the nature of the truth in geometry and mechanics.[32] It is, therefore, difficult to conclude categorically that Kant was not at some time just prior to 1770 familiar with the Clarke-Leibniz Controversy, particularly the section in which Clarke affirmed that space is indivisible in spite of the fact that we imagine it to be divided and, more especially, with the passage in which Clarke denied that space is an idea because it is infinite while we can frame ideas of it only as finite.

[30] Kant, *Inaugural Dissertation*, § 15, B, C.
[31] *Ibid.*, § 15, B.   [32] Cf. below, Chapter VI, § 3.

An even more important reason for considering that Clarke may have had an influence upon Kant's thinking just prior to 1770 lies in the wider problem which Clarke raised in rejecting the contention that space is an idea. While it is true that Clarke's view raised more explicitly the possibility that space is neither an idea nor a substance nor an attribute nor a relation, it is also true that he raised the wider problem of the possibility of a new kind of conception (of which space would be an example but only one example). If there should be a kind of conception other than substance, accident, relation, or idea, why should space and time turn out to be the only examples of this type? If space and time should turn out to have a new logical status and to be dependent upon principles different from principles of analytical reasoning, and if, in addition, space and time are the forms of a world, would it not follow that they are possibly not the only examples of such a conception, or the only forms of that world? Furthermore, if there should be other examples of this new kind of conception and yet space and time are the only examples of it which are forms of one world, perhaps there are other examples of it which are forms of another world. If Newton's view of the metaphysical reality of space should turn out to be correct and space is a form of the real world, perhaps other (undiscovered) conceptions would turn out to be other forms of that same world. On the other hand, even if Leibniz's specific theories of space should turn out to be false, perhaps space, as an example of such a new conception, may be metaphysically ideal, not the bearer (as an attribute of God) of things in themselves, but merely of appearances, while certain other (undiscovered) examples of the new kind of conception might turn out to be the forms of a non-spatial world of things in themselves.

I do not maintain that Kant followed through any such line of thinking in reference to the views of Clarke and Newton. But it is true that in 1770 he came to the following conclusions. Space is not a substance, attribute, or relation, but a kind of conception different from the usual general conceptions. Space (and time) is, furthermore, the form of the world of sensible objects (appearances). There is, furthermore, an intelligible, real world, with intellectual forms of the same logical status as space and time. He attempted to reduce the world of space, which Newton had called the world of things themselves, to a world of appearances and to discover forms of another world, the intelligible, real one. He hoped to find other conceptions, which, like space and time, are forms of a world and different from general conceptions whose particulars are ordered *under* them according to the principles of thought. Therefore, though it cannot be definitely concluded that Kant was familiar with Clarke's contention that space is not an idea, yet that contention surely contained the seeds of many of Kant's doctrines.

§ 4

To COMPLETE our account of Clarke's theories of space, it is necessary to anticipate to some extent our analysis of the views of his opponent, Leibniz: first, by considering the next portion of Clarke's summary, which is an attack upon the theory that space is a relation; and secondly, by referring further to Leibniz's views concerning the inadequacy of Clarke's conclusion that space is a property of God. Clarke attacked the theory that space is a relation, first, by claiming that it is a quantity and hence cannot be a relation, and secondly, by contending that the finitude of the universe implies extramundane space.[33] The first of these arguments hinges upon the difference between the extension of a thing and its relation to other things. As we shall discover,[34] Leibniz's views of the nature of space sway between two different accounts: first, that it is a sort of abstraction from extension; and secondly, that it is a relation of bodies to each other. In his dispute with Clarke, however, only the second view is upheld. In this view, one body without other bodies would have extension but would be non-spatial. This conclusion is false, Clarke meant, for one body has quantity, namely, that portion of absolute space which it occupies.

In the light of twentieth-century mathematical physics, the ver-

[33] Clarke, Paper V, § 46 *n*.: "That it is not *a bare Relation of one thing to another*, arising from their *Situation* or *Order among themselves*, is no less apparent: Because *Space* is a *Quantity*, which *Relations* (such as *Situation* and *Order*) are not. . . . Also because, if the material Universe *is*, or *can possibly be*, Finite; there cannot but be, *actual* or *possible*, Extramundane Space. . . ."

[34] Cf. below, pp. 52–55.

dict on this question would seem to be for the side of Leibniz, but in a sense this is not the case. Clarke's theory that space is a quantity was tied up with the Newtonian theory of space and with the doctrine that space is a property of God. Leibniz showed unanswerable difficulties in the latter doctrine, and the former has lately been called into question in mathematics and physics. Yet minus its theological appendage and stripped of its Euclidian simplicity, the theory that space is a quantity and not a relation may . very well still bear great significance. In the first place, even if quantity is merely a relative term, even if bodies have extension only relative to other bodies, such a dependence of the nature of space upon bodies in no way establishes the Leibnizian theory that space is the relation of coexistence. The spatial relation of a body to another considered as a unit measure is much more than mere coexistence. It is different also from the relations—equal to, less than, or greater than. It is a much more specific, numerical relation of one quantity (length) to another considered as a unit (whether relative or absolute). Logically, the difference between relative quantities and relations of coexistence is as sharp as that between absolute quantities and such relations, and it was this difference that Clarke was insisting upon, admittedly with reference to absolute space. Quantities, even relative quantities, are not quantities of relation. Again, even if some relational theory of space should hold in mathematics and physics, this fact would not, as Mr. S. Alexander has pointed out,[35] preclude the possibility (upon which indeed his whole position is worked out) that the things related are themselves in some more fundamental sense based upon the nature of space and time (or perhaps space-time). Consequently, Clarke's contention that space is a quantity and not a relation may turn out to retain significance in the face of twentieth-century relational theories of space, either by forming the core of some absolute theory of space or by indicating some aspect of space presupposed by the relational theories. Upon the outcome of these issues we are not here in a position to decide.

Clarke's second criticism of the Leibnizian theory of space as the relation of coexistence is of greater historical significance than

[35] Alexander, *Space, Time and Deity*, I, 174.

the first. Raising, as it does, the problems of vacuums in nature, of extramundane space, and of the spatial infinitude of the universe, it involves important points of conflict between the Newtonian and Leibnizian general philosophies and deals with the problem of Kant's first antinomy. Writing to Garve in 1798, Kant held that it was from the problems of the antinomies that he set out.[36] We should bear these facts in mind as we turn to Clarke's second criticism.

"If the material Universe *is*, or *can possibly be*, Finite; there cannot but be . . . ," Clarke held, "Extramundane Space. . . ."[37] Is the material universe finite or infinite? This question had very different meanings for Clarke and Leibniz. For the former, it meant: is the amount of gross matter in the infinite spatial container a maximum, or could there be more than there is? Two empirical considerations suggested to Newton that the amount is less than it might be. First, the nature of planetary motion, with the absence of resistance to it.[38] This fact demonstrated as clearly as any empirical evidence can that there is no gross matter outside of planetary atmospheres to make the planets languish. Secondly, the observed and calculable nature of the density of the atmosphere of the earth.[39] The facts about atmospheric density likewise show that the interstellar spaces are empty of gross matter. Yet Newton's method prevented him from generalizations about these questions, and he mentioned the possibility of a thin fluid ether. Therefore, Clarke was not concerned to establish in any categorical sense the finitude of the universe, with the accompanying theory of vacuums. He was interested, however, in elaborating the high probability of these doctrines as a refutation of Leibniz's theory that space is a relation. Furthermore, he believed that the finitude of the universe, as he conceived it, militated in favor of the theory of a creation of the universe in time by God, as well as a retention by Him of the power to intervene to alter its constitution. Assuming that space and time are both infinite, he believed that a universe infinite in mass (as favored by Leibniz) would also necessarily be eternal, in the past and in the future. It would

[36] Kant, *Briefwechsel, Phil. Bib.* Bd. 52 b., pp. 779–80.
[37] Clarke, Paper V, § 46 *n.*
[38] Newton, *Optics*, pp. 341–42.   [39] *Ibid.*, p. 343.

be uncreated and indestructible; God would not be able to alter the amount of its matter. Therefore, Clarke contended for a finite universe, spatially, temporally, past and future, and in mass, such finitude being, of course, within the infinite spatial and temporal framework.[40]

What was Leibniz's view of this question? Is the material universe finite or infinite? For him this question meant: is the material universe finite or infinite, including, as it does, all space and time?[41] As we shall find, space and time are, according to Leibniz, inextricably bound up with material bodies.[42] Consequently, to maintain, as Clarke had done, that space and time are infinite meant to contend for the infinitude of the universe. An infinite time in the past would involve, according to Leibniz, an uncreated material universe that has always existed. Such a doctrine would run counter to the theory of God's creation, to which Leibniz was committed.[43] Similarly in regard to the future, infinite time would mean an eternally existing material universe. This conclusion, however, he accepted. In regard to space, infinitude could mean only a certain condition in the nature of matter; the idea of spaces without matter is meaningless. There are no vacuums whether terrestrial, interstellar, or extramundane. In sharp contrast to the question of temporal and spatial finitude or infinitude, Leibniz considered the quantity or mass of the material universe to be indeterminate or incalculable, that is, no quantity of matter may be assigned to it.[44] In this sense, the universe is necessarily infinite or indefinite. The greater the amount of matter, the greater the power which God has exercised upon the universe. Leibniz had in mind a sort of maximum and minimum density, an absolute vacuum and absolute plenum, neither of which in his opinion exists. The perfection of God's creation is

[40] Clarke, Paper IV, § 7; Paper V, § 41.

[41] Leibniz, Paper IV, § 41; Paper V, § 47.

[42] Leibniz, Paper IV, § 41: Space "est cet *Ordre* qui fait que les corps sont *Situables,* & par lequel ils ont une Situation entre eux en existant ensemble, comme le *temps* est cet *Ordre* par rapport à leur position successive." Cf. below, pp. 61–62.

[43] Leibniz, Paper V, § 74; cf. below, pp. 44–48.

[44] Leibniz, Paper IV, § 21: "Il n'y a point de raison *possible,* qui *puisse limiter* la quantité de la matière. Ainsi cette limitation ne sauroit avoir lieu." Paper IV, P.S.: "Il n'est *point possible* qu'il y ait un Principe de determiner la Proportion de la matière, ou du rempli au vuide, ou du vuide au plein."

not involved in the amount of matter that there is in the universe. But the amount of matter reflects the amount of power that He has seen fit to exercise. If a vacuum is granted in or beyond nature, then with reference to that vacuum, God has exercised no power; such a course is incompatible with the principles of His nature as worked out by Leibniz, which we have yet to consider.

For the purposes of our study, the debate between Clarke and Leibniz takes on, therefore, two significant aspects. (1) Clarke's attack upon the relational theory of space as incompatible with the findings of Newton, set over against Leibniz's defense of that theory. (2) Their respective stands on the highly ambiguous question of the finitude or infinitude of the universe. On this second question, Clarke held that the universe is probably finite spatially, temporally, and in mass; that in any event it is either finite in all or in none of these respects;[45] that in any event space and time, themselves, are infinite and eternal respectively, the latter in regard to both the past and the future. Leibniz held that the universe is limited in time *a parte ante,* eternal in time *a parte post,* infinitely relational in space, and indeterminate in mass. Each believed that the views of the other shattered the theory of divine creation: Clarke because a universe infinite in any respect is infinite in every respect: Leibniz because an infinite time in the past would mean a universe existing eternally from the past. According to Clarke, space and time, being bound up with God's essence, transcend the conditions of creation and form a divine framework necessary to creation and within which creation has occurred.[46] According to Leibniz, such space and time would derogate from God's perfection and make Him anthropomorphic; while space and time, correctly conceived, are merely aspects of created nature and as such can in no sense transcend matter.

It is, of course, not justifiable to claim categorically that Kant's thinking in those crucial years about 1769 centered about this

[45] Clarke, Paper V, §§ 73–5: "If the *Material Universe* CAN *possibly* . . . be *Finite* and *Moveable* . . . then *Space,* (in which That Motion is performed,) is manifestly *independent* upon *Matter.* But if, on the contrary, the *material Universe Cannot* be *finite* and *moveable,* and *Space cannot* be *independent* upon *Matter;* then . . . it follows evidently that God neither *Can* nor *ever Could* set Bounds to *Matter;* and consequently the *material Universe* must be not only *boundless,* but *eternal* also, both *a parte ante* and *a parte post.* . . ." Cf. Clarke, Paper IV, § 7.

[46] Clarke, Paper IV, § 15; Paper V, § 45.

sharp conflict of ideas. Bearing in mind, however, his letter to Garve[47] and the other likenesses between his views and Clarke's, it is at least possible that the road to his own antinomy concerning the spatial and temporal finitude or infinitude of the world was paved by this clash between these two important predecessors. Possibly Kant realized that before him lay the unique spectacle of two men holding antithetical views of space and time, each of whom looked upon the other as holding a mutually repudiated view (namely, the theory of an uncreated material universe). The spectacle may have led him to examine quite profitably the question of the infinitude of the world.[48] He may have pursued some such line of thinking as the following: Clarke holds that space and time cannot be inextricably bound with matter unless the material universe is eternal *a parte ante, a parte post,* and infinite spatially. Newton's findings seem to support him in this contention. Yet Leibniz shows grave difficulties in the doctrine that space and time are properties of God and parts of the divine essence. Is it not possible that they are both correct? Cannot Clarke's denial of the link between matter and space be retained without leaping to a further link between space and God? Does not the difficulty lie in the ambiguity of the question? "Infinitude" may refer, on the one hand, to the mass of the world, its past time, its future time, or its space; or, on the other hand, to space and time themselves. Such ambiguities as these may have very readily led him to suspect that some kind of sham conflict was involved.

In the concluding arguments of his summary,[49] Clarke held that space is neither body nor any other kind of substance. Believing that he had finally eliminated all other possibilities, he concluded that space must be a property. It was this conclusion that Leibniz attacked. Before turning to the latter's general philosophy, let us trace briefly his criticisms of Clarke on this point. In the first place,[50] Leibniz held, space is in part commensurate with bodies. If space is God's immensity, then God is in part commensurate with bodies. In the second place,[51] if infinite space is a property

---

[47] Cf. above, p. 36.
[49] Clarke, Paper V, § 46 *n.*
[48] Cf. below, pp. 161–63.
[50] Leibniz, Paper V, § 36.
[51] Leibniz, Paper V, § 37: "Ainsi l'Espace occupé par un Corps, sera *l'Etendue de ce Corps:* Chose absurde, puisqu'un Corps peut changer *d'Espace,* mais il ne peut point quitter *son Etendue.*"

of a Being (or Substance) who is everywhere, namely, God, then finite spaces will be, likewise, a property of beings or substances which are somewhere, that is, a property of bodies. If space is a property of bodies, it must be their extension. A body, however, retains its extension even when moving, but it changes its space. Hence space and extension are different. Here Leibniz held the same ground for the difference between space and extension which Euler, an advocate of absolute space,[52] later held. If, then, space and extension are different, what quality of a body can space be? If finite space is not a quality of body, upon what grounds can it be held that infinite space is a property of God?

If infinite space, he asked thirdly,[53] is a property of God, and if some finite spaces are properties of bodies, of what substances would those empty, finite spaces, in which Clarke and Newton believed, be properties? Would it follow, he asked, that square or round empty spaces would be properties of God? His own view was that there is no such thing as an empty space, but if such a thing exists, and if space is a property of God, would not such round or square, empty spaces be properties of God? He did not consider the possibility of God's being, in such a view, three-dimensional, but he quite justifiably asked whether certain shapes of an empty space would not be, in that view, divine qualities. Would there be immaterial, extended substances, he asked, in these empty spaces, of which such spaces would be qualities? Would a space be successively the property of matter, spirits, and God?

Fourthly,[54] he held that if infinite space is a quality of God, and if bounded spaces are properties of finite substances, it would follow that God is composed of the properties of these substances. Such a conclusion could be avoided, he held, only by denying that bounded space is a property of bounded things. But if this denial is made, then, along the same lines of reasoning, infinite space would have to be denied to be a property of an infinite being.

Leibniz's fifth and last argument is strongest of all.[55] The im-

---

[52] Cf. below, p. 129 n.   [53] Leibniz, Paper V, §§ 38–39.   [54] Leibniz, Paper V, § 40.
[55] Leibniz, Paper V, § 45: "L'immensité de Dieu, fait que Dieu est dans tous les Espaces. Mais si Dieu est *dans* l'Espace, comment peut on dire que l'Espace est *en* Dieu, ou qu'il est sa proprieté? On a bien öui dire que la Proprieté soit dans le

mensity of God means that God is everywhere. If space is real,
then omnipresence means presence everywhere in it. Hence God
as well as everything else would be in space. But if God is in space,
how can space be in God? A quality may be said to be in a substance, but can a substance be said to be in its property? All substances except God are, Clarke held, in space. God is, he held,
not in space, but space is in God. He confused two types of inclusion. Logical inclusion means the adherence of qualities to a
substance. If space is, in this sense, included in God, then in the
same sense, it would be included as a property in other substances.
On the other hand, physical inclusion means the inclusion of a
substance with all of its properties in a medium which lies outside
of it, and in which it can, with all of its properties, move. It was
this type of inclusion that Newton assumed in his formulation of
the laws of the motion of bodies in space. Bodies do not move in
a space which is the property of one or more of them or in a space
which is the relation between two or more of them. Bodies move
in a space which includes them all physically with all of their
properties and relations. It was with this type of inclusion in mind
that Newton formulated his theories of the nature of space and
its relation to bodies. In considering the relation of space to God,
he reversed the procedure, and, instead of claiming that space
contains God physically as it does bodies, he held that God includes space logically. Such logical inclusion, Leibniz rightly held,
refers never to the presence of a subject (God) in its quality
(space) but always the reverse. If space has the same relation to
all substances that it has to God, and if it is a property of God,
then it must be a property of other substances, the bodies which
move in it, and hence those bodies are in their property. If Clarke
had maintained consistently that everything is (physically) in
space, then it would follow that God is also in space, and hence
space cannot be a property of God. If he maintained consistently
that everything is (logically) in God, then it would follow that
space is a property of God, and hence parts of space are (logically)

Sujet, mais on n'a jamais öui dire que le Sujet soit dans sa Proprieté. De même,
Dieu existe *en* chaque Temps: Comment donc le temps est il dans Dieu; & comment peut il être une Proprieté de Dieu?"

properties of other substances. If infinite space is a quality of one substance, then a finite space would be the property of another. If Clarke had merely held that bodies are in space and had not gone on to hold that space is in God, none of the objections which Leibniz brought up concerning the latter theory would have been relevant. Against this latter theory, Leibniz's criticisms were, however, valid on the various counts mentioned, and this fact may have influenced Kant in 1770 in his criticisms of the Newtonians.[56]

[56] Cf. below, pp. 147–49.

CHAPTER III

SPACE AND SUBSTANCE IN LEIBNIZ

§ 1

NEWTON'S VIEWS of space were, for the most part, assumptions, elaborated only incidentally in his treatment of natural philosophy (physics). On the other hand, Leibniz's philosophy of space is the definite outcome of wider, explicitly adopted, metaphysical principles. In spite of this fact, if any of Leibniz's various views of space are adopted (and this study proposes now to point out several that he formulated), the significance of space becomes definitely limited to its role in computations in mechanics. Such is not the case in the views of Newton, however uncritical and fragmentary those views may have been. In other words, of the two men, Leibniz worked out a system of metaphysics, while Newton avoided such a study as if it were the plague; yet the very nature of Leibniz's system of monads precluded any philosophy of space apart from a consideration of the spaces of mechanics; whereas despite the fragmentary nature of Newton's examination of space, he leaves open the possibility of a metaphysics of space. As Cassirer has pointed out in reference to Descartes,[1] Leibniz's general metaphysical dualism between monads and phenomena (involving space and time) ought not to obscure from us the fact that with reference to nature or phenomena, he formulated a monistic view. Nature, in his opinion, is not bifurcated into "container and contained" but is merely a realm of mechanical objects, one abstract feature of which is space. No aspect of nature is in any sense cut off, and capable of being treated apart, from the whole. In reference to nature, it was Newton, not Leibniz, who was a dualist and who alone held forth the possibility of an immovable object, separable from matter. Leibniz's theory of monads, as a somewhat

[1] Cassirer, *Substance and Function and Einstein's Theory of Relativity*, pp. 395–99.

Aristotelian type of metaphysics, ought not to blind us to this fact. If philosophy of space is considered the type of first philosophy that this study is contemplating (along lines later worked out by S. Alexander),[2] it was Newton and not Leibniz who left the door open to such a study. If Descartes's and Leibniz's theories of nature are considered apart from their doctrines of immaterial substances, physics and mathematics become first philosophy in a far more absolute sense than Newton would allow. To the extent that Kant (like Newton) made space prior to the bodies moving in it and more intrinsic to nature than they, he may be said to have retained the possibility of a metaphysics of space;[3] whereas, to the extent that he relegated space to a role dependent upon, and derivative from, the objects in it, his philosophy of nature, like Leibniz's and like Broad's today,[4] reduces philosophy to a critical analysis of the findings of the special sciences, which alone provide any clue to nature and thus become first philosophy.[5] We must bear these considerations in mind in working out the particular sort of metaphysics for which Leibniz stood. In spite of his elaborate scaffolding, it was he, rather than Kant's other main predecessor, whose views precluded a philosophy of space.

All possible universes are governed, Leibniz held, by the principle of contradiction. This universe is governed in addition by the principle of sufficient reason. God's infinitely continuing, free choice or act of creation of this universe is limited by the former principle; it expresses the latter. To break through the show of things to their essence is to trace everything back to the principle of contradiction; to return from this principle to the contingent facts of experience is to discover an additional principle in operation—the principle of sufficient reason. God's nature is revealed in the latter; conditions by which even He is determined are revealed by the former. The realm of essence is the realm of possibilities; the realm of existence is the realm of actualities. God is limited, in His vision, by the realm of possibilities; He is limited in His act of creation also by the conditions of His own free choice or nature. On the plane of essence, the principle of contradiction

---

[2] Cf. below, Chapter IX, § 1.
[3] In 1770 and in the *Aesthetic*, cf. below, Chapter VI, § 2; Chapter VII, §§ 1, 2.
[4] Cf. below, Chapter IX, § 3.   [5] In the *Analytic;* cf. below, Chapter VIII, § 2.

operates independently of the nature of God; a violation of that principle even by God is impossible because of conditions external even to God's nature. Such a violation is unthinkable because it is precluded by the nature of possibilities, by the nature of possible structures in the realm of essence. By the absolute necessity[6] involved in the law of contradiction, possible worlds are what they are and not otherwise. On the plane of existence, God operates according to the principle of sufficient reason; a violation of that principle is impossible, not because of conditions external to God's nature, but because of conditions involved in His free choice of the "best" from among the possibilities. He is bound by conditions which He Himself imposes freely upon Himself. A violation of these conditions is thinkable, because no contradiction is involved; but it is impossible because it would involve an imperfection in God's nature. Such a violation is not precluded by the nature of possibilities—by the nature of possible structures in the realm of essence—but merely by the nature of the train of actualities which demands no gaps or breaks, that is, no reconsiderations on the part of the Divine Author. By the hypothetical necessity involved[7] in the law of sufficient reason, our actual world is what it is and not otherwise and has assumed a part of this definite evolutionary plan and not of some other. No patching is required. The hypothetical necessity flowing from God's nature is within the framework of the absolute necessity determining possible worlds and imposes upon our actual world the additional set of conditions lying in His nature.[8] A possible thing is determined only by the law of contradiction; an actual thing is determined in addition by the law of sufficient reason.

A possible beginning of a universe is determined merely by the absolute necessity of the law of contradiction. In accordance merely with such necessity, the universe might have begun at some other point in time than the point at which it actually began. Such a possibility is thinkable because not violating the principle of contradiction.[9] But this possibility does not mean that there is an empty continuum of real time inside which the universe begins

---

[6] Leibniz, Paper V, §§ 4, 5, 76.   [7] Leibniz, Paper V, §§ 4, 5.
[8] God's will is different from his power; Leibniz, Paper V, § 76.
[9] Leibniz represented it in a diagram; Paper V, § 56.

and continues to exist. Such a possibility merely means that any universe must conform to the conditions of possible universes, that is, to the principle of contradiction. No actual universe begins merely in accordance with the laws governing possible universes, but also in accordance with the laws governing an actual beginning; never merely in accordance with the law of contradiction, but also in accordance with the law of sufficient reason; never merely in accordance with the nature of possibilities, but also in accordance with the nature of God's free choice from among those possibilities. To admit that it is thinkable for this universe to have begun at some earlier time than it actually began is merely to admit that upon the removal of the law of sufficient reason, the nature of one beginning would not violate the law of contradiction any more than the nature of another. Far from proving time to be real, this admission shows only all the more clearly, Leibniz held, that time apart from actual conditions is an ideal order, the nature of which imposes no further conditions upon a beginning of a possible universe than those imposed by the law of contradiction itself. Judgments concerning time are (as Kant later called them) analytic. To admit that it is thinkable for a universe to have begun at some earlier time than it actually began is merely to admit that the law governing possible universes imposes no conditions which preclude the full operation of the law of sufficient reason, that is, of God's free choice of the best. To conclude, on the other hand, that time is an empty, eternal framework in which all possible universes must begin, is to subject all possible universes to laws other than that of contradiction, namely, the laws bound up with the nature of such an eternal, empty, temporal, framework. In such case, the actual beginning of this universe could occur in accordance with the principle of sufficient reason only to the extent that that law did not violate the conditions bound up with the nature of time. Temporal conditions would, in such a case, be absolutely necessary, even more necessary than the hypothetical necessity involved in God's act of creation. God would thus be made anthropomorphic and finite. Such a view, Leibniz maintained, is a palpable confusion of the absolute necessity determining possible worlds and the hypothetical necessity determining this world.[10] A possible universe may be thought of as beginning earlier rather than later; that is, there is nothing in the nature of a possible universe to require it to begin at one time rather than another. Such temporal indefiniteness among possibilities in no way implies any actual time with reference to them. For all possible universes, although as such, determined only by the law of contradiction, are subject in becoming actual to an additional law—the law of sufficient reason. But our universe is not only a possible universe; it is also a universe which has become actualized. Therefore, our universe is determined by the law of contradiction, and also by the law of sufficient reason, which precludes any beginning other than the actual beginning which has occurred.

In other words, the beginning of the universe involves the operation of the law of sufficient reason: God has a free choice. A free choice is not one free from inner motives but free from external compulsion.[11] No choice is absolutely free except one which is the result of complete insight, and the only condition limiting such insight is the principle of contradiction. Within the bounds of that principle the operation of the principle of sufficient reason involves an original vision on the part of the Creator into every possible sequence of events. Freedom is based upon absolute vision, not upon a lack of determination by motives. Freedom begins with insight; a free choice is an action based upon such insight. Complete insight exhausts all of the possibilities within the limits of the law of contradiction. In this initial insight into all possibilities, God gets His freedom of action; nothing that He subsequently does can be regarded as a limitation of that freedom. As a universe becomes actualized, its qualities are better or worse than the rejected possibilities to the extent that the act of creation involved is based upon insight into all possibilities. But God's act of creation is based upon such insight. Hence the qualities of the universe created by Him are the best from among all possibilities. Hence it lies in God's nature not only to be free—that is, to foresee all possible sequences of events—but also to choose the best.

[10] Leibniz, Paper V, §§ 4, 5, 76.
[11] Leibniz, Paper III, § 8; Paper IV, § 2; Paper V, §§ 9, 15, 17, 69, 70.

When the principle of sufficient reason begins to operate, the actualization of a universe sets in. Following upon His complete insight into all possibilities comes God's eternal act of creation, the process of actualization of the universe. All contingent events are within this eternal process of actualization and are limited by both the principle of contradiction and the principle of sufficient reason. All contingent events are both absolutely and hypothetically necessary: absolutely necessary because they do not violate the nature of possible structures, hypothetically necessary because they belong to that particular chain of events and manifest those particular structures which reflect the continuing choice of God of the best from among the possibles. The adaptation of means to ends among a series of contingent events reflects the motive of God in His free choice of the best. A completely mechanistic, physical universe reflects this motive, as does the harmony of that universe with the acts of purposive creatures. The choices of the latter, based upon imperfect insight, frequently involve what seems to be the less perfect. In the wider perspective of God's original, continuing, free choice, such imperfections are portions of the best possible plan. God's freedom is preserved, in spite of the apparent imperfections, because of the original perfect insight on His part. Man is bound, but not because his actions are motivated actions: in this regard his actions are like divine actions.[12] Man is bound because, prior to his actions, he lacks sufficient insight to reveal the best and so to furnish the motive for choosing it. God is free not because His eternal act of creation is unmotivated, but because the complexity of His motive follows upon the complete insight which makes such a motive possible. God is free because, prior to His action, He has sufficient insight to reveal the best and so to furnish the motive for choosing it. There is a sufficient reason for every contingent event when viewed from the perspective of the whole.

Sufficient reasons are, however, never available for a choice between two absolutely identical possibilities.[13] There must be a discernible difference between two alternatives upon which a suf-

---

[12] Leibniz, Paper IV, § 2.
[13] Leibniz, Paper III, § 5; Paper IV, § 3; Paper V, §§ 17, 21, 23, 66.

ficient reason may be based; if such a difference is lacking, there can be no sufficient reason, and, hence, no choice. A discernible difference is not a discerned difference, except in the case of God's choice.[14] In all cases of human choice, the differences discerned fall short of the differences discernible; human choices are based upon limited insight; the motives in such choices do not involve an insight into all consequences. God's eternal act of choice is, however, based upon complete insight, and He discerns, therefore, all discernible differences. In cases lacking any discernible differences, God could not act with sufficient reason. God's action is, however, always the result of a sufficient reason. The alternatives presented to Him, therefore, never lack discernible differences. Hence two realities (substances) cannot be identical, and there is never among the nature of possible structures an indiscernible difference. Space and time are, however, by definition, composed of parts with indiscernible differences.[15] They cannot, therefore, belong to the structure of any possible universe, including this one. Hence, space and time are ideal.

§ 2

WITHIN THE created universe, there are an infinite number of simple substances or monads, and the essential nature of each is active force. Such force is something midway between a mere faculty of action and action itself.[16] It differs from a faculty of action because it is not merely completely unexercised potentiality; instead, it involves an actual attempt on the part of a substance to carry out in motion the principle of its own nature. It differs from action in so far as expressed action always involves, in addition to the operation of the active nature of the substance, the presence of the phenomenon, motion. Leibniz illustrated this theory by the case of a heavy body stretching a rope on which it is hung and by a taut bow. A mere faculty of action is the formal possibility of action, involving nothing actual in the nature of

[14] Leibniz, Paper V, § 52.
[15] Leibniz, Paper III, § 5; Paper IV, § 18; Paper V, §§ 27, 58, 60, 67.
[16] *On the Reform of Metaphysics and on the Notion of a Substance*, in *The Philosophical Works of Leibniz*, edited by Duncan, p. 76.

bodies. But in the case of the heavy body on the string and in the case of the taut bow, there is the actual straining, although in neither case is there motion. Leibniz believed that there is no intrinsic difference in a substance when its force has passed over into motion, and when it has not. Nothing new is added to its nature when it moves. Consequently, all of the elements which enter into the computation of its motions are extrinsic to its nature. Such elements as time, place, extension, etc., do not refer to the essential nature of a substance but merely to its phenomenal aspect. Formally, every substance except God is linked with a sort of passive force or primary matter, but such matter is intrinsically different from the secondary, or clothed, matter which a substance wears as a portion of a mechanical, phenomenal realm. The essence of every substance is active force; in addition, all created substances have passive force or primary matter.

On the other hand, within the realm of phenomena, Leibniz formulated the very different distinction between living and dead forces.[17] All substances are, as such, active. A dead force refers to nothing intrinsic to their nature but, rather, merely to a condition in one substance as a phenomenon relative to a condition in another substance similarly considered. A condition involving motion in the one is merely relative to a condition called rest in the other, and if the relation is considered in the reverse direction, the first is at rest and the second moving; or, again, with reference to a wider group of phenomena, both may be considered moving. A dead force refers merely to the absence of motion, which is always relative to other substances and hence does not concern the active nature of substance as such. Similarly, a living force refers to the presence of motion in relation to other things. Space and time, being relative to the living or dead forces in phenomena, are not merely ideal in relation to substances but are even abstractions from them in their phenomenal aspects. Consequently, there are several different fashions in which space is ideal.

There are, in the views of Leibniz, four different and distinct meanings of the term "ideal." (1) Immaterial subjects (monads)

[17] Leibniz, *New Essays Concerning Human Understanding*, edited by Langley, p. 674.

and their qualities are alone real, that is, metaphysically real, consisting of active force; material subjects (phenomena) and their qualities and relations are ideal, that is, metaphysically unreal. (2) Material subjects (phenomena), their qualities and relations are alone real, that is, concrete; abstractions from these (place and space) and their qualities are ideal, that is, abstract. (3) Particular abstractions from phenomena, namely, places, are alone real, that is, nonfictitious, not being based upon the assumption of absolute rest, which is impossible; generalized abstractions from phenomena, namely space and time, are ideal, that is, fictitious, being based upon the assumption of absolute rest, which is impossible. (4) Material subjects (phenomena), their qualities and relations, including relations of situation, are alone real, that is, objective; feigned identities among relations of situation (places and spaces) are ideal, that is, subjective or arbitrary. In the first sense, "ideal" is the opposite of metaphysically real; in the second, of concrete; in the third, of nonfictitious; in the fourth, of objective. In the first sense, "ideal" means metaphysically unreal although concrete and existing; in the second, it means abstract although nonfictitious and objective; in the third, it means fictitious although objective and nonarbitrary; in the fourth, it means subjective and arbitrary.

The criterion of "ideality" in the first sense, is the lack of active, spiritual force; in the second sense, the abstraction of materiality; in the third sense, the assumption of absolute rest; in the fourth sense, the feigning of an identity between two relations. Leibniz held space to be ideal in the first sense in all of his writings. He held it to be abstract (ideal in the second sense) in all of his writings, although he tells us[18] that he gave up the belief in a vacuum early in his life, implying that at one time he had believed in it. In one part of the *Nouveaux essais* and in the *Examen des principes du R. P. Malebranche*, he held it to be the abstraction of extension, or three-dimensionally extended place. In another part of the *Nouveaux essais,* he held it to be fictitious (ideal in the third sense) involving the assumption of absolute rest, which is

---

[18] *On Locke's Essay on Human Understanding*, in *New Essays Concerning Human Understanding*, edited by Langley, p. 16; cf. Leibniz, Paper IV, P.S.

impossible. In another part of the *Nouveaux essais* and in one part of the Controversy with Clarke, he held it to be abstract (ideal in the second sense), but objective (not ideal in the fourth sense), claiming that it is the order of possible coexistences. In another part of the Controversy with Clarke, he held that it is subjective (ideal in the fourth sense) involving the feigning by the mind of an identity between two relations of situation.

In 1702, in his *Réplique aux reflexions de Bayle*, Leibniz described extension as the order of possible coexistences. Since this account is identical with his later views of space, and since he never again referred to extension in this fashion, it seems safe to conclude that he equated extension and space at that time.[19] Extension is, he held, not merely a concrete property of phenomena and an abstract order of actual coexisting bodies but also an abstract order of possible coexisting bodies. This is clearly a statement of the abstractness of extension. But extension is likewise a property of bodies, and bodies and their properties, while metaphysically unreal, are concrete. How, then, can extension be both a property of bodies and an order? It is, he held, like number. "One" is a property of "one" chair and also a member of an order (one, two, three). "Two" is a property of "two" chairs and also a member of the same order. Similarly, "this extension" is a property of a chair and also a member of an order of extensions. While this analogy may show that extension can, in some sense, be both a property and an order, it is difficult to see how it shows it to be the particular order that Leibniz claims it to be, namely, an order of coexistences. If one chair has the property "one" in reference only to a possible group of two chairs, one body would, on the analogy, have the property "extension" only in reference to a possible second body. Whatever are its difficulties, this view of extension is clearly in line with his later view of space. It is probable that in 1702 he either inadvertently confused space and extension or deliberately equated them.

One year later, in 1703, in the *Nouveaux essais,* he distinguished

---

[19] *Leibnitii Opera Philosophica Omnia,* edited by Erdmann, p. 189: "l'étendue est l'ordre des *coéxistences possibles* . . . de sorte que ces ordres quadrent non-seulement à ce qui est actuellement, mais encore à ce qui pourroit être mis à la place, comme les nombres sont indifférens à tout ce qui peut être *res numerata.*"

between space and extension, but he did so in such a way that, while he considered extension to be a property and not a relation, he treated space ambiguously: on the one hand, as a property, actualized only in the extension of things; on the other, as a relation, actualized only in coexisting things. He retained this confusion, possibly because he compared space with number and because he confused the cardinal numbers (one, two, three . . .) and numerical relations or ordinal numbers (first, second, third . . .) . A body has its own extension, but it is not always determined by, or equal to, the same space.[20] Extension is a characteristic of body in a way that space is not. Did Leibniz mean that space is the order of possible coexistences, which he had, a year before, called extension? Did he mean that the extension which a body possesses is a quality which it retains in moving from one place to another in an order of coexistences (space) ? Did he mean that the places in the order of coexistences (space) have an extension different from that of the bodies moving into and out of them? It is true, he held, that body is more than space, but it does not follow that there are two extensions, one of body, and the other of space.[21] Did he mean that space has no extension of its own because it is only the order of coexistences, possible and actual, and hence, like numbers, relational only; or did he mean that it has no extension of its own, because it is the ideal, abstract quality, extension, which is actualized only in the concrete extensions of bodies? Not realizing that these two doctrines of space are different and contradictory, he set out to show both that space is a system of relations and that it is an abstraction from the concrete extensions of individual bodies.

He made the same comparison between space and number that he had the year before made between extension and number.[22] In conceiving several things at a time, the mind, he held, never con-

[20] *Ibid.*, p. 229.

[21] *Ibid.*, pp. 229–30: "Cependant, quoiqu'il soit vrai, qu'en concevant le corps, on conçoit quelque chose de plus que l'espace, il ne s'en suit point qu'il y ait deux étendues, celle de l'espace et celle du corps. . . ."

[22] *Ibid.*, p. 230: "Car c'est comme lorsqu'en concevant plusieurs choses à la fois, on conçoit quelque chose de plus que le nombre, savoir *res numeratas*, et cependant il n'y a point deux multitudes, l'une abstraite, savoir celle du nombre, l'autre concrète, savoir celle des choses nombrées. On peut dire de même qu'il ne faut point s'imaginer deux étendues, l'une abstraite de l'espace, l'autre concrète du corps; le concret n'étant tel que par l'abstrait."

siders number by itself, but always with reference to things numbered. There are not two sets of entities, numbers and things
numbered; numbers refer only to things numbered. The concrete
numbered things gain their numerical characteristics by means of
the abstract numbers. Similarly, extended bodies gain their extended nature by means of the abstract, extended space. The latter
is nothing but an ideal order which gives certain characteristics
to the former. In this analogy, there is a serious difficulty. Does a
thing get the characteristic "one" with reference to an abstract
"one" or "oneness"; or are two things required to give one of them
that quality, the two of them gaining thereby the quality of "two"?
If one thing gains "unity" from an abstract "one," without any
relation to a second thing, and if number and extension are alike,
would not one body similarly gain concrete extension from abstract extension or space without any relation to a second body?
In this case, space would not be the order of coexistence, for one
body can coexist only with another. Hence, if space is compared
with "one," it would follow that it is ideal, having no existence
apart from concrete bodies, but it would not follow that it is a
relation, since it might be actualized in one body no less than in
more than one. Leibniz tried to avoid this conclusion by comparing space not with numbers (one, two, three . . .) but with numerical positions (first, second, third . . .).[23] Numbers and numerical positions are quite different from each other. Number refers
to the extent of an order, one thing (actual or possible), two
things, three things, four things, etc. Numerical position refers to
the place (la place) in an order, the first, second, third, or fourth
place, etc. A thing may be in the first place in a group of four
things; it may take over the second place in that group, the thing
in the second taking over the first; it may become the fourth, the
fourth becoming the second. Yet during these changes and all possible ones, the number of things in the group remains four; each

---

[23] Ibid.: "Et comme les corps passent d'un endroit de l'espace à l'autre, c'est à
dire qu'ils changent d'ordre entr'eux, les choses aussi passent d'un endroit de l'ordre
ou d'un nombre à l'autre. . . . En effet le tems et le lieu ne sont que des espèces
d'ordre et dans ces ordres la place vacante (qui s'appelle vuide à l'égard de l'espace)
s'il y en avoit, marqueroit la possibilité seulement de ce qui manque avec son
rapport à l'actuel."

of the things in the group remains one thing; each two remain two things; and each three remain three things. Leibniz confused the place of a thing as the first in an order, which it may lose by passing to another place, with its unity, which it does not thereby lose. One thing remains no less one thing on becoming the second of an order rather than the first. "One" and "first" are not the same. In claiming that space is an abstraction of extension, he compared it to "one"; in trying to show that it is a relation, he compared it to "first." If space is like "first," it is a relation and not the abstraction of extension. Unless there were two or more things coexisting, there would be no space; in the same way that one thing becomes first only with reference to another. If space is like "one" it is an abstraction from extension, but it is not a relation. One thing existing alone would have space in the same way that one thing is one without any relation to another. Either space is an abstraction of extension, and it is concrete only as a quality of bodies, in which case it resembles "one"; or it is a relation but is not the abstraction of extension or any other quality, in which case it resembles "first." It cannot be both.

Although Leibniz gave these two contradictory views of the abstractness of space, both of them are compatible with his wider contention that space is neither metaphysically real with reference to monads nor a concrete feature of phenomena. Whether it is a relation of coexistences or the abstraction of extension, it is not concrete like matter and its extension, and *a fortiori* it is unrelated to substances. Again, neither of these views involves the fictitiousness or the subjectivity of space (the third and fourth meanings of "ideality").

He proceeded in the same paper to formulate the quite different doctrine of the fictitious nature of space. Space, he held, is universalized place. Both space and places are metaphysically unreal; both are abstract; but space, involving a certain presupposition which contradicts the nature of phenomena, is, in addition, fictitious.[24] Place is particular with reference to certain bodies and universal with reference to all. Place depends upon change. Particular places are determined by the changes of particular bodies;

[24] *Ibid.*, p. 240.

universal place, or space, by those of all bodies. The determination of universal place, or space, requires that one body be absolutely fixed. If no body is fixed, universal place, or space, could not be determined even by a perfect recording of all changes. But no body is absolutely at rest. There can be no actual places, therefore, except particular places, that is, places determined with reference to a body which is relatively at rest but actually (in a wider context) moving. Universal place (space) presupposes a condition which the active nature of all bodies precludes, namely, a condition of absolute rest.[25] Hence there is no universal place, or space. Space is ideal, not merely in the sense of being an abstraction from the nature of bodies, but also as fictitious, involving the incorrect assumption of absolute rest.

From this argument, Leibniz could validly conclude that space is fictitious but not that it is, therefore, a relation. Yet it is precisely this additional conclusion that he went on to draw.[26] If space is universal place and (unlike particular places) fictitious, its fictitious nature is no evidence that it is relational. If places are particular relations of coexistence, and not abstractions from extensions, space or universal place would be relational; but if place is an abstraction from particular extensions, then universal place, or space, is merely an abstraction from all extensions. The fictitiousness of universal place is no evidence that it is a relation, except in so far as particular places are assumed to be relational. Space or generalized place is either the abstraction of extension or the relation of coexistence, but not both. Leibniz elaborated the former view in his *Examen de Malebranche,* and the latter in the Controversy with Clarke.

§ 3

In 1712, in his *Examen des principes du R. P. Malebranche,* Leibniz proceeded to develop the view that space is the abstraction of extension. Extension is a necessary characteristic of bodies;

[25] *Ibid.*
[26] *Ibid.:* "C'est un rapport, un ordre, non seulement entre les existans, mais encore entre les possibles comme s'ils existoient."

hence if it were annihilated, they would be annihilated.[27] Extension alone is not body but would be space without body, if there were such a thing. If extension is abstracted from body, only the "subject" or "nature" of body would remain. It would be ideal and would become actual only upon being extended in body. If from an existing body materiality (that which is extended) is abstracted, extension, as an abstract, ideal characteristic, would remain. In body, that which is extended is prior to extension. Extension is an abstraction and demands something extended. It requires a subject and is something relative to this subject; something prior is presupposed in this subject—some quality, attribute, or nature in this subject which is extended. If extension were removed by abstraction, this subject would remain and would then be quite ideal. Yet apart from a subject which is extended, extension is also an abstraction. The nature or quality of the subject is extended or diffused. Extension is the diffusion of this nature or quality. In milk there is an extension or diffusion of whiteness; in diamond there is an extension or diffusion of hardness; in body in general there is an extension or diffusion of the antitype of materiality.[28] In milk there is never whiteness which is not extended; in diamond there is never hardness which is not extended; in body in general there is never materiality which is not extended. Yet in none of these is extension a subject or substance but merely a quality (admittedly essential) of each. The nature of milk or diamond or body in general is not extension; but in milk, whiteness is extended; in diamond, hardness is extended; in body, materiality is extended. Extension is the diffusion of each of these subjects.

Extension bears the same relation to space as duration bears to time.[29] Extension is an attribute of things, but space is considered as outside of things, and it serves to measure them. Extension is not the materiality of body but the diffusion of materiality. In the same way that extension is the actual diffusion of materiality (from within) of body, so space is the diffusion of body considered

[27] Ibid., p. 691: "Dieu détruisant l'étendue détruiroit le corps; mais en ne produisant que de l'étendue, il ne produiroit peut-être que l'espace sans corps. . . ."
[28] Ibid., p. 692.   [29] Ibid., pp. 692–93.

abstractly (from without) and serves to measure it. In other words, space is the extension of body with materiality abstracted. Strictly speaking, Leibniz went on to hold, space is only three-dimensional extension considered without materiality; while two- and one-dimensional extensions without materiality are places, but not spaces. Furthermore, all spaces are abstract extensions: but some places, namely points, are not extended.

In spite of his admission that extension without matter would be space, and that extension is not the same as body, Leibniz denied that space is a substance. He went on to say that even if he should admit that there is a substance other than body, extension would not be that substance but would adhere to its nature[30] in the same way that it adheres to the whiteness of the milk and the hardness of the diamond. Let us assume, he said, that the abstraction of materiality from body leaves more than something merely ideal, namely, some real subject other than body. Even on this assumption, there would be a difference between the extension of such a subject and the attribute which is extended. This attribute would be the situation, location, or place, and it would be extended; but would not be extension. Even if place were the attribute of some nonmaterial substance (a line, surface or solid), extension would not be that substance but would be the diffusion of place, just as it is the diffusion of the materiality of bodies; and space (in the case of a solid) would be the three-dimensional diffusion of such a subject. The diffusion of place would form space. By means of space, the extension of material things could be measured. Extension as an attribute of space would be the diffusion or continuation of situation or locality in the same way that the extension of bodies is the diffusion of the antitype of materiality.

Since a point as well as space is a place or locality, some places lack extension or diffusion.[31] Similarly, a point in matter is no less material than body. Matter is in a point just as place is in a point. In neither case is there any extension. It is not clear whether Leibniz meant that all places except points are spaces, or only those which are three-dimensionally diffused. He would seem to imply the former contention in mentioning space as a kind of

[30] Ibid., p. 693.   [31] Ibid.

place in opposition to points as another kind of place. However, in drawing a parallel between matter and place, he contrasted a point (one kind of matter) with body (another kind). Since it would hardly seem that bodies are ever extended merely in one or two dimensions, Leibniz would seem to mean that only three-dimensionally extended place is space. In any case, lines are places or matter extended in one dimension; while surfaces and solids are places or matter extended in two and three dimensions respectively.

In holding that there is some matter which is not extended, namely, in a point, did not Leibniz contradict his view that there can be no subject (except monads) which lacks extension? Even in the view that places are ideal, that is, abstract, if matter can be in a point, such points would seem not to be ideal, that is, abstract, but real (because material), and yet by definition a point lacks extension. Would it not follow, therefore, that some subjects (other than monads) lack extension? In spite of this apparent discrepancy in Leibniz's views, there is no contradiction here. He would seem to mean that, apart from monads, only body is a genuine subject, that it is material and extended three-dimensionally. Consequently, not only places and space are abstractions, but material planes, lines, and points are also. There is materiality in a surface, a line, and a point, no less than in a solid; but only in the last case is there anything existing concretely. Beginning with a body, there may be abstraction in two ways. First, materiality may be abstracted, in which case, an abstract, three-dimensional, geometrical solid (space) remains. From such a solid, one dimension may be abstracted, leaving a two-dimensional place (a geometrical surface); from that place, another dimension may be abstracted, leaving a one-dimensional place (geometrical line); and from that place the one dimension may be abstracted, leaving a dimensionless, unextended (geometrical) point. Such solids (space), surfaces, lines, and points, lack materiality and are abstract; but they are all extended, except the points. On the other hand, beginning with body, there may be abstraction in another way. Without abstracting materiality, one of the three dimensions of the body may be abstracted, leaving a two-dimensional, material figure (a material surface). Such a figure has the characteristic, materiality; but it is abstract, since it never exists except as body, that is, in conjunction with a third dimension. Again, another dimension may be abstracted, leaving a one-dimensional, material figure (a material line). Such a figure has the characteristic, materiality, but it is abstract, since it never exists except as body, that is, in conjunction with a second and a third dimension. Again, the third and last dimension may be abstracted, leaving a dimensionless, material figure (a material point). Such a figure has the characteristic, materiality, but it is abstract, since it never exists except as body, that is, in conjunction with extension in three dimensions. All three of these abstract figures are material, and only the last (a material point) is not extended.

Summing up, there are eight different kinds of things, only the first of which is concrete, the rest being abstractions. (1) A body which is a subject with three-dimensional materiality; (2) a three-dimensional (geometrical) solid without materiality, which is space; (3) a two-dimensional, material figure, a material surface; (4) a two-dimensional figure without materiality (a geometrical surface); (5) a one-dimensional, material figure, a material line; (6) a one-dimensional figure without materiality (a geometrical line); (7) a dimensionless, material figure (a material point); and (8) a dimensionless figure without materiality (a geometrical point). A body is material and is spatial (extended in three dimensions). In the light of these distinctions, Leibniz could hold consistently that there is no subject except monads which lacks extension and yet admit that some things which lack extension (material points) are material.

There is an assumption underlying this theory of the nature of a body. The qualities of body are not different in kind, and any one of them may be abstracted in the same way that the others are abstracted. Extension may be abstracted from body, and what remains is admittedly abstract, namely, materiality. Similarly, materiality may be abstracted from body, and what remains is likewise abstract, namely, three-dimensionally diffused place (space). Leibniz clearly holds that materiality and extension never exist apart. Extension is the diffusion of materiality. But he overlooks a possible difference in kind between an abstract, material point, that is, body with extension abstracted; and an abstract place, that is, body with materiality abstracted, or (except in the case of a geometrical point) extension treated as existing without something extended. He overlooks the possibility that the abstracting of materiality from body might be different in kind from the abstracting of extension from it.

§ 4

IN HIS Controversy with Clarke, Leibniz discarded all of these accounts of space, except the one that space is an order of coexistences[32] and proceeded to formulate this view along objective and subjective lines.[33] Space is metaphysically unreal; it is abstract, not as three-dimensionally extended place, or universal (fictitious) place, or a subjectively feigned order, but as an order of situation. He did not mean that the mind has imagined or feigned anything. There are existing bodies (phenomena) with actual properties and relations. These are all concrete rather than abstract. There is a set of not merely possible, but actual, relations. He made two assumptions: A body changes its relation to a number of others. The others do not change their relations to each other. It is not that the observing mind assumes or feigns changes of relation between the first and the others. It is not that the observing mind assumes or feigns a fixity of relation between the others. Place is the name which we give to the relation which one had to a set of others, and which a new one assumes with reference to that same set. But we have named a relation which is genuine, and not one which we have feigned or read into the pattern of bodies. Motion is the name which we give to the change in the relations of one body to the others. Again we have named a change which is genuine, and not one which we have feigned or read into the body. If more than one should alter their relation of situation to

---

[32] Leibniz, Paper III, § 5; Paper IV, § 41; Paper IV, P.S.

[33] Leibniz, Paper V, § 47: "Voicy comment les hommes viennent à se former la notion de *l'Espace*. Ils considèrent que plusieurs choses existent à la fois, & ils y trouvent un certain *ordre* de coexistence, suivant lequel le rapport des uns & des autres est plus ou moins simple. C'est leur *Situation* ou distance."

others according to laws of motion, the relation of situation of each one to every other one may be determined. Such a determination is not a subjective alteration by the mind. Place is abstract because it includes possible as well as actual relations of one body to a set of others. It is not subjective in the sense of being something imposed by the observing mind, but is an objective determinant of bodies (phenomena). Relations possible and actual are objective conditions of the various bodies in question, and not merely assumed to be in them by the observing mind. Admittedly these relations are not in substances, as such, but with reference to phenomena they are real.

Leibniz shifted his position, however, and proceeded to describe places as feigned identities of relations.[34] Instead of holding that all the bodies (phenomena) save a few have remained fixed, he held that the mind merely assumes this to be the case. Instead of holding that place is the actual relation of situation which first one and then another body has with reference to a group, he held that these relations are feigned by the mind to be the same and are named the place first of the one and then of the other. He directly contradicted himself. In the first view, place is a relation between bodies, observed by the mind and not feigned by it. A set of fixed bodies is observed, not feigned. A change of one body with reference to them is observed, not feigned. A change of more than one body with reference to them is observed, not feigned. All their changes are observed, not feigned. Even changes which do not occur are possible, not feigned, changes. In his second view, place is a feigned identity of the relations of situation between bodies. It is feigned that a set of bodies remains fixed, and if this fixity is feigned, any relation of one body to such a set of fixed bodies must also be feigned. Place (in its generalized form, space) is not merely metaphysically unreal, and an abstract order, but also subjective. It is not a condition (even abstract) of the objective nature of phenomena, but a subjective condition imposed by

[34] *Ibid.:* "Et supposant ou feignant que parmy ces coexistens il y ait un nombre suffisant de quelques uns, qui n'ayent point eu de changement en eux; on dira que ceux qui ont un rapport à ces existens fixes, tel que d'autres avoient auparavant à eux, ont eu la même *place* que ces derniers avoient eue. Et ce qui comprend toutes ces places, est appellé *Espace.*"

the observing mind. The places (and hence spaces) first of body A and then of body B with reference to C, D, E, etc. are feigned to be identical; their respective relations of situation to C, D, E, etc., are never identical but are merely in agreement.[35] The mind, overlooking this mere agreement, reads into the picture an identity. Place (and space) is not the two agreeing relations of situation but is merely the feigned identity between them. This view is out of harmony with all of Leibniz's previous theories of space.

Why are the relations of situation merely in agreement? Why do the actual relations of bodies merely agree and never become identical? Why are relations of situation never places or spaces? Why does the mind never apprehend place as a feature of the structure of nature, even considered as phenomena, but merely read place into nature? Possibly in the heat of his debate with Clarke, Leibniz forgot that the bodies between which there are relations of situation are in his own more considered opinion, not substances but phenomena. As such they have no genuine inner constitution which must be different in each one of them, for actually they consist of precisely those qualities—motion, place, time, etc.— which may be considered identical in several. Forgetting that he was considering relations of situation not between substances, but merely between phenomena, he proceeded to apply his doctrine of substance to them. Every substance is the source of all its determinations. All these determinations are inner, and no two substances have identical qualities. Consequently, it is, of course, impossible that one substance could take over the relation of another to a third. This inability is due, however, not to the fact that relations of situation can merely be in agreement but to the nature of substance *per se,* and to the fact that relations of situation refer never to substances but to phenomena. Forgetting these distinctions, Leibniz proceeded to hold that a body, *qua* phenomenon, is the source of all of its determinations. If first body A and then body B is next to C, the characteristic "next to" is, in each case,

[35] *Ibid.:* "Et il est bon icy de considerer la différence entre la Place, & entre le rapport de Situation qui est dans le Corps qui occupe la place. Car la place d'A & de B est la même; au lieu que le rapport d'A aux corps fixes, n'est pas precisement & individuellement le même que le rapport que B (qui prendra sa place) aura aux mêmes fixes; & ils conviennent seulement."

an inner quality of each. A, in being next to C, possesses a different characteristic from the one possessed by B in being next to C. Precisely what the quality of A is can be determined only by treating A in a wider context, namely, in relation to other bodies, D, E, F, etc., and eventually in relation to the whole universe. Yet the characteristic "next to" as well as all of A's qualities, although capable of clarification only by a consideration of bodies other than A, is, nevertheless, an inner characteristic of A. The same condition obtains in the case of the qualities of B. Hence, if first A and then B is treated as next to C, D, E, etc., it is clear that the two relations can never be identical but merely in agreement. Consequently, identity of situation or relation is outside things, and even with reference to phenomena, such identity is feigned by the mind,[36] and named place or space. Space is not a relation of situation, but a distortion by the mind of relations of situation as they are. It is not merely an abstract order, but subjective and arbitrary.

This shift in Leibniz's account of space is due to his mistaken application of his principles concerning the nature of substance to bodies, which, in his own theory, are phenomena, and have no "inner" nature. As realities, substances have relations of situation as little as they have places or spaces. Motion, rest, place, and time are extrinsic to them. Yet as phenomena they possess these features, not because any of them are feigned by the mind, but because they are discovered as objective features of a mechanical universe. In such a universe there may be identities of relations of situation precisely because such identities, as well as motion and rest, are not genuine features of related substances but aspects of objects of an entirely different sort, objects whose very nature consists in such identities and differences. Leibniz's more considered account of the nature of phenomena finds a marked parallel in the present-day view of Whitehead, while his lapse into subjectivism and his denial of identities of situation finds its modern counterpart in the views of Poincaré.[37]

---

[36] *Ibid.:* "Mais l'esprit non content de la convenance, cherche une identité, une chose qui soit veritablement la même, & la conçoit comme hors de ces sujets; & c'est ce qu'on appelle icy *place* & *Espace.* Cependant cela ne sauroit être qu'ideal, contenant un certain *ordre* où l'esprit conçoit l'application des rapports. . . ."

[37] Cf. below, pp. 246–50.

CHAPTER IV

NEWTON vs. LEIBNIZ ON PERCEPTION

§ 1

THERE ARE three general problems involved in an examination of sense perception: the problem of the nature of the object of perception; the problem of the nature of the act or process; the problem of the nature of the perceiver or perceiving subject. A philosophy of space has important connections with each of these questions, but more directly with the first. The nature of the object perceived, its status as metaphysically real or ideal, phenomenal or subjective, hinges upon its relation to space, and the nature of space as metaphysically real or ideal can be fully worked out only by an examination of the nature of the objects of perception. Furthermore, the doctrines of space of Newton and Leibniz can be understood only by tracing their theories of the nature of perception.

Newton, as we have found, formulated doctrines of space chiefly as a basis for his application of mathematical principles to nature in calculating the motions of bodies. His departure from this strict procedure in the *Principles* was found in certain Scholia, of which one was appended in the second edition (1713). But in the *Principles,* and to an even greater extent in the *Optics,* he acknowledged the dependence of all scientific method upon the data of sensation and upon the assumption of the uniformity of nature. He held that sensation shows us that all bodies are extended, hard, impenetrable, movable, and inert.[1] It does so by putting us in contact not with all bodies whatsoever, but merely with some. He held that all bodies have these qualities because nature must be assumed to be simple and uniform. Far from this being an unjustified hypothesis at variance with the inductive method, it is, he held, the very basis of the operation of that method. Upon this

[1] Newton, *Principles,* pp. 384–85.

assumption all philosophy is founded,[2] and by philosophy in this sense Newton meant physics. Consequently, all mechanics rests, Newton held, upon an explicit theory of the data of sensation, the theory that all bodies are extended, hard, impenetrable, movable, and inert.

Nor did Newton halt his theory of knowledge at this point. In spite of the fact that this assumption was sufficient for his scientific investigations, he proceeded to raise the deeper, metaphysical question: what is the nature of the objects whose qualities we discover in perception? He held that we do not know what the real substance of anything is.[3] He went on, in explaining what we know of bodies, to make an important addition to the group of sense data over and above those which he had treated in his foregoing analysis of matter. Whereas in explanation of the validity of the scientific method he had mentioned only the qualities of extension, hardness, impenetrability, movability and inertia, he added, in this later analysis, figures, colors, sounds, outward surfaces, smells, and tastes. From the fact of our perception of the first set of qualities, we may infer that all bodies possess them; from the fact of our perception of the second, we may make, in Newton's opinion, no corresponding inference. In neither case can we by sensation or by inference know the nature of outward objects. To understand Newton's theory of the nature of sense data and their relation to space, we must distinguish between two questions. (1) Do processes of sense perception have as their outer termini qualities of external substances, in spite of the fact that neither those processes nor acts of inference from them yield a knowledge of *what* those substances are? (2) Does our ignorance concerning *what* substances bear the qualities perceived justify the conclusion that those qualities are images perceived by us in our sensoriums? It was because Newton failed to distinguish between these two questions that his theory of perception involves two incompatible points of view. He was able to ignore this discrepancy only by

[2] *Ibid.*

[3] *Ibid.*, p. 506: ". . . what the real substance of any thing is we know not. In bodies, we see only their figures and colours, we hear only the sounds, we touch only their outward surfaces, we smell only the smells, and taste the savours; but their inward substances are not to be known either by our senses, or by any reflex act of our minds. . . ."

arbitrarily limiting his attention to those qualities which he assumed to be found in all bodies. Such a limitation is satisfactory enough, perhaps, in an uncritical pursuance of mechanical computations, but it is in no way satisfactory in trying to understand the nature of the objects of all our perceptions and their relation to space.

The first of these two points of view in Newton's theory of perception is "realistic," that is, according to it, the objects of perception (sensible species of things) are portions of an order of external reality (things themselves) and lie in external space. The second of these points of view is "subjectivistic," that is, according to it, the objects of perception are only images of an order of external reality and lie, not in external space, but in the sensoriums of perceiving subjects. According to the first view, the processes of sense perception have as their outer termini qualities of external substances, in spite of the fact that neither those processes nor acts of inference from them yield knowledge of what those substances are. According to the second, in spite of our ignorance of the substances bearing the qualities perceived, those qualities are images perceived by us in our sensoriums. The first of these views is implied in the *Principles,* although not explicitly worked out there. The second is the view of the *Optics.*

In the *Principles,* Newton formulated neither view of perception explicitly. In our attempts to know the substance of sensible things, we are thrown back upon colors, tastes, and the like. What an object is, we know not, for we know only its sensible qualities. The fact that we do not know *what* an object is does not imply that we perceive either real objects or images. Yet Newton would seem to have meant the former. He nowhere formulated the distinction which he made in the *Optics* between sensible species of things and things themselves. He nowhere mentioned his theory (stated in the *Optics*) of a sensorium or place of perception. He nowhere denied that the place of perception is in the public space in which objects lie. He nowhere contrasted human perception with divine perception except to say that the latter is "in a manner not at all corporeal, in a manner utterly unknown to us."[4] He no-

where stated the theory of human perception by immediate presence. All of these doctrines, which are parts of his subjective view,
he worked out only in the *Optics*. The absence of these specific
subjective doctrines which he elsewhere worked out, while not
showing that he held the realistic view in the *Principles*, would
seem to imply a definite leaning in that direction.

He completed his theory of perception in the *Principles* by dealing with the problem of the nature of the perceiver and of the act
of perception. Since the perceiver is in the various organs of perception, and since these are in space, hence the perceiver, like the
objects perceived, is in space.[5] This fact is no ground for denying
a continuing personal identity during the whole of life or for
denying that the person is indivisible. Far from maintaining that
there is a special place of perception, the sensorium, Newton contended that the perceiver is in all and each of his organs of sense
and remains the same, indivisible man in them at different times.
Nothing could have been farther from his mind than the theory
that the self is in some unique way present in a special part of
the body, a sensorium, spatial or nonspatial.

Furthermore, Newton formulated a suggestive theory of sensation. There is a subtle spirit pervading all gross bodies.[6] By the
force and attraction of this spirit, the particles of bodies mutually
attract one another, sensation is excited, and bodily members move
at the command of the will, namely by the vibration of this spirit
from the organs to the brain and thence to the muscles, but we are
not yet in a position to determine by experiment the laws by
which this electric spirit operates. So far as this suggestion of the
application of scientific method to sensation is a prelude to modern
physiology it is interesting in many other connections. For us, the
question is rather, did he mean here to acount for the same phenomenon which he had previously called the presence of a perceiver to "each and all" of his organs of sense? Was he referring to
what he described in the *Optics* as the conveyance of the sensible
species of objects through the sense organs and brain to the sensorium? Was he maintaining that the spirit causing the sense
organs to operate is the same in kind as that causing the attraction

[5] *Ibid.*   [6] *Ibid.*, p. 507.

of bodies, the phenomena of light and heat? He in no way explained how the perceiver is present in the organs or how the latter operate in the act of perception. He mentioned the presence of the person in the organs of motion as well as in the organs of sense. The person, who is, in some acts, the perceiver, is present in organs of motion as well as in those of perception. It is difficult to distinguish except in degree between the various types of organs in which he is present. In perception and in the motion of the body by will, there is the passage of a spirit through the organs; in the case of acts of will, along sense organs, brain, and muscles. How, in this view, is the immaterial substance brought into contact with the objects? Did Newton propose to give an account of sensation and voluntary motion in terms of sense organs, brain, and muscles with no reference to the presence of the perceiver? Would the "accurate determination and demonstration of the laws"[7] by which the electrical spirit moves—to which Newton made no pretension—result in the perceiver dropping out? I think not. Newton admitted that the nature of gravitation is unknown, although he showed that its effects can be observed and accurately calculated. He would seem to mean that a similar, unknown "spirit" operates in perception. He probably meant that a thorough demonstration, in terms of observable phenomena, of the operations of this spirit in sensation and will would leave us as much in the dark concerning the nature of that spirit as his investigations in physics had left him concerning the nature of gravity. A complete description of the nature of the motion of an organ or muscle no less than of a planet would tell us nothing about the nature of the forces or their relation to a perceiver human or divine.[8] In the same way that gravity penetrates bodies, propelling them according to laws, and yet God's omnipresence is uninterfered with, so the spirit operating along the sense organs, brain, and muscles, according to other (undiscovered) laws would, Newton held, in no way interfere with the presence of the person (as the perceiver, willer, etc.) in each and all of the organs.

[7] *Ibid.*

[8] *Ibid.*, p. 505: "In [God] are all things contained and moved; yet neither affects the other: God suffers nothing from the motion of bodies; bodies find no resistance from the omnipresence of God."

The discovery of the laws according to which the organs of sensation and movement operate, propelled by the spirit, would in no
way detract from the immateriality of the perceiver and his presence in each one of those organs. The spirit would turn out to be
an unknown force, operating upon the organs in the same way
that that other unknown force, gravitation, operates. In neither
case is there a mechanical process.[9] We are as little able to say
that gravity is a mechanical principle as we are to say that the
spirit operating in sense organs is mechanical. In the same way
that there is no *a priori* reason for denying the possibility of an
alteration of the nature of the laws of gravitation,[10] since their
validity has been discovered *a posteriori,* so there would be none
for denying the same possibility with reference to the principle
according to which the spirit in the organs of sense operates. Unlike Leibniz's view of pre-established harmony, mind could act
upon matter.

§ 2

UNLIKE THE *Principles,* Newton's *Optics* contains an elaborate
theory of sense perception, the subjective theory that we perceive
images.

Is not the Sensory of Animals that place to which the sensitive Substance is present, and into which the sensible Species of Things are
carried through the Nerves and Brain, that there they may be perceived by their immediate presence to that Substance? [11]

The meaning of this passage hinges, in my opinion, upon the
meaning of the phrase "sensible species of things." Was this phrase
intended to mean one kind of things set over against another kind,
namely, some nonsensible species? If this is the case, then probably
Newton meant this other kind of things when he referred to
"things themselves." In this case, there are two orders of things:
the sensible, phenomenal, or unreal, in opposition to the nonsensible or real. This subjective view receives confirmation in the
passage which follows: "Of which things the Images only carried
through the Organs of Sense into our little Sensoriums, are there

---

[9] Cf. Newton, *Optics*, pp. 344–45.   [10] *Ibid.,* p. 380.   [11] *Ibid.,* pp. 344–45.

seen and beheld by that which in us perceives and thinks."[12] Here
Newton stated a purely subjective position. Only the images pene-
trate to a human sensorium. The realities are perceived only
by God. The order of genuine reality is obscured to us because only
images of that reality may pass into our ken. Whatever is the
nature of our organs of sense, when the process of the conveyance
of the sensible object into our sensoriums is completed, only an
image is there.

In one other passage, Newton made the same distinction between the species of things perceived by man and things themselves.

. . . he [God] is no more the Soul of them [bodies], than the Soul of
Man is the Soul of the Species of Things carried through the Organs
of Sense into the place of its Sensation, where it perceives them by
means of its immediate Presence, without the Intervention of any third
thing. The Organs of Sense are not for enabling the Soul to perceive
the Species of Things in its Sensorium, but only for conveying them
thither; and God has no need of such Organs, he being every where
present to the Things themselves.[13]

These passages clearly show that Newton was formulating the
subjective theory of the nature of the perceived objects. The process of perception must be carefully distinguished, he held, from
whatever processes are necessary to bring the image of the object
from the external, public space into the sensorium. Such processes
require sense organs and nerves. But the process of perception is
immediate and direct and involves the intervention of no third
thing between the perceiver and the perceived. The process of
conveying the external object into the sensorium interferes with
its nature sufficiently to change it into an image. But once the
image is in the sensorium, no assisting medium is necessary for
perception by immediate presence. Sense organs are not used to
perceive with, but merely to bring together the sensible species
of things (images) and the sensitive substance (perceiver).

Is the doctrine of perception by immediate presence compatible
with any view of perception other than a realistic one? Can a
process of perception be immediate if it involves the immediate
presence of the perceiver merely to an image and not to the object

[12] *Ibid.*, p. 345.   [13] *Ibid.*, p. 379.

itself? The only way to attempt this combination would be to maintain that the immediate presence of the sensible object has nothing to do with the nature of that object; in other words a real object or an image could, either one of them, be perceived by immediate presence to the perceiving substance. If the former is present, there is a type of perception realistic as well as immediate. If the latter is present, then there is a type of perception subjective as well as immediate. Realism would concern only the nature of the object perceived and would have no reference to the nature of the act of perception; whereas the immediacy or mediacy of perception would have nothing to do with the nature of the object, being concerned only with the nature of the act. Newton was contending that perception is immediate and subjective.

There are several possible ways in which such a subjective theory of a perceived image may be stated. First, the object out in public space before being conveyed to the sensorium is not real but an image. Secondly, the object out there is real, it remains real in passing through the organs of sense, and yet is perceived as an image by the sensitive, perceiving substance. Thirdly, the object out there is real, but the effect of its passage through the organs of sense is a transformation of it into an image. The first possibility would render superfluous Newton's statement that only the images are carried into the sensorium. If only images are out there then obviously nothing else *could* be carried into the sensorium, however accurate the sense organs might be in the act of conveyance. The second possibility obviously contradicts the meaning of the doctrine of immediate presence. For if the real object is immediately present after being conveyed into the sensorium by the organs of sense, then only that object, and not an image of it, would be perceived. To hold otherwise would make the immediate presence of the object a meaningless phrase. Newton held that the immediate presence of things themselves to God is the basis of His intimate, thorough perception of them. If those objects which are able to get into the immediate presence of a human perceiving substance should turn out to be perceived as mere images, why would not the objects which God is able to perceive thoroughly and intimately because of their immediate presence to

Him also turn out to be only images? This question is not answered by Newton's fuller description of God, which, as we shall see, turns out to contain its own difficulties. The third formulation of the subjective view is Newton's. Granted that a real object is out there, granted that immediate presence to it would involve a perception of it as real; human perception requires, nevertheless, the passage of the object through the sense organs into a limited human sensorium and the nature of that passage involves its transformation from a real object into an image.

Newton doubtless considered that the transformation of an object into an image during its passage through the sense organs to the sensorium is essential to a theory of immediate perception. Human beings lack the characteristic of omnipresence and must be somewhere when they perceive. They are not, however, in the parts of public space where objects are; hence they are not able directly to perceive such objects. Therefore, they can perceive only what is in their sensoriums, namely, images. In the *Principles,* Newton had denied only that we know the nature of objects, but he had not denied that we have perceptual contact with them. In his doctrine of images he took the further step of cutting the mind off from objects entirely. He seems to have assumed that either the doctrine of immediate perception or the doctrine of any contact with objects at all would have to be given up.

He did not realize that he might have retained a theory of perception which is realistic and also immediate with or without the theory of sensoriums. Retaining the latter theory, he might have maintained that quantitative limitation is not the same as qualitative alteration. Not all objects are conveyed to a human sensorium; not every aspect of any one object is conveyed there. In being conveyed to a sensorium, objects are not conveyed in their entirety but in part. In this way, there is an alteration (by limitation) of objects by the sense organs. Such an alteration must be admitted, but it is not incompatible with—in fact, it is an ingredient of—a realistic theory of perception. We perceive only some things and some aspects of those things. We do not perceive the other side of the moon, but this fact is no evidence that the part of the moon which we see is an image and not the moon itself. The sensible species of things would be a portion of things themselves. The theory of images leaves its proponent at once open to the question: what is the evidence that there is any unperceived object other than the perceived image? This question must be faced by any defender of the theory that there is for every percipient a sensorium or place of perception different from public space and that there is a qualitative alteration of the object in public space into an image as it passes through the organs to that sensorium. The theory of the immediate perception of the image once it is there in no way solves the difficulty.

Also, Newton did not consider the possibility of a theory of perception that is at once realistic and immediate without the doctrine of a sensorium. Assuming that the only type of alteration possible for an object on its way to the sensorium is qualitative, if there is no such thing as a sensorium, then there is no passage to one required and, hence, no alteration. It might be objected that immediate perception without a place of perception, such as a sensorium, is impossible unless the perceiving self, being nonspatial, can be nowhere. Without making this highly questionable assumption about the self, it might nonetheless be held that immediate perception is possible. The self no more needs to get through the organs to the object than the object needs to get through them to the self.

Where then is the place of perception? It is twofold, depending upon which aspect of perception is being considered. If it is asked where is the place of the perceived object, the answer is that the object has as its place whatever portion of external space it happens to occupy. That place, if you like, is the sensorium. Or, if it is asked where is the place of the perceiving subject, the answer is that the subject is in each and every organ of perception, as Newton had contended in the *Principles*. If it is asked where is the process, the answer is that to some extent the question is meaningless, for in the same sense that the perceiver and the object are somewhere, the process is probably not; but, to the extent that the question has a meaning, the process would seem to be where the object is, where the perceiver is, and in whatever portion of space between them that is necessary for the relation to be established.

But it will be asked whether such a process is immediate. Certainly it is not mediate in the sense that conceptual inference is mediate, and, moreover, it would seem to be just as immediate as an alleged contact in a portion of space (the sensorium) that is arbitrarily allowed to include an image but not an object. Such immediacy would, of course, not mean timelessness or instantaneousness. Varying lengths of time would be necessary for the process of perception to occur. To the extent that perceiving is subsequent to the conveyance of the object through the organs of sense, it is linked temporally with sets of physiological changes. To the extent that these are preceded by physical processes in space, such as the passage of a ray of light from an object, the process of perception is bound up with such physical processes in the outside world involving longer or shorter intervals of time. For example, a ray of light from a distant star may have required years to traverse the space between it and the perceiver's eye on the earth. Yet such a process, as well as the physiological one in the eye, optic nerve, etc., while a necessary antecedent of the process of perception, does not constitute that act, and the temporal length of the former in no way implies that the latter is mediate. Even though the process of perception occupies a much shorter span of time than the physical and physiological processes necessary to it, it nevertheless occupies some time. But its occupancy of this short span of time is not evidence that it is mediate, and the occupancy of a longer span of time by its antecedent conditions is also not evidence of such mediacy. Moreover, the dependence of the process of perception upon those physical and physiological conditions involving longer or shorter spans of time is no evidence that the object of perception must be an image. The difficulties which the subjectivist claims to have overcome in this connection by his contention that only images are perceived, remain, in fact, just as acute in terms of his own position. Let us grant that the length of time required to perceive an image in the brain, or any other assumed sensorium, is infinitesimal in comparison to the span of time it takes a ray of light to reach the human eye from a distant planet. The time required for the perception of such an image is, nevertheless, a portion of time. If instantaneousness or timelessness is the test of immediacy, such a process is quite as mediate as the perception of a real object in distant space. It would be quite as difficult to explain how an immaterial perceiver could perceive such an image in its sensorium as to account for the apparently weird procedure of perceiving in the present a planet as it was years ago.

The subjectivist would have to face all of the difficulties involved in the process of perception which the cautious realist is willing to admit to be there, plus the additional difficulties of explaining where the image is and how it became an image. Physical science tells us much about the objects of perception, if the realistic theory is held; it tells us nothing of the subjectivist's realm of images. Physiology tells us much about processes following upon the physical processes in the world of objects; it tells us nothing about the formation of any images. Neither science tells us what constitutes the process of perception, but both tell us much about the nature of its termini, if those termini are, as the realist holds, external objects. Granting our lack of information concerning the inward nature of external objects, physics yields much information concerning the qualities of those external bodies, if the assumption of the uniformity of nature is made. Such information is most exact in reference to those (primary) qualities which are most difficult to consider as images, and our ignorance is deepest in reference to those secondary ones, which, after experience with genuine images in mirrors, on photographic plates, etc., seem to be imagelike.

Another grave difficulty lies in Newton's subjective theory of perception. Not only does the theory jeopardize our knowledge of the external world, but, more seriously for his own position, it calls into question the doctrine of the metaphysical reality of space. If a mind perceives only images in its sensorium and if no inference can be made from these images to the nature of substances in the external world, not only is it difficult to see upon what grounds the mind could apprehend (or infer the existence of) any external things themselves, but a similar difficulty would confront it in attempting to apprehend or infer any external space whatsoever. Even if Newton did not mean to go to such lengths in the direction of subjectivism as to deny the spatial nature of the sensoriums (and I do not believe that he did), the fact that images are immediately perceived in a sensorium, spatial in nature, is no more grounds for assuming that such space extends beyond the part apprehended than for assuming that such a sensible species of things extends beyond the range of perception (in the sensorium) out into the real world. In fact, Newton's general position, particularly his theory of space, is incompatible with the subjective theory of perception which he formulated in the *Optics*. In reference to extension, hardness, impenetrability, inertia, motion, etc., he contended that we could assume all of the bodies of nature to be like the ones perceived in that they possess these primary qualities. Even the secondary qualities of smell, color, etc., he spoke of in the *Principles* as being on the objects, not on images. After all, images and qualities, however much Newton may have intended to equate them in the *Optics,* are not the same. His theory of our perception of qualities and our ignorance of the nature of substances is quite different from his theory of our perception of images. We may perceive qualities of external objects without necessarily knowing what the inner nature of those objects is, and yet such objects may be the termini of the perceptual process. The view of the *Principles* in no way squares with the theory of God's immediate presence to things themselves and our immediate presence only to their images. In the *Principles,* Newton did not mention sensoriums, human or divine. The view of the *Optics* in no way squares with the theory that we perceive qualities and merely lack a knowledge of *what* substances are. These sets of distinctions work at cross-purposes. Newton could hardly have meant that we perceive qualities of an image but that we do not even know what is the nature of the image *qua* image. If we perceive the quality "green," does this quality adhere to an unknown nature which is the image of another unknown nature, an external object? "Green" is not an image of a tree, but at best of another external, unseen green.

To combine his two sets of distinctions, Newton would have to hold that outside in public space there are unknown objects with unknown qualities. In perception, neither the objects nor the qualities, but only their images, get into human sensoriums. Such images would be correspondingly twofold: the images of the objects and the images of the qualities. These twofold images, let us assume, get through the organs into the sensorium. Once there, the images of the qualities are perceived. Are the images of the objects also perceived? If, on the one hand, they are not, they remain quite as unknown as the objects themselves. In this case, there is no evidence that anything more than the qualities of objects themselves has entered the sensorium, and the doctrine of images falls. If, on the other hand, the images of the objects are perceived in the sensorium, Newton has abandoned his contention (as stated in the *Principles*) that we know only qualities. If we know that a given sense datum is not a quality but an image, we know to that extent what its nature is. In no way can the quality-substance distinction of the *Principles* be combined with the image-object subjectivism of the *Optics*. The distinction between objects and qualities of objects is very different from that between objects and images. Images, no less than objects, have a substantial nature to which qualities adhere.

In spite of these discrepancies in Newton's theories of perception, his doctrine of a sensorium or place of perception, stripped of the subjectivistic theory of images, may be combined with the more realistic theory of the *Principles*. It may be held that human beings immediately perceive those real objects (things themselves) which have been conveyed by organs of sense to the sensorium, and yet that the nature of those objects remains unknown. The real object is present to the perceiving self in the sensorium, and yet the self does not know what the inner nature of that object is. The distinction between the substance and the qualities of objects is a portion of the realistic theory of perception, if it is held that those qualities are qualities of real objects and not of unreal images. In spite of the fact that we do not know *what* real objects are, we know *that* they are there, that is, we perceive them there and know *what* their qualities are. We perceive that they are there without knowing what they are. We know the sensible species of things by their immediate presence in the sensorium; they are conveyed to the sensorium by the sense organs. Such conveyance does not constitute the act of perception, and, in fact, is not needed in the case of God's omnipresent act of perception in his sensorium (the whole of space). Do we perceive realities? Yes, but only some of them. Do we know *what* their substance is? No; of this we are, and remain, in ignorance, as we are also in regard to the nature of gravity and the nature of the electric spirit operating in perception. Does this limitation mean that those qualities of real objects which we know are, therefore, images in the brain? No. To reduce them to images in the brain is to confuse again the fact that we perceive objects with the fact that we do not know *what* they are. To equate the qualities *that* we know with images of what we do *not* know is to be as presumptuous as to say that we know *what* substances are. To claim that we know the entity perceived to be only an image is to be as presumptuous as to maintain that we know it to be a real, external object. In terms of Kant's critical view of this question, it is as uncritical to maintain that you perceive only an appearance as it is to maintain that you perceive a thing in itself.[14] This precise distinction emerges in Newton's view. In the *Principles,* he claimed that we know only qualities and implied that we perceive the real objects of which they are qualities. He affirmed our complete lack of knowledge of the inner substance of objects. With this contention the claim that we are able to perceive only images is incompatible. In the *Optics,* he contradicted the view of the *Principles,* and held not only *that* we perceive an entity (substance and qualities) which has been conveyed to our sensoriums by the sense organs, but also that we know *what* its substance is, namely, an image.

§ 3

Just as was the case with Newton's theory of space, his theory of perception was elaborated by Samuel Clarke in the exchange of papers with Leibniz. Those papers began with a discussion of the question of whether Newton had claimed that space is God's organ or medium of perception. Newton made no such claim, Clarke contended.[15] Perception by immediate presence is inde-

---

[14] Cf. Kemp Smith, *A Commentary to Kant's 'Critique of Pure Reason,'* p. 114.
[15] Clarke, Paper I, § 3; cf. Newton's *Optics,* pp. 344–45.

pendent of any co-operating medium or organ. In the same way
that human beings perceive by immediate presence without any
interference with that act either by organs or by space, so God
perceives by immediate presence (omnipresence) without any
dependence upon space. For perception, nothing beyond the immediate presence of a perceiver (human or divine) to the perceived image or object is required. Clarke clearly worked out
Newton's subjective theory of perception.

In order to make this [view] more intelligible, he [Newton] illustrates it by a *Similitude:* That as the Mind of Man, by its immediate
Presence to the *Pictures* or *Images* of Things, form'd in the Brain by the
means of the Organs of Sensation, sees those *Pictures* as if they were
the Things themselves; so God sees *all Things,* by his immediate
Presence to them: he being actually present to the *Things themselves,*
to all Things in the Universe; as the Mind of Man is present to all
the *Pictures of Things* formed in his Brain.[16]

Clarke made two additions to, if not changes in, Newton's theory.
First, he made the brain the place of human perception. Secondly,
he made the sense organs the means of the formation of the images
or pictures in the brain. Newton, as we have found, alternated
between the theory that a self is in each and every organ of sense
and the theory that organs play solely a conveying role, bringing
images into the sensorium. Clarke was expounding the latter view.
In that view, however, Newton nowhere held that the sensorium
is the brain. Again, whereas in that view, Newton held that an
object, in passing through the organs, is qualitatively altered, he
did not hold that such alteration occurs in the brain or that images
are formed by sense organs. The function of the organs is, according to Newton, that of conveyance and not of formation. Since
objects are altered into images in the passage through the sense
organs, it might be held that those organs are, in a fashion, organs
of formation. But with reference to the objects they would seem
rather to be organs of deformation. Clarke[17] distinguished between the process of forming images or pictures and the act of
perceiving them once they are formed. The brain and the sense
organs assist in the first process, but they play no role in the sec-

[16] Clarke, *loc. cit.*   [17] *Ibid.*

ond. The act of perception is different from, and set over against, such a formative activity. Perception occurs by immediate presence in spite of the fact that the entities perceived (in the case of human perception) are images or pictures. There are two distinct processes in different intervals of time: first, the transformation of things themselves into images by the organs and the brain; secondly, the act of perception unimpeded by, and unconnected with, such transformation. Like Newton, Clarke failed to consider the possibility that a realistic theory of perception might be built upon the same distinction. In the first process, realistically interpreted, there would be the conveyance of the sensible species of things, one portion of things themselves, through the sense organs; in the second, the act of perception would have those objects as its termini and would itself be unimpeded by, and unconnected with, the process of conveyance.

Clarke's[18] more significant elaboration of Newton's view concerned the nature of divine perception. As in the case of human perception, space, the place of divine perception, is a medium which does not interfere in the formation (by God) of the things themselves or in His act of perceiving them. God (in his creative act) forms things themselves; human sense organs form the images perceived by men: space interferes in neither case. Human minds are present to images in their sensoriums without space interfering with their act of immediate perception; God is present to all things themselves without space interfering with divine perception.

There is a grave difficulty in Clarke's account of divine perception. If men by limitation see pictures "as if they were the things themselves," and God is present to all things themselves, is God present only to things themselves? If images or pictures constitute a class whose denotation lies entirely outside of the denotation of things themselves, is God present only to the latter, and does this fact constitute a lack in His nature, perhaps even a denial of His omnipresence? If we perceive images or pictures in our brains, does God perceive these images or not? If He does not, is He omnipresent? If He does, is He not as dependent as we are, upon

[18] *Ibid.*

the sense organs which aid in conveying, if not in forming those images? If God is present no less to the images than to objects, can He apprehend the former except as human beings do? Things themselves are things unaltered by sense organs. Images are entities altered or formed by sense organs. If God perceives images, He perceives things altered or formed by sense organs. Such alteration or formation would have to be either by sense organs of His own or by organs of human beings. In either case, He, no less than human perceivers, would require, in some cases of perception, organs for forming images: which is precisely what Clarke and Newton deny. Therefore, if the distinction between objects and images is made, either God is not omnipresent or He is dependent on sense organs for some of these perceptions. Neither Newton nor Clarke considered this difficulty.

Newton maintained, furthermore, in the *Optics,* that God is "in infinite Space, as it were in his Sensory."[19] Clarke altered this doctrine in two ways. He admitted that Newton meant that God "perceives all Things by his immediate Presence to them, in all Space wherever they are. . . ." God is present, both he and Newton claimed, in infinite space. In his first alteration, he laid a stress upon the meaning of the term *"as it were."* Newton meant by this term, Clarke claimed, that God is "actually present to the *Things themselves,* to all Things in the Universe; as the Mind of Man is present to all the Pictures of Things formed in his Brain."[20] Again: "And this *Similitude* is all that he [Newton] means, when he supposes Infinite Space to be (*as it were*) the *Sensorium* of the Omnipresent Being." Again: "Sir *Isaac Newton* does not say, that *Space* is the Sensory; but that it is, by way of Similitude only, *as it were* the Sensory."[21] Clarke's first interpretation consists in admitting that God is in space and that God has a sensorium, but claiming that space is not literally but figuratively such a sensorium. Space is God's sensorium in a way similar to the way that we, as human perceivers, have such places of perception. This interpretation of Newton's meaning is a possible one. Possibly Newton meant that space is only figuratively and not literally God's sensorium. It seems quite as probable, however, that Newton meant

[19] Newton, *Optics,* p. 345.   [20] Clarke, Paper I, § 3.   [21] Clarke, Paper II, § 3.

what Leibniz took him to mean, namely, that space is literally God's sensorium, and parts of space are literally our human sensoriums. In any event, Newton meant that God is literally in space.

Clarke went on, however, to work out another interpretation of Newton.

God does not exist *In* Space and *In* Time; but *His Existence causes Space and Time.* And when, according to the *Analogy* of *vulgar Speech,* we say that he exists *in All Space* and *in All Time;* the Words mean only that he is *Omnipresent* and *Eternal,* that is, that *Boundless Space and Time* are necessary *Consequences* of his Existence; and not, that Space and Time are Beings distinct from him, and *in which* he exists.[22]

Here Clarke departed from both views of Newton. He held neither that God exists literally in space which is literally His sensorium nor that He exists literally in space which is figuratively His sensorium. Clarke referred to the opinion of those who claim that God is literally in space as the opinion of vulgar speech. Without realizing it he called Newton's position,[23] including his own first interpretation of it, the view of vulgar speech. He no longer maintained that space is figuratively the sensorium of God but held it to be only figuratively where God is. Literally, space is caused by God or is a consequence of God. God is not omnipresent in the sense of being everywhere in space; He is everywhere only in the sense that his creation is everywhere.

§ 4

WHEREAS NEWTON's theories of perception, even with Clarke's elaboration of them, involve an account of the nature of objects without shifting the center of emphasis entirely from man to God, it is otherwise in Leibniz's views. His philosophy of nature is a definite outcome of the wider principles involved in his metaphysics of monads; his theory of perception is definitely an appendage to his account of the nature of thought and creation. The seeming passivity of perception is, for him, merely an apparent

[22] Clarke, Paper V, § 45.
[23] Newton, *Principles*, p. 505: "Since every particle of space is *always,* and every indivisible moment of duration is *every where,* certainly the Maker and Lord of all things cannot be *never* and *no where.*"

eddy in the stream of creative activity or expression and the "objects" of such a process are phenomena. This view can best be explained by an analogy. In perceiving objects, human beings usually seem to be confronted with a set of "hard" ready-made materials which they have not themselves created. But the artist takes a very different, and, according to Leibniz, a truer, view. The sculptor views a piece of marble, not as something unalterably given, but as material for the creation of a statue according to principles worked out by him. His perception of the marble as something given is by far the least significant feature of his activity. He proceeds to shape it in a certain way and the statue results. Similarly, all apprehension of the external world involves actually a kind of shaping of it by the human mind, and for God, as an absolute creator, the apprehension of anything as given drops out completely and the entire process is one of creative effort. Human apprehension of the external world contains to some extent this creative, rather than perceptive, attitude, and upon examination, what remains of the latter can be reduced to the former. Perception and its objects must be treated, therefore, as not differing in kind from the processes of thought and creation and their moulded objects. The human mind is the sculptor of the world, and God is the perfect artist.

Our task is not to appraise Leibniz's account of substances as active spiritual force or even to evaluate his reduction of perception to a sort of active, self-expressive thought, but rather to consider his account of the "objects" of perception within the realm of phenomena. If perception is in the last analysis identical with thought and will, does it, nevertheless, in any sense involve a contact of the mind with features of objects as phenomena? Does a monad which mirrors the universe most clearly by means of its own conceptual thought also mirror in its perceptual processes any features of that universe as phenomena? Does a monad which has no windows towards the universe yet have windows towards phenomena—windows through which the thought of the monad can pierce in the weakened form of a perceptive gaze? Depending upon the answer to these questions, Leibniz's view of perception will turn out to be realistic or subjective.

For a realistic account of perception several features of Leibniz's view militate: his attack upon Newton's distinction between images and realities; his rejection of the theory of a sensorium; and his refusal to draw any distinction in kind between perception and the simpler processes of sensation and appetition. Furthermore, in spite of his ontological distinction between monads and phenomena, he does not distinguish, within the realm of phenomena, between things themselves and a sensible species of things or between primary and secondary qualities. The whiteness of milk is not different in kind from its extension. Again, except in his subjective theory of space, which is out of harmony with his other views, his contention that space is abstract, whether as a quality or an order, cannot be considered as evidence of subjectivism. While space is not a real, concrete feature of phenomena, extension is, and whiteness is. Indeed, the ultimate reducibility of the entire realm of phenomena to a metaphysically unreal status is no evidence that, within its own limits, it does not have a genuine, nonsubjective, existential status, and its primary and secondary qualities may be said to share in this status. Such epistemological realism would be representational, for thought not only enters into and determines the perceptual process but in the last analysis swallows it up.

The clue to his theory of perception lies, however, in his description of thought: "Les âmes connoissent les choses, parce que Dieu a mis en elles un *Principe Representatif* de ce qui est hors d'elles."[24] In each monad there is a principle representative of things outside. The process by which a mind knows those things is not perception, in the usual sense of the term, for the process is indirect or representational, and it is active rather than passive. If we remember that Leibniz was describing all processes of knowledge, including the less "clear," perceptual type, we are justified, nevertheless, in considering his description as covering perception. The only genuine knowing process, he means, reduces without remainder to active thought, but such a process, inadequately examined, involves in some cases a representation of "something" in terms of "something else" according to a certain principle. This

---

[24] Leibniz, *A Collection of Papers with Clarke*, Paper IV, § 30.

process, apart from Leibniz's reduction of it to creativity and thought, is perception. Does his view explain it or explain it away? He continued:

Elles [the souls] sentent ce qui se passe *hors* d'elles, par ce qui se passe *en* elles, repondant aux choses de dehors; en vertu de *l'harmonie* que Dieu a préétablie . . . qui fait que *chaque substance simple* . . . est . . . une *concentration* & un *miroir vivant de tout l'Univers* suivant *son point de veue*.[25]

Leibniz's description must be tested in two ways, first admitting, and secondly denying, his contention that perception is reducible to thought. If this contention is admitted, there are in the total situation: (1) the knowing monad; (2) the known object; (3) the knowing relation between the two according to (4) a principle in the monad representative of the object in such a way that the monad actively mirrors the object (as well as the rest of the universe) according to its own point of view; and finally (5) the wider principle of pre-established harmony, of which the principle in this monad is a special aspect. The principle of pre-established harmony is the sole guarantee that the mind knows an object outside itself; which, in effect, begs the .question. The mind knows an object merely because it knows it. Consequently, even admitting the highly questionable assumption that there is nothing unique in perception, even admitting that it can be treated as a less "clear" case of active thought, Leibniz's account of the relation of the mind to the external world involves a *petitio principii* of the most obvious sort. If no such admission is made, the situation is even more precarious. As a description of the perceptual process, the total situation would involve: (1) the perceiving monad; (2) the perceived object; (3) the perceptual relation between the two according to (4) the same representative principle, resting in turn upon (5) the same principle of pre-established harmony. In such a case, the question immediately arises: in terms of what is the object represented according to the principle in the mind? Leibniz has confused the principle *according to which* the object is represented, and the "something" *in terms of which* it is represented. If X is represented as Y according to principle Z,

[25] Leibniz, Paper V, § 87.

then Y and Z are very different.[26] In such a representation, the "something," Y, representing the object, X, is itself either in the mind or in nature (phenomena). If the entire process is one of thought, there is no difficulty involved, for the "something," Y, is merely a conception, perhaps a symbol. It is in the mind in the same sense as the principle according to which it represents the object. But if the total situation is described in perceptual terms, the representation, Y, must be something more than a conception and, therefore, must be either in the mind or outside. If, however, it is inside, Leibniz thereby falls into the same error for which he criticized Clarke and Newton, for he thus sets up a realm of ideas, images, or copies. If, on the other hand, it is outside, it is entirely superfluous, since objects could themselves be equally well given to the mind, and it (the Y) would not be required to represent them. Since Leibniz can hardly be considered to have meant this last alternative, his view reduces to subjectivism. If his view is not considered as explaining perception entirely in terms of thought, that is, as explaining it away, the necessary outcome of his contentions is that some sort of images, copies, or ideas are in the mind, as Newton and Clarke held. Moreover, Leibniz's words suggest precisely this result. The mind does not think of a symbol or label, which represents the object (according to the principle). Something "occurs" inside corresponding to what is outside. Something "se passe en elles." The narrower principle in the monad and the wider principle of pre-established harmony merely guarantee a conformity of what occurs inside (idea or image) with what occurs without (object). As a theory of representative conception, this view rests solely upon the assumption of a pre-established harmony; as a theory of representative perception it has a similarly weak basis, and involves, in addition, an inner realm of "given" images or ideas, quite as difficult to account for or to relate to the outer world, as those of Clarke. In the one case,

---

[26] Cf. Cunningham, "Meaning, Reference, and Significance," in *The Philosophical Review*, Vol. XLVII, No. 2, p. 162. Mr. Cunningham distinguishes between (1) the knowing mind, (2) the referend, "something which is said to refer," and (3) the referent, "something which is said to be referred to." In these terms, Leibniz may be said to ignore the referend. But if the mind represents the object (referent), a referend is implied.

perception is not explained but explained away; in the other, it
is explained in subjective terms.

In spite of the fact that Leibniz's theory of perception, to the
extent that he has one, reduces to subjectivism, it might be made
the basis for a representational realism. If the principle in the
monad is considered to guarantee a representative relation between what is within and what without not in an absolute, but
merely in a functional, sense, the same distinction results which
the critical realists have brought to the fore.[27] There is no inner
realm of "ideas" or images of objects but merely a distinction between the content and the object of perception. Leibniz's attack
upon Newton's doctrine of images re-enforces this result. The
mind perceives the objects, but only in terms of contents. The
guarantee that such objects are known rests not upon the nature
of what is immediately given but upon inference. Such inference
would be in terms of the sort of principle that Leibniz had in
mind. The chief difficulty in this view lies likewise in the problem
of the precise ontological status of the contents. If they are a part
of the object, then the object is known immediately and not indirectly by inference. If they are in the mind, what is the evidence
that anything outside of the mind is known at all? Is such evidence
sufficiently strong to answer the subjectivist's claim that from such
contents it is as difficult or impossible to infer the existence of an
external object, as to make the same inference from given "ideas."
If the contents are neutral, being both inside and outside, is the
view representational at all? Merely to make some principle the
basis of such inference is perhaps no less unsatisfactory than Leibniz's theory of pre-established harmony. Even if such a view could
be satisfactorily worked out, it would differ from Leibniz's views
in its attempt to treat perception "on its own feet" rather than
as reducible to active thought.

[27] Pratt, *Personal Realism*, Chapter XIV.

CHAPTER V

KANT ON SPACE AND SUBSTANCE: HIS EARLIER VIEWS

§ 1

WE CAN NOW turn to Kant's first published work,[1] and begin to collect the various threads of thought of his predecessors as they were united and altered by him. At the outset he stated that the common-sense view, as well as the view of all philosophers except Aristotle, the Schoolmen, and Leibniz, was that a body in motion has force, while a body at rest does not. Kant held that, in spite of the teachings of Aristotle and his followers, Leibniz was the first to set up the doctrine that "in body there inheres a force which is essential to it and which indeed belongs to it prior to its extension."

Kant went on[2] to attack Leibniz's followers (he mentioned no names) for attempting to define active force as a moving force because it generates only motions. In his *Specimen Dynamicorum*,[3] Leibniz had distinguished between active and passive primitive forces as the two aspects of substances. Substance is formed of primitive force and primary matter, but moving bodies are quite differently formed, and this distinction concerns solely the nature of substance. After turning from the metaphysical portion of his theory, Leibniz discussed, in the same paper, the problem of the computation of motion and the various types of forces involved. In this discussion, he set up the quite different distinction[4] between living and dead forces. Whereas active and passive forces refer to substances as such, living and dead forces refer

[1] Kant, *Thoughts on the True Estimation of Living Forces*, selected passages in Kant, *Inaugural Dissertation and Early Writings on Space*, translated by Handyside, pp. 3–15.
[2] *Ibid.*, pp. 4–5.
[3] Leibniz, *New Essays Concerning Human Understanding*, edited by Langley, p. 672.
[4] *Ibid.*, p. 674.

solely to phenomena. His example was a ball in a glass tube which is whirled around the end in which the ball lies. He pointed out that as the ball begins to move towards the other end propelled by its own centrifugal force, it is dead, while after it has begun to move, it is living. This distinction is not to be confused, he held, with the difference between primitive active and primitive passive force. Primitive active force was impressed upon substances at the creation and never manifests itself in its pure form in phenomena (the ball in the whirling tube). Primary matter (primitive passive force) was similarly impressed upon substances at the creation and likewise never manifests itself in its pure form in phenomena. The primitive active forces of groups of substances manifest themselves in phenomena always as derivative active forces; while in phenomena primary matter always appears as clothed or secondary matter, involving motion, space, and time. The increase of derivative forces in one group of phenomena and the corresponding decrease in another is motion, viewed from the point of view of the one group or the other. The force involved in an aggregate prior to its motion is called a dead force, although from a metaphysical point of view it is, even then, formed of substances active in nature. The force involved in the aggregate during its motion is called a living force, although from a metaphysical point of view it continues to be formed of the same substances active in nature. In other words, the active force for which Leibniz contended, is a conception different from, yet underlying, the distinctions between living and dead forces formulated solely with reference to moving phenomena. The active forces of which substances are composed have, as such, nothing to do with the distinction between living (moving) and dead forces.

Kant was quite justified in protesting against any confusion of these distinctions. He did not realize that Leibniz, himself, in later papers, fell into the same confusion. Instead of retaining his doctrine of substance as a reality implicit in, yet more fundamental than, the phenomenon of motion, Leibniz, in his paper *On Nature in Itself,*[5] and his *Letter to Wagner,*[6] worked out his doctrine of an

---

[5] *The Philosophical Works of Leibniz,* edited by Duncan, pp. 119–134; esp. p. 128.
[6] *Ibid.,* p. 279.

active force as a theory of mechanics. He no longer claimed that active force with primary matter completes substance but held that it completes the phenomena (secondary matter) which move. Therefore, Kant would have been justified in accusing Leibniz (as well as his followers) of departing from his strictly metaphysical teachings and bringing the conception of active force rather than moving (living) force into his discussion of mechanics.

In 1747 Kant combined the Leibnizian theory of substance with a theory of interaction between mind and matter—instead of the theory of pre-established harmony as its author had done. He did not, however, hold that there are moving forces. To describe the cause of motion as due to a moving force is, he held, to resort to the same kind of artifice as did the Schoolmen, "who in their inquiry into the grounds of heat and cold took refuge in a *vis calorifica aut frigifaciens*."[7] The fact that motion is the only observable manifestation of active force is no ground for holding that an active force is a moving force. The fact that dead force or secondary matter is the only observable manifestation of passive force or primary matter is, likewise, no ground for holding that a passive force or primary matter is a dead force or secondary matter.

Proceeding to follow out Leibniz's own earlier hypothesis in regard to primitive active force, he set up a new account of motion.

A body to which an infinitely small opposition is made, and one which therefore hardly acts at all, has motion in an especial degree. The motion is only the external phenomenon of the state of the body; for the body is not here acting, and yet is striving to act. If, however, through [meeting] an object, it loses its motion suddenly—that is, in the moment in which it is brought to rest—it is then active.[8]

A body should not be considered as initially at rest and then beginning to move, but initially moving and suddenly brought to rest. According to Leibniz, a body in motion has a living force. According to Kant, on the other hand, a moving body to which no resistance is being made is not acting at all. If there is a very small resistance being made to its motion, it is acting only to a very

[7] Kant, *Inaugural Dissertation and Early Writings on Space,* translated by Handyside, p. 5.
[8] *Ibid.*

small degree. It begins to act when, suddenly meeting another resisting body, it is brought to rest. At the moment in which it is brought to rest it is active but not so long as it is moving in an unimpeded way.

Let us return to Leibniz's own example of the ball in the tube. Let us assume that the far end of the whirling tube is sealed. When the body is moving in an unimpeded fashion along the tube, it would be, in Leibniz's terms, endowed with a living, in opposition to a dead, force. While so moving, it would not, however, in Kant's opinion, be acting. Upon striking the end of the tube and being blocked and suddenly brought to rest, it would at that moment be acting and only then, although at that moment it would be losing, instead of gaining, motion. Kant meant that, far from the nature of an active force being discoverable in a resting body which is trying to move and then begins to move—in other words in a body whose dead force is becoming a living force—precisely the opposite is the case. An active body is one which acts in losing the motion which it possesses.[9]

Leibniz's examples to illustrate the difference between a force which is trying to act and one which has passed over into action (motion) were a weight hanging on a thread and a taut bow. The weight, he held, is trying to fall; the bow is trying to move. Kant claimed that the procedure must be reversed. We would have to consider the weight as it is falling and the bow as it is passing from its taut position to the loose one. We must not consider, he said, a sphere resting on a table as trying to fall. In all of these examples, an active force expresses itself not in the passing over of the body from a condition of straining rest to one of motion, but from one of unrestrained motion to rest. The weight falling would not be acting during its fall; only in the process of being impeded would it be active. The bow in motion after its release would not be active. It would be active at the moment of its being

[9] *Ibid.*: "We should not, therefore, take our title for the force of a substance from that which is not an action; and still less should we say of the bodies which act while they are at rest (e.g. a sphere which through its weight presses upon the table on which it lies) that they strive to move. For since in moving they would not be active, we should have to maintain that in so far as a body is active it strives to fall into the state in which it does not act. Accordingly *vis activa* is a much more appropriate title for the force of a body than *vis motrix*."

impeded and ceasing to move. Active force expresses itself in the passing over into rest. For this reason the expression "moving force" is highly inaccurate, and active force is something different. What Leibniz called a living force, that is, the force in a moving body, is not an active force. What he called a dead force is not one trying to become living by moving. A living force is not active until it is impeded, at which moment it tries to become dead. A dead force is not trying to become active but becomes active only to the extent that it is merely relatively dead (relatively at rest). With respect to a wider group of phenomena it is still moving and can, by other phenomena, be brought to a more absolute (less relative) state of rest. In other words, even after the ball in the tube has been brought to rest at the end of the tube and has acted at that moment, it would still be moving as a portion of the whirling tube, and, as a part of the tube, it would act still further in being brought to rest with reference to the earth.

Kant held that in being brought to rest the body is active, meaning that the active force is within the body. But he implied that an external impediment is requisite to such action. He did not hold that matter is inert: force cannot be reduced to motion, nor is motion the result of forces operating upon a body from without by attraction and repulsion. He retained the idea of active force in a body, but he made an external impediment the sole occasion of its operation. Newton held that a body at rest remains at rest until acted upon by an external force, and that a body in motion in a straight line continues in that straight line until acted upon from without. Kant, like Leibniz, avoided the assumption of a complete rest, with the accompanying doctrine of an absolute space and time. He assumed, however, that a body relatively at rest acts to become less relatively at rest only upon the occasion of an external impediment. One body interacts with another by being the impediment which causes the other to act, but no body is—as Newton held to be the case—merely acted upon from without. Both Newton and Kant describe the way in which a body comes to rest (Kant to relative rest, Newton, in some cases, to absolute rest). They differ in regard to the question of whether the body itself acts in coming to rest, Kant holding the outer impediment to be the occasion of its inner action, Newton holding the body to be merely acted upon from without. Kant retained Leibniz's theory that substances consist of inner force. He maintained, however, that this force acts to bring a body to rest and not to make it move, and that the occasion of an external impediment is required.

In his reformulation of the theory of an active force, he proceeded, both in the realm of metaphysics and in that of mechanics, to speak of interaction. If there is a genuine interaction between bodies (omitting the even more difficult question of an interaction between soul and body) is the external impediment merely the occasion upon which the body itself exercises force? Either the body (as inert matter) is brought to rest, as Newton held, entirely by the action of the external body, in which case Kant's theory of the action of the body itself in coming to rest is incorrect, or, as Leibniz held, no external force acts upon a body at all. In the latter case, the action of one body is perhaps the occasion of a change of motion by another, but there is no interaction. Kant's account swayed between these two views.

He turned[10] to the problem of the action of the body upon the soul and concluded that the only hindrance to such action is removed with the rejection of the theory of a moving force. In the same way that the action of one body does not manifest itself by an increase in its motion, but only when it is impeded by another, so the effects of the body upon the soul are not manifested in the soul's motion, but in some other fashion. A similar situation obtains in reference to the influence of the soul upon the body. The effects of that influence are not manifested in the motion of the body. The chief point at issue in regard to such interaction, is the question of "whether [the soul's] essential force can be determined to an outwardly directed action, that is, whether it is capable of acting on other beings outside itself, and so of producing changes in them."[11] Kant claimed that the soul has position in space and must be capable of acting outside itself. He held also that such position refers to the mutual action of substances. Again his view was a compromise between those of Newton and Leibniz. With Newton, he held that a body or a soul may act outside itself

<hr>

[10] *Ibid.*, pp. 5–6.   [11] *Ibid.*, p. 7.

and that both of them have position in space. With Leibniz, on the other hand, he tried to avoid the conclusion that space is itself anything more than a resultant of the actions of various bodies in it. He rejected Leibniz's distinction between substances and phenomena and held that substances are in space; but he held that the nature of space is dependent upon those substances. He was arguing in a circle, claiming that the force in bodies (or in souls) lies in their outwardly directed acts. For this to occur, a body or a soul must have a position in space. Its position in space is, however, nothing but the resultant of its outwardly directed actions upon other bodies and souls, and the actions of the others upon it. Kant began by using position in space as a condition of the interaction of substances and went on to hold that such position is dependent upon the interaction.

Kant's account of the interaction between substances, whether bodies or souls, jeopardizes the theory that every substance is the source of all of its inner determinations. Yet he tried to retain this latter theory.

Matter, when set in motion, acts upon everything that is spatially connected with it, and therefore also upon the soul; that is, it changes the inner state of the soul in so far as that state stands related to what is ouside [the soul].[12]

A body has inner force, yet it interacts with other bodies. Similarly, the essential nature of the soul is inner force, yet bodies act upon it. Matter acts upon the soul, as one body blocks another; yet in both cases inner activity is called forth in the substance affected. Could Kant retain this compromise? Can there be genuine interaction and yet the nature of substances be considered to consist entirely of inner force? Can one body act upon another and the effect upon the second be reduced without remainder to active, inner changes? Can a body act upon a soul and the effect upon the soul be similarly reduced completely to such inner changes? In both cases, if the action of the affecting substance is merely the *occasion* of the changes in the substance affected, the latter may be said to be the source of all its inner determinations. But in this case, there is no interaction. If, on the other

[12] *Ibid.*

hand, the action of the first substance is the occasion for the changes in the second and also interacts with it, the second substance cannot be the source of all its inner determinations. The theories of inner force and interaction are incompatible.

Kant showed that he was aware of this difficulty. "Either substance is in a connection and relation with others outside itself or it is not."[13] Following Leibniz, he held that each substance can exist independently of all of the rest. Each of them "contains within itself the complete source of all its determinations. . . ."[14] Can there be more than one such substance? If so, can one of them have any relation to another without violating its own independent nature? Leibniz claimed to have avoided the conclusion that there is only one substance, as well as the theory of a *Deus ex machina* to co-ordinate a plurality of them, by means of his theory of pre-established harmony. Kant rejected this view. He held that position in space is the basis of interaction between substances. Therefore, according to him, all substances which have position in space mutually interact, while those which lack position contain within themselves the complete source of their determinations. Some substances would, therefore, have no position and be nowhere (in what he was going to define as the world), while others, having position, interact and are somewhere in the world. He overlooked or deliberately rejected Leibniz's distinction between substances and phenomena. Substances, according to Leibniz, have no position (even in relative space); phenomena, not being real, are not parts of the real world of substances and have position in space only as coexisting. On the other hand, Kant claimed that some substances (souls and bodies) interact and hence have position in space, while others do not interact and hence have no position in space: these are, strictly speaking, nowhere.

The necessary result of his view, Kant realized, is a limited definition of a world. "Only that which stands in an actual connection with the other things which are in the world can be reckoned as belonging to the world."[15] The world includes only those substances which interact, that is, have position. Other substances, containing the complete source of their own determinations, are

[13] *Ibid.*, p. 8.   [14] *Ibid.*   [15] *Ibid.*, p. 9.

not related to the substances in the world. Each of them having no connection with any other substances would itself be another world; while if some of them are related to others, such a group would form another world. In either case, more than one world can exist.

§ 2

FROM THIS DEFINITION of the term "world," based upon the inter-action of substances, and hence upon their position in space, Kant proceeded to discuss the nature of space:

If the substances had no force whereby they can act outside themselves, there would be no extension, and consequently no space.

It is easily proved that there would be no space and no extension, if substances had no force whereby they can act outside themselves. For without a force of this kind there is no connection, without this connection no order, and without this order no space. But it is somewhat difficult to comprehend how, from the law in accordance with which this force in substances acts outside them, the plurality of the dimensions of space follows.[16]

Here he returned to a strictly Leibnizian view of space, although he stated a different reason for it. Space is dependent upon an order. As we have found, space, according to Leibniz, is the order of coexistence of bodies. But bodies are, in his view, phenomena. Substances are not next to each other. Primary matter involves extension, but only secondary matter involves position and motion, and space. Kant, however, attributed such an order not to phenomena, but to certain substances. Substances, Leibniz held, do not interact, and there is no real connection between them. Some substances, according to Kant, interact; that is, they act outside themselves. Such action is indirectly the basis of the order which is space. Without interaction, there would be no connection between substances, and without this connection no order, and without this order no space; but space is, in the last analysis, not merely this indirect resultant of interaction; it is in some way a condition of the interaction. Can space (and position) be bound up with interacting forces without imposing upon them certain

[16] *Ibid.,* pp. 9–10.

qualities of its own nature, for example, its three-dimensionality?
If it does this, can it be maintained that some forces do not involve space? If all forces involve space, can a substance have an
active force in its nature without being in space? If space is essential to substance, is not space more than an order? Can substances
interact in a space that is merely their order? Kant did not face
all these questions, but he realized that one aspect of space could
not be readily deduced from force, namely, its three-dimensionality.

"The ground of the threefold dimension of space is still unknown."[17] Leibniz's derivation of spatial three-dimensionality
from the number of lines which can be drawn at right angles to
each other from a point involves, Kant held, circular reasoning.
The very three-dimensionality which is supposed to be proved by
such a procedure is presupposed by it. Furthermore, nothing in
the fact that certain numbers can be squared and cubed accounts
for such spatial three-dimensionality. It is true that the fourth
power of a number is the square of the square, and hence differs
in kind from the square and the cube; but

in anything representable through the imagination in spatial terms,
the fourth power is an impossibility. In geometry no square can be
multiplied by itself nor any cube by its root. The necessity of the
threefold dimension does not, therefore, rest upon the fact that in
assuming additional dimensions we should be doing nothing else but
repeat the others (as occurs in the powers of numbers), *but rather
upon a certain other necessity which I am not as yet in a position to
explain.*[18]

A line may be compared to a number, and the square of the number may be represented by a square formed upon the line; the
cube of the number may be, furthermore, represented by a cube
formed upon the line. In arithmetic this procedure may be continued by forming the fourth power, etc., of the number. In
geometry, the mind is blocked. Why? Kant replied that there are
certain conditions governing the way in which anything is representable through the imagination in spatial terms. What is the

[17] Kant, *Inaugural Dissertation and Early Writings on Space*, translated by Handyside, p. 10.
[18] *Ibid*. Italics ours.

nature of these conditions? Does the threefold nature of spatial dimensions depend upon a set of conditions mental in their origin? Does it depend merely upon the imagination? This question was beyond the scope of Kant's investigation in 1747. He held that the three-dimensionality depends: (1) not upon the number of lines which can be drawn at right angles to each other through a point; (2) not upon the kind of necessity involved in arithmetic; (3) but upon some kind of necessity, the nature of which he had not yet determined.

He did not then consider the following questions which he later treated. (1) Does the three-dimensionality of space (and its other qualities) flow from the analytical laws of thought? (2) Is it determined by induction, by the method which Newton called that of analysis? (3) If the three-dimensionality of space is apprehended by the imagination, is space necessarily three-dimensional? (4) If the nature of space can be determined only by the inductive method, is space necessarily three-dimensional? (5) If space is necessarily three-dimensional, and yet that quality is derived neither from the laws of thought nor from experience, what is its source? Kant's conclusions in 1747, in so far as they committed him to an answer to these questions, are contradictory. He concluded[19] that the three-dimensionality of space is based upon some kind of necessity, without claiming to know what it is. He proceeded,[20] however, to derive that quality from the laws governing the forces acting between substances, and, hence, in the last analysis, from observable phenomena. Any necessity which is so derived, he admitted, can not be greater than that which experience yields. "It is probable that the threefold dimension of space is due to the law according to which the forces in substances act upon one another."[21] In spite of the theory of interaction which he was formulating, he held that a substance and all its qualities must be capable of being deduced from a ground lying in the substance. Since this ground is active force, all qualities including the three-dimensionality of space are traceable to the active force in a substance. It "will be grounded in the qualities of the force which the substances possess in respect of the things with which they are

[19] *Ibid.*   [20] *Ibid.*, p. 11.   [21] *Ibid.*

connected."[22] He overlooked the conclusion which Leibniz drew from this principle, namely, that between genuine substances there can be no interaction. If the force of one substance directly affects other substances, then the principle lying in the second substance cannot be held to determine its action completely: for the principle lying in the first will do so at least partially.[23] He did not show how the law according to which substances act upon each other can be in the nature of one of the substances (as the ground of all its determinations) and, at the same time, can operate outside that substance in its action upon others. It is even more difficult to show how such an inner ground could (as the principle of action of one substance) be related to the action of another substance upon it. Interaction is possible only if the ground of the interaction lies, not exclusively in any one of the substances, but in all of the substances in the world. In this case, no part of the world could be the source of all its determinations, and none of the parts would be true substances. If there is interaction, the principles must lie in the group, in which case they will not be substances; if they are genuine substantial natures, the principles must lie in each substance and would be hence incapable of governing any interaction. In the first case, space (and its various qualities) would not be determined by the nature of substances; in the latter case, space would refer only to phenomena and not to substantial nature as such.

Assuming that a principle of interaction is involved in a collection of substances each of which retains its own nature as active force, the necessity involved in the three-dimensionality of space becomes, Kant admitted, dependent upon experience. In the last analysis, the principles of a certain type of interaction depend upon the observed tendency of bodies to act upon each other in a certain way. "The threefold dimension seems to arise from the

[22] *Ibid.*

[23] *Ibid.*: "The force, whereby a substance acts in union with others, cannot be thought apart from a determinate law which reveals itself in the mode of its action. Since the character of these laws according to which the substances act upon one another must also determine the character of the union and composition of a multiplicity of them, the law according to which a whole collection of substances (that is, a space) is measured, in other words, the dimension of the extension, will likewise be due to the laws according to which the substances by means of their essential forces seek to unite themselves."

fact that substances in the existing world so act upon one another that the strength of the action holds inversely as the square of the distances."[24] The principle of interaction from which the three-dimensionality of space seems to flow is an observed fact. In basing the nature of space upon observed phenomena, Kant adopted the Newtonian method of analysis or induction. Newton, as we have found, deduced the laws of motion simply from a wide range of empirical findings and admitted that there can be no demonstrative certainty ascribed to those laws. He assumed, however, that the elements of space and time have an absolute nature. Clarke held that God can alter the laws of motions at will. Those laws are not necessarily what they are and not otherwise; different laws may hold in distant parts of space and time. At the same time that Newton and Clarke affirmed the contingent nature of the laws of motion, they set up an absolute nature of space. The very basis for the contingency of the laws of motion is, in Newton's opinion, the eternity and fixity of the nature of space. The empirical nature of the laws of motion requires that space be eternally and necessarily what it is.

Kant reversed the order of this procedure. No absolute space forms the basis for the laws of motion. The nature of space (including its three-dimensionality) is derived from the observed nature of those laws. Kant carried Newton's inductive or analytic method one step further than Newton himself had done. From the observations of the actions of bodies upon each other, is derived both the law[25] governing that interaction, and the three-dimensionality of the space in which that action occurs. It can be readily conceived, he claimed in accord with Newton, that some other law of motion might hold, but he went on to claim, in opposition to Newton, that it is also conceivable that such other laws would involve types of space different from the kind in which the present motions occur. Forces of another sort operating between bodies would yield other (non-three-dimensional) types of space.

In consequence of [the way the threefold dimension has arisen] I hold that the substances in the existing world, of which we are a part,

[24] *Ibid.*

[25] Newton held that bodies attract each other in direct proportion to their masses and in inverse proportion to the squares of their distances.

have essential forces of such a kind that in union with one another they extend the sphere of their actions according to the inverse square of their distances; secondly, that owing to this law the whole which thence arises has the property of threefold dimension; thirdly, that this law is arbitrary, and that God could have chosen another, for instance the inverse threefold relation; and lastly, that from a different law an extension with other properties and dimensions would have arisen.[26]

The three-dimensionality which he had held in the preceding section[27] to be based on a kind of "necessity which [he was] not as yet in a position to explain," he now turns around and explicitly calls arbitrary. Substances act upon each other according to the law of the inverse square of the distance. The resulting space is three-dimensional. Since that law, however, is arbitrary and may be supplanted by another, therefore other kinds of space are possible.

In fact, Kant was not sure whether space has a necessary nature or not. He was looking for the basis of such necessity; but his deduction of the nature of space from the laws of motion led to the opposite result. Unlike Newton, he did not claim that the contingency of the laws of motion requires a fixity in the nature of space. By claiming that even the nature of space is dependent upon observed motions, he raised the possibility of different kinds of space. If there can be other kinds of space, then space possesses no necessary qualities and is determined solely by the nature of observed motions. From this view Newton had drawn back. To assure any exactitude, he held, in the application of the inductive or analytic method to nature, space must have a necessary nature. This inductive method, if carried out strictly, shows perhaps the same dependence of space and time upon particular observations as the laws themselves, but this possibility was not considered by Newton, and it was definitely precluded by Clarke. Kant raised the possibility because he did not assume a fixed nature of space independent of the nature of observed motions. His theory that all of the determinations of a group of substances must lie in the forces operating between them led him to deduce

---

[26] Kant, *Inaugural Dissertation and Early Writings on Space*, translated by Handyside, pp. 11–12.
[27] *Ibid.*, p. 10.

space from force. Since the law governing the forces is arbitrary, space has a contingent nature, in spite of Kant's previous claim to the contrary.

In arriving at the conclusion that space may have a contingent nature, and that other kinds of spaces are possible, Kant admitted that he was tentatively formulating his views and searching, at the same time, for the source of a genuine necessity in the nature of space. He was committed either to the theory that space is dependent upon the arbitrary nature of the actions of bodies upon each other or to a further search for the source of its necessity. Either there may be spaces of other sorts called into being by changes in the laws of interaction, in which case the nature of space is arbitrary, or, those laws retaining their contingent nature, there is some other source of the necessary nature of space. It was this second possibility which caused him to re-examine his theory of substance. The nature of interacting substances turns out to be dependent not upon a law lying in their natures, but upon the way that they are observed in experience to interact. The necessary nature of space can be retained either by rejecting the theory that substances interact and returning to the theory of a pre-established harmony and referring space only to phenomena; or by preserving the theory of interaction with its empirical basis and seeking the necessity of space outside the nature of substances. Following this latter alternative, Kant came some years later to accept the theory of an absolute space. Pending his investigation of the nature of the necessity of space in comparison with the necessity flowing from the laws of thought, he took the Newtonian position.[28] It was even later that he arrived at his own theory of a type of necessity differing both from that flowing from the laws of thought and from the relative certainty flowing from the generalizations involved in induction.[29] In 1747 he had groped far enough in his theory of space to realize that if the source of its three-dimensionality is the nature of active substances, then that quality is arbitrary. Perhaps, in the light of post-Kantian mathematical developments,[30] his conclusion of 1747, although strangely arrived

[28] Sometime just before 1768.   [29] About 1769.
[30] Cf. below, pp. 250–53; Broad, *Scientific Thought*, pp. 27–32.

at, is more correct than his own more developed views. Perhaps Newton ought to have concluded that the nature of space is as arbitrary as the laws of motion which he assumed to occur in an eternal, homaloidal space. Just as Newton was unable, however, to reduce the nature of space to an arbitrary status, in spite of his cautious inductive theory, so Kant, in another way, was unable to abide by his conclusions of 1747, both in reference to the nature of substance and of force, and also in regard to the possibility of other sorts of space.[31]

§ 3

WITH KANT's later views available to us, it is tempting to claim that in 1764 in his *Prize Essay*[32] he had made great advances towards them. He set out in that paper to point out the difference between the kind of truth in mathematics and in metaphysics. In the former, definitions are reached synthetically; in the latter, analytically.[33] A synthetic process is an arbitrary or random conjunction of conceptions and a rejection of the process of conceptual analysis. In the process of analysis, a conception is given, admittedly in a confused form, and is broken up by abstracting characteristics from it and comparing them with all other particular examples of the same conception. In synthesis, a conception is treated as singular, and clear results are obtained.

"[Die Aufmerksamkeit hat] nicht die Sachen in ihrer allgemeinen Vorstellung, sondern die Zeichen in ihrer einzelnen Erkenntnis, die da sinnlich ist, zu gedenken. . . ."[34] Knowledge in mathematics is singular knowledge. In that science, we do not establish general truths by proceeding inductively from a number of given instances; nor do we begin with a general principle and deduce particular facts. Some of our knowledge of Socrates is obtained by examining the relation of "a man" to "man." In induction we proceed from the common nature of individual men to

---

[31] This feature of Kant's development will be expanded below, pp. 121–26; pp. 176–78.

[32] *Untersuchung über die Deutlichkeit der Grundsätze der natürlichen Theologie und der Moral; Phil. Bib.*, Bd. 46 a.

[33] *Ibid.*, p. 118.   [34] *Ibid.*, p. 136.

establish the nature of "man." In deduction, we reverse the process and derive our knowledge of individual men from the already known nature of "man." But in experience, we know more about Socrates than those facts about him which are also facts about all men. This additional knowledge may be said to lie in Socrates as a singular conception. In 1764, Kant meant that our knowledge in mathematics is like this additional knowledge about Socrates.

Did Kant have in mind two distinctions which we know that he later worked out? Did he mean that the truths of mathematics, on the one hand, carry a kind of nonempirical necessity, in opposition to the truths of experience, while, on the other hand, they fail to conform to the conditions of conceptual analysis, and are hence synthetic? In a word, had he already discovered that mathematical truths are *a priori* and synthetic? This account of Kant's thinking seems so plausible, as Cassirer says, that "man eben darum gegen ihn misstrauisch werden, dass man in ihm eher eine begriffliche Konstruktion, denn eine Beschreibung der geschichtlichen Tatsachen vermuten könnte."[35] This caution is well grounded. Kant proceeded in 1764 to hold that all true propositions are derived from experience; in mathematics general conclusions are reached in the concrete,[36] in metaphysics, in the abstract. In mathematics, singular figures are taken in the concrete and treated synthetically. But Kant calls this procedure random (*willkürlich*). The procedure which Kant called "synthetic" is the procedure of experience. "Synthetic" and "empirical" are identical terms. Kant did not realize that three conclusions which he drew implicitly are incompatible. (1) The procedures of mathematics and experience are identical (i.e. both are synthetic). (2) There are no necessary conclusions in experience. (3) There are necessary conclusions in mathematics. If the synthesis of experience and of mathematics is one and the same, then it must yield necessary conclusions in both fields or in neither. If there are necessary conclusions in mathematics and there are none in experience, then the synthetic procedures in the two cases must be separate procedures and not one. If a synthetic procedure is actually a random (*willkürlicher*) one, then both in mathematics

[35] Cassirer, *Das Erkenntnisproblem*, II, 613.   [36] *Phil. Bib.*, Bd. 46 a, pp. 120–21.

and in experience there would be no necessary and universally valid conclusions. If, on the other hand, a synthetic procedure yields clear and complete conclusions in mathematics, and if it is, at the same time, the procedure in experience, then both in mathematics and experience, necessary and universal conclusions would seem to be reached.

In the paper of 1764, Kant did not consider these issues. He praised the clarity and completeness of mathematical demonstrations. He held that in that science the procedure is synthetic and that such a procedure is empirical, but he did not raise the question of the basis of the necessary truth of mathematical propositions. Hence, in spite of his identification of the methods of mathematics and experience and his failure to deny that there are necessary conclusions in the former field, he did not raise the question of the possibility of *a priori*, synthetic truths.

The clearest evidence that in 1764 Kant identified the synthetic procedure of mathematics with that of experience is his explanation of the treatment of the symbols of mathematics *in concreto*. What is the nature of such symbols? "Denn da die Zeichen der Mathematik sinnliche Erkenntnismittel sind, so kann man mit derselben Zuversicht, wie man dessen, was man mit Augen sieht, versichert ist, auch wissen, dass man keinen Begriff aus der Acht gelassen. . . ."[37] Far from meaning that the synthetic procedure in mathematics guarantees a validity greater than, and different from, experience, Kant considered that the symbols of mathematics are sensuous tools of knowledge and held that this very fact assures a certainty and completeness to mathematical calculations equal to that involved in visual experience. The synthetic procedure in mathematics yields thorough and accurate results because at every stage it is the procedure of experience. The kind of thoroughness which Kant had in mind was the thoroughness of Newton's empirical method. In 1764 Kant was either unaware of Newton's admission that his method always falls short of demonstrative certainty, or he was aware of this fact and considered such certainty to be in any case, ephemeral. He called the method of mathematics and experience the synthetic method and appealed

[37] *Ibid.*, p. 136.

to Newton as the formulator of that method.[38] As we have found, Newton called his method the method of analysis in opposition to that of composition. It would seem, then, that Kant was unaware of Newton's own description of his method at the end of the *Optics*.[39] For Kant's empirical "synthetic" method is identical with Newton's method of analysis. In any case, Kant's contention that the symbols of mathematics are sensuous is sufficient evidence[40] that in 1764 he equated the synthetic method of mathematics with the method of experience. Hence he did not realize that, if such an equation is justified, either the necessity of mathematical truths is no greater than that of experience or empirical truths are necessary, like those of mathematics. Until he realized these two alternatives, he could not have been aware of the possibility of truths which are both synthetic and *a priori*.

The doctrine that mathematical symbols are sensuous is very important in a chronological account of Kant's development because of its unique relation both to his earlier and his later views. It marks the development of his view of space of 1747 in a decidedly empirical direction. In that earlier year, as we have found, he derived the nature of space from a tendency of the imagination to represent it in a certain fashion. This view left its nature uncertain, but did not base it upon sense experience. Yet, at the same time he derived the nature of space from the laws of motion which he admitted to be arbitrary. Again, he might have gone a step further and concluded that both those laws and space are derived from sense experience; but he did not take that step. In 1764, he explicitly drew this conclusion. The nature of the symbols of mathematics are sensuous; therefore, the space embodied in those symbols is sensuous.

This contention is also important in relation to his later views. As we shall find, he contended in 1770 that space is a singular representation (*singularis repraesentatio* or *Einzelvorstellung*). At that time he developed this view in a more adequate fashion. In

---

[38] *Ibid.*, p. 117: "Ich werde daher sichere Erfahrungssätze und daraus gezogene unmittelbare Folgerungen den ganzen Inhalt meiner Abhandlung sein lassen."

[39] Cf. above, pp. 11–13.

[40] Cassirer, *ibid.*, II, 613–14, cites *Reflexionen* No. 292, 296, 499, 500, and 726 to support this view.

addition, however, he departed sharply from the contention that the symbols of mathematics are sensuous. Space is singular, but it is nonempirical. It is not given in experience. The figures of geometry are given in some fashion outside sense perception. These two facts are the basis for the synthetic, *a priori* nature of mathematical truth. His contention in 1764 that the symbols of mathematics are sensuous shows indubitably that he was unaware of that special kind of truth in that year. The synthetic method is that part of the empirical method which deals with the singular features of objects in opposition to the method of deductive analysis. Space is a singular, sensuous representation. Kant never returned completely to this view, although his final conclusions in the *Analytic* resemble it.[41]

As final evidence that in 1764 Kant was unaware of the leading features of his later views of space, let us notice what he has to say about the problem of its necessary nature. In seeking to analyze its nature, we find ourselves faced with the problem of its three-dimensionality and other qualities. Consider the proposition: space has three dimensions.

Dergleichen Sätze lassen sich wohl erläutern, indem man sie in concreto betrachtet, um sie anschauend zu erkennen; allein sie lassen sich niemals beweisen.[42]

Here again Kant may seem to be formulating his later views. In 1770, one of his leading theses was that space is an intuition (*Anschauung*). It is given, he held, outside experience and has a necessary nature. Was this his meaning in 1764? There is an ambiguity in the term *betrachtet*. In the above quotation, he was referring to a proposition: space has three dimensions. Now an object is "viewed" in a very different fashion from the way that a proposition is "considered." Yet *betrachtet* sometimes means "viewed" and sometimes "considered." Which did Kant mean? He would seem to have meant that the propositions are viewed, for he says that they are *in concreto betrachtet*. He meant that we may consider the three-dimensionality of space in the concrete in the sense that space is so viewed (*anschauend erkannt*). While this statement is quite compatible with his later treatment, there is

---

[41] Cf. below, pp. 218–20.   [42] *Phil. Bib.*, Bd. 46 a, p. 124.

one main difference. In 1770 and 1781 when he contended that space is immediately viewed in the concrete, he believed that its necessary nature (including its three-dimensionality) could be established because it is given outside sense experience. In 1764 he would seem to have meant that it is immediately viewed in the concrete, but that its necessary nature cannot be established, because, like anything else that is given in the concrete, it is given in sense experience. The fact that he specifically referred to mathematical symbols as sensuous would seem to make this even more probable. However, even if he meant by the terms *in concreto . . . anschauend erkennen . . .* something similar to his later doctrine of a pure intuition, he had not yet formulated a single one of the major arguments in defense of that doctrine.

§ 4

LET us turn now to his paper of 1768.[43] The leading thesis of that paper was: "*. . . that absolute space has a reality of its own, independent of the existence of all matter, and indeed as the first ground of the possibility of the compositeness of matter.*"[44] Kant did not explicitly state what he meant by the "absolute" nature of space. He said, however, that he intended to show the geometers "a convincing ground for asserting the actuality of their absolute space." He would seem to have meant that the absolute nature of space is different from certain more specific characteristics which he proposed to show it to have. Its absolute nature is constituted neither by its reality or concreteness nor by its existence independent of all matter nor by its basic relation to all matter as the first ground of the possibility of the compositeness of the latter. There would seem to be only one meaning in Kant's mind for the term "absolute." Space is absolute, if, in opposition to "relative" space, it has a necessary nature. He was proposing to describe that "necessary" space in which he had said in 1747 that he believed.

At that time, he had held that spaces are possible with other

[43] *On the First Ground of the Distinction of Regions in Space,* in Kant, *Inaugural Dissertation and Early Writings on Space,* translated by Handyside, pp. 19–29.
[44] *Ibid.,* p. 20.

dimensions than three, but he had admitted that this conclusion seemed to involve consequences to which he did not feel himself permanently committed. If there are spaces with other natures than the one under consideration, all such spaces must be "relative." If space need not have the characteristics which it has but can take on other, different characteristics, thereby becoming another kind of space, it is relative. The relative nature of space has nothing to do with the question: Is space a substance, accident, or relation? but only with the question: Can there be various kinds of spaces? If, on the other hand, space has a necessary nature—if, in other words, space must be as it is and not otherwise—there can be only one kind of space, and space is absolute. In this sense of the term, Kant held in 1768 that space is absolute.

The necessary or absolute nature of space was, however, not by any means the only issue which he proceeded to consider and discuss. In the first place, he went on to hold that absolute space has a reality of its own; it is actual. It is significant here that Kant expressly calls such space the space of the geometer. He assumed that only an extremely empirical view of geometry would deny the necessary nature of its conclusions. Even Hume had admitted that the propositions of geometry are necessary.[45] Kant turned purposely to the kind of space which was generally admitted to yield necessary conclusions, that is, to the kind of space that was admitted to be absolute or necessary, and claimed, in addition, that such space has reality or actuality. In other words, the space of the geometer is not merely a necessary or absolute space, but it is, in addition, a real, that is, concrete, space. What could Kant have meant by the reality or actuality of space? It would seem probable that he meant that geometrical space is physical space, that the conclusions of geometry (about spherical triangles, for example) and the conclusions of experience (and possibly mechanics, although he did not mention that science) are about the same space. But the conclusions of geometry are admitted to be necessary; while the space encountered in experience (and in mechanics) is assumed to be actual. Hence, Kant concluded explicitly, the space of geometry is real space, and, he implied, al-

[45] Hume, *An Enquiry Concerning Human Understanding*, Chap. IV, p. 23.

though he did not explicitly conclude, that some of the propositions of experience (possibly those of mechanics) are necessary.
These conclusions, although the second is only implied, are very
far-reaching. Kant would seem to mean that the propositions of
mechanics are necessary. Why would he otherwise distinguish between "absolute" space and its "reality"? If he meant merely that
the axioms of geometry are necessary and concern an absolute
space, while the conclusions of experience are, in every case, contingent, why did he specifically maintain that the space of the
geometer is real? He could have set up a theory of the absolute
nature of space without going on to add that it is a real space.
By specifically concluding that the space of geometry shares the
"reality" of physical space, he implied that some of the propositions about real space are necessary. If the propositions of geometry and mechanics concern the same real space, are not both of
them necessary? If there are propositions in geometry which are
necessary and concern real space, are there not other necessary
truths about real space, perhaps in mechanics, contrary to Newton's contention?

In addition to his theory that there is a necessary or absolute
space and that it is a reality, Kant went on to claim that such space
is independent of the existence of all matter and that it is the
first ground of the possibility of a characteristic of matter, namely,
its compositeness. This step marks a complete break with the
views of Leibniz. Whether matter is considered as phenomena
or as substances themselves, it was Leibniz's opinion that its nature is traceable to the nature of substances. A substance is the
source of all its determinations, including its determinations in
relation to other substances, that is, as a set of phenomena. Space
and time and motion are determinations of secondary matter and
impose no conditions directly or indirectly upon substances. Kant
proceeded in 1768 to claim that space is the source of the compositeness of matter. Far from being the result of the fact that
parts of matter exist outside, and simultaneously with, other parts,
space is the cause of this fact. The teachings of Euler,[46] which had
an influence upon Kant in the formulation of his own views of

---

[46] Cf. below, Chapter VI, § 2.

space in 1769, possibly influenced him in reaching this conclusion in 1768.

In general, then, Kant maintained four theses in 1768 concerning space. These were: (1) there is necessary or absolute space; (2) it is real or actual; (3) it is independent of the existence of matter; and (4) it is the first ground of the possibility of the compositeness of matter.

He collected a number of examples from nature and geometry to show that a body is not the source of all its inner determinations.

. . . [T]he complete ground of determination of the shape of a body rests not merely upon the position of its parts relatively to one another, but further on a relation to the universal space which geometers postulate—a relation, however, which is such that it cannot itself be immediately perceived.[47]

If space is, as Leibniz had held, the relation of coexistence of bodies, there would be no space in a universe consisting of one body. In such a universe, the body would have, however, in Leibniz's view, a definite nature, with certain qualities flowing from that nature, such as shape, size, etc. Kant proposed to show that space is independent of the nature of body, and also that in a nonspatial universe bodies could not possibly have the natures which they have in this universe. In a universe with only one body, there would have to be space in order that the body might have qualities which we would know it to have. Kant proposed to point out certain qualities which we know that one body existing alone would have and which it could not have unless it were related to space. Some qualities in a body cannot be discovered directly in the body, but only by comparing that body with another.[48] In a universe containing only one body, those qualities could not be discovered in this way. If we can know, however, that those qualities would have to be in that body, it would follow that some qualities of a body are dependent neither upon its own nature nor upon its relation to others, but upon its relation to space.

[47] Kant, *Inaugural Dissertation and Early Writings on Space*, translated by Handyside, p. 25.
[48] *Ibid.*, pp. 125–26.

What are examples of such qualities? A right-handed and a left-handed screw; a pair of equal but incongruent, spherical triangles; a pair of human hands or human limbs—these may, in each case, be identical in every regard so far as inner shape, structure, and determinations are concerned, but they cannot be superimposed. These are the examples of incongruent counterparts. In each case, the surface bounding the physical space of one member of the pair cannot be made to bound the surface of the other. Hence the difference rests upon an inner ground. "This inner ground cannot, however, depend on any difference in the mode of connection of the parts of the body relatively to one another; for . . . in this respect everything may be completely identical. . . ."[49] Each body has, therefore, a characteristic which is independent of the relation of its parts to each other. For every relation of the parts of a right hand to each other, there is an identical relation of the parts of the corresponding left hand to each other. If the sum total of the inner determinations of a hand were merely the entire mode of connection of the parts relatively to each other, there would be no difference between a right hand and a left one. But there is such a difference, hence some other mode of explanation is required to account for all the inner differences between the two hands.

Kant's argument here proves only that the nature of a body is determined partially in some way other than by the relations of the inner parts to each other. It in no way shows what the new or additional principles of explanation are. It may be that the conception of a body is an abstraction from some wider context in such a way that the complete explanation of the nature of the body requires a reference to that wider context. It may be that some relations between bodies rest upon principles different from those determining the qualities of any of the bodies considered singly. There is, however, no justification for Kant's additional conclusion that certain characteristics of bodies are dependent upon the relation of those bodies to absolute space. All that he could justifiably conclude is that some characteristics of bodies are not dependent merely upon the inner arrangement of the

[49] *Ibid.*, p. 27.

parts. Upon what these characteristics are dependent the examples of incongruent counterparts in no way show.

His negative conclusion is, however, unanswerable. In bodies there are characteristics which are not dependent upon the relations of the parts to each other. These characteristics are dependent upon some other principle of explanation. Nothing in the nature of body explains them. A body is not the source of all its inner determinations. If there were only one body in the universe, it could not possess characteristics which bodies in our universe possess. These characteristics, Kant went on to hold, are dependent upon the relations of bodies to space. Because of the fact that there are more bodies than one in the universe, we are able to perceive differences in bodies which indicate their relations to space, in spite of the fact that we cannot perceive those relations directly. These differences are dependent upon, and subordinate to, the relations of the bodies to space, yet we perceive the latter only in terms of the former. Consequently, if there were only one body in the universe, while it would have relations to space, we would not be able directly or indirectly to apprehend those relations, since there would be no other body in which we could discover differences dependent upon, and indicative of, such relations. "If we conceive the first created thing to be a human hand, it is necessarily either a right or a left. . . ."[50] Such a hand would be related to universal space in such a way that it would be either a right or a left. As in our universe of many hands, such a relation would not be directly discoverable. In addition, however, it would not be indirectly discoverable, although it would exist. For not having any other hands or objects with which to compare the one hand, there would be no discernible difference between it and any other object: and it is only in terms of such a discernible difference that its relation to space could be discovered.

Consequently, Kant appealed to the Leibnizian principle of indiscernibles to establish his theory of absolute space. Leibniz had held[51] that space is ideal, since its parts are homogeneous and involve no discernible difference from each other, while bodies, created according to the principle of sufficient reason, have dis-

---

[50] *Ibid.*   [51] Cf. above, pp. 48–49.

cernible differences (although not necessarily discerned by human beings). Kant pointed out certain discerned differences between bodies which are based solely upon the relation of these bodies to universal space. Granting Leibniz's central contention that bodies must have discernible differences, he proposed to turn that contention against its proponent by showing that, in some cases, a real space is at the basis of those differences. Leibniz held that the principle governing differences in the structure of two bodies had been implanted inside those bodies by God in his act of creation; that is, it lies entirely within the body. No two bodies are precisely alike (according to the principle of indiscernible differences) and the principles determining those differences must lie, according to Leibniz, entirely within each. In each body lie the principles governing its complete nature, including its difference from the other body. But in the examples of incongruent counterparts, as brought out by Kant, two bodies, in so far as they are determined from within, are identical. Yet between the two there are not only discernible differences undiscerned by men, but differences discerned by men and requiring an explanation. Instead of rejecting the principle of indiscernibles, as Clarke had done in his attempt to show that space is not a relation between bodies, Kant accepted the principle and went on to show that it forces us to conclude that there is a real, absolute space, in order to account for its operation in reference to certain differences in bodies. ". . . [To] produce the one [hand] a different act of the creating cause is required from that whereby its counterpart can come into being."[52]

God, in implanting in each substance the principle of all future determinations (including those as body), created no two substances identical, that is, he created discernible differences in each of them. If the first created thing were a human hand, and if God implanted in it the principle of all future determinations, it could be neither a right hand or a left hand, for the difference between these two can lie in neither. If the principle of all future determinations lies in each substance, either there would be only one hand created which would be neither right nor left but indeter-

[52] Kant, *Inaugural Dissertation and Early Writings on Space*, translated by Handyside, pp. 27–28.

minate, which is contrary to the facts,[53] or two hands would be created, each containing in it the principles of all its inner determinations. But the difference between right and left not being determinable by such an inner principle, there could be no discernible difference between the two hands, and the principle of indiscernibles would be violated. Hence, in order to create the right and the left hands, either the principle of indiscernibles would have to be violated, or the two hands would have to lie in absolute space.

Whatever is the weakness of Kant's positive argument here for an absolute space, his use of the examples of incongruent counterparts to show the incompatibility of Leibniz's theory of substance and his principle of the lack of indiscernibles is unanswerable. Whether or not the examples of incongruent counterparts offer effective support to the theory of an absolute space, they show, at least, that there are some characteristics of bodies which cannot be accounted for by an inner principle determining the arrangement of parts. If such an inner principle should account for all of the determinations of a body, then equal, incongruent bodies would have no discernible differences, and, according to Leibniz's other principle, would be identical. Not being identical, the discerned differences must be accounted for in some way other than by an inner principle. Perhaps they may be accounted for in some way other than by reference to a universal space. Two years later, Kant was constrained for other reasons to account for them in another way. But even then he retained his negative argument against Leibniz although he drew other, different, positive conclusions from it.

The dispute among the commentators concerning Kant's theory of space in 1768 has arisen chiefly from two sentences of Kant's towards the end of his paper.

Since absolute space is not an object of an outer sensation, but a fundamental concept which first makes all such sensations possible. . . .

[53] *Ibid.*, p. 28: "[If] space consists only in the outer relations of the parts of matter existing along side one another, in the case before us all actual space would be that which this hand occupies. But since, whether it be right or left, there is no difference in the relations of its parts to one another, the hand would in respect of this characteristic be absolutely indeterminate, i. e., it would fit either side of the human body, which is impossible."

And:

There is, indeed, no lack of difficulties surrounding this concept, if we attempt to comprehend its reality—a reality which is sufficiently intuitable to inner sense—through ideas of reason.[54]

Chiefly because of these two quotations, Riehl[55] and Fischer[56] claim that Kant did not maintain in 1768 that space is absolute and real but held (as he did two years later) that it is an intuition. Why? In the first sentence, he applied to space two of the tests which he later applied to a pure intuition. It is not an object of outer sensation but is a fundamental conception which makes such sensation possible. In the second sentence, he formulated the distinction between intuitions and conceptions, in the same way that he did in 1770.[57] For these reasons, Riehl and Fischer hold that the main doctrine in the paper of 1768 was the view that space is an intuition. It is obvious from Kant's use in 1770 of the example of incongruent counterparts, with the same negative interpretation, but with a new positive interpretation, that this example can be used as a basis for the doctrine that space is an intuition. But it is my view, in agreement with Vaihinger and Kemp Smith,[58] that in 1768 Kant's chief concern was to show that space is absolute and real. In that year, he meant that space is absolute and real in spite of the fact that it is "not an object of outer sensation." Far from attaching significance to the fact that space is not an object of outer sensation and can be grasped only with many difficulties through ideas of reason, Kant merely noted these facts as difficulties in his doctrine. He did not conclude that space is an intuition because it is not an object of outer sensation but held that it is a fundamental conception. He made this statement incidentally in claiming that the relations of bodies to absolute space can be apprehended only through comparison with other bodies. He did not claim that the facility with which the reality of space is intuitable to inner sense is evidence that it is nonconceptual,[59] but that in contrast to such facility there are

[54] *Ibid.*, pp. 28–29.   [55] Riehl, *Der Philosophische Kritizismus*, I, 339.
[56] Fischer, *A Commentary on Kant's Critick of the Pure Reason*, pp. 30–31.
[57] Kant, *Inaugural Dissertation*, § 15 A, B, C.
[58] Vaihinger, *Kommentar zu Kants Kritik der reinen Vernunft*, II, 525; Kemp Smith, *A Commentary to Kant's 'Critique of Pure Reason,'* p. 163.
[59] Kant, *Inaugural Dissertation*, § 15 B, C.

difficulties in treating space by means of ideas of reason. The two arguments are very different, and nothing in the one, as stated in 1770, suggests a likeness to the other, as stated in 1768. Perhaps the doctrines are not incompatible, but this did not occur to Kant in 1768, if it ever did.[60] Not only did he take over the Newtonian theory of space in that year, but he even implied that the necessary nature of geometrical truths refers to such real space, and hence the truths of mechanics concerning moving bodies in it are necessary rather than contingent. He held forth, at least by implication, the possibility that the laws of gravitation rest upon a necessary basis, in a way that Newton himself did not claim. Even after Kant developed his own, different views of space in 1769, he retained this view of the necessary nature of truth in mechanics. He followed Newton in 1768 in regard to the nature of space, and he seems to have outstripped him in that year in regard to the nature of the validity of truths in mechanics.

[60] Vaihinger, *op. cit.*, II, p. 310.

CHAPTER VI

KANT'S THEORIES OF SPACE
ABOUT 1769

§ 1

IN TURNING to Kant's theories of space after 1768, one general remark is necessary. About 1769 Kant worked out such developments in his philosophy of space that all of his subsequent thinking on the subject was more or less by way of elaboration or retraction of these views. Before entering upon our discussion of these views, we must remember that they involve a definite theory of perception. What is the relation of space to the objects of sense? In answering this question, Kant used the wider term "experience" to cover the act of sense perception. In other parts of his general philosophy, such as his doctrine of the categories, "experience" turns out to be a wider term than "perception," but in his theories of space he equated the terms. If we bear this identification in mind, we can deal with Kant's theories of space directly, and also in relation to the problems of perception.

To understand in detail the changes which Kant made in his views of space between the paper of 1768 and the *Inaugural Dissertation* of 1770, three distinct phases of his thinking at that time must be kept separately in mind during the examination of his views. (1) In the first phase he arrived at his original formulation of the doctrine that space is a pure intuition and a pure form of empirical intuition. This formulation was the result of an analysis of the conception of space, undertaken under the direct influence of Leonhard Euler. (2) In the second phase, he elaborated his views of space as a pure intuition, retaining his original evidence for those doctrines but supplementing it by the fact that the truths (not judgments) of geometry and mechanics are synthetic and *a priori*. (3) In the third phase, he supplemented his already formulated views of space with the different and independent—and as

I shall contend, extrinsic—doctrine that space is metaphysically unreal. These three structures of thought were worked out and superimposed upon each other sometime between the publication of the paper of 1768 and the *Dissertation* of 1770, roughly within 1769, the year which, he later said, gave him much light.[1]

His views of space about 1769 can be understood only if these three phases and all their implications are considered separately, although in sequence. His views can be understood in their first phase only if the facts are borne in mind (1) that he had not yet formulated the theory of the synthetic, *a priori* nature of truth in geometry and mechanics, and (2) that he ignored, or at least postponed, the problem of the metaphysical reality or unreality of space. His views can be understood in their second phase only if it is remembered that in discovering that truth in geometry and mechanics is synthetic and *a priori* (1) he had previously formulated the doctrines of space as a pure intuition and a pure form of intuition, and (2) that he still ignored, or at least postponed, the problem of the metaphysical reality or unreality of space. Finally, his views can be understood in their third phase only if we realize: (1) that he had already formulated his doctrines of the first two phases, and (2) that he superimposed upon them the quite different doctrine of the metaphysical unreality of space.

We can best keep these various issues clear by recalling the various meanings of the term "ideal" which we have already considered. Leibniz held that space, like other relations between phenomena is ideal, that is, metaphysically unreal, in opposition to monads which are metaphysically real. Newton held that space is metaphysically real, as a property of God. Kant ignored this entire issue in the first two phases of his thinking in 1769. Leibniz held, in addition, as we have found, that space is ideal, that is, abstract; that is, it is an abstraction from phenomena and their qualities, which are real, that is, concrete. Newton held that space is concrete as the container of bodies. It was with Newton's theory of the reality of space, as elaborated by Euler, that Kant was concerned in his first phase about 1769. The fictitiousness and the subjectivity of space, in the senses of the term "ideal" as used by

[1] Erdmann, *Reflexionen Kants*, No. 4.

Leibniz in specific portions of his writings, may be ignored in considering Kant's views of 1768–70.

In the first phase of his thinking in 1769, Kant, as we shall find, held that space is a pure intuition and a pure form of intuition; that is, ideal in a specifically Kantian sense of nonempirical or pure; yet real or concrete in comparison with abstract conceptions. In the second phase, he re-enforced these contentions with the fact that truth in geometry and mechanics is "synthetic" and "*a priori*," terms whose meanings we shall explain. In the third phase, he added the different doctrine that space is metaphysically unreal. His final result in 1770 was that space is real, that is, concrete; ideal, that is, nonempirical or pure; and ideal, that is, metaphysically unreal. Let us turn to the views of Euler, which were the immediate cause of Kant's development of these views.

§ 2

IN HIS *Reflexions sur l'espace et le temps,* Euler had defended the conception of an absolute, real, that is, concrete, space. The main body of his proof consisted in an appeal to the nature of mechanics as evidence for such a space. There was, however, a significant difference in portions of his paper. Instead of appealing to the nature of motion to show that space is absolute, he undertook an analysis of the conception of space.

Il est vrai que les sens ne sont pas capables de nous fournir les idées abstraites, semblables aux idées des genres & des espèces, qui n'existent que dans notre entendement, & auxquelles il ne repond aucun objet réel.[2]

There are, he held, certain conceptions which are abstract, existing only in our minds. Such conceptions (for example, conceptions of genera and species) are not furnished by the senses and correspond to nothing real: they are ideal, that is, abstract. Here Euler distinguished between the source of a conception and its reference, or lack of reference, to an object. There are two quite different questions which must be raised concerning conceptions.

[2] In *Histoire de l'Académie Royale des Sciences et Belles Lettres* for 1748, § XIV. Cf. *Lettres à une princesse d'Allemagne,* Letters CXXII, CXXIV, CXXV.

First, what is their source? Secondly, do they refer to anything real, that is, concrete: are they real, that is, concrete, or ideal, that is, abstract? He proceeded to analyze space and place with reference to the first question.

> . . . la manière, dont on parvient à l'idée de l'espace & du lieu, est bien différente de celle, dont nous nous formons les idées des genres & des espèces.[3]

"Space" and "place" are formulated or reached by the mind in a way different from the way "genera" and "species" are reached. The source of the conceptions of space and place is different from the source of the conceptions of genera and species. The source of "genera" and "species" is not the senses. Did Euler mean, by implication, that the source of the ideas of space and place is the senses? Turning to the second question, Euler held:

> Et on se tromperoit fort, si l'on vouloit soutenir, qu'il n'existe pas des choses, dont nous n'avons d'autres idées que par réflexion.[4]

Admitting the existence of things apprehended through the senses and admitting the existence of genera and species in the mind as products of reflection, are the only things which exist those which are apprehended in the one way or the other? It would be a mistake, Euler meant, to make such a claim. There may be real, that is, concrete, things which are neither genera nor species nor the objects of sense. There may be other ways of having ideas· furnished than by the senses and by reflection. "Genera" and "species" are not apprehended through the senses but by reflection. "Space" and "place" are not apprehended in the same way that "genera" and "species" are apprehended; that is, "space" and "place" are not apprehended by reflection. But if conceptions are not apprehended by reflection, it does not follow that they are apprehended by sensation. Only if sensation and reflection are the sole possible sources of conceptions, and if the conception of space is not arrived at by reflection, only then must it be arrived at by sensation. This had been Kant's view in 1765. Euler meant, in contrast, that the conception of space is arrived at in neither way. In 1768, Kant had

---

[3] Euler, *Reflexions sur l'espace et le temps*, § XIV.   [4] *Ibid.*

admitted that there are difficulties in the view that space is apprehended by reflection but had held, incidentally, that it is sufficiently clear to inner sense. Now, in 1769, he faced squarely for
the first time the problem, how is space apprehended? Euler raised
this question for him.

The conception of extension, Euler continued, is formed by
taking away from the conception of a body all of the determinations except that of the extended.

C'est ainsi que nous nous formons l'idée de l'étendue en général, en
retranchant des idées des corps toutes les déterminations, hormis
l'étendue.[5]

But, he went on to say, the conception of the place (or space)
which a body occupies is obtained quite differently. It is gained
not by taking away determinations from a body, but by taking
away the body itself with all of its determinations. Place and space
remain after this has been done, and, therefore, they cannot be its
determinations.

Mais l'idée du lieu qu'un corps occupe, ne se forme pas en retranchant
quelques déterminations du corps; elle résulte en ôtant le corps tout
entier: de sorte que le lieu n'ait pas été une détermination du corps,
puisqu'il reste encore, après avoir enlevé le corps tout entier avec
toutes ses qualités.[6]

A quality of a body may be obtained by abstracting all other
qualities from that body, leaving the quality in question. On the
other hand, the conception of space is gained by abstracting the
body with all its qualities. When this is done, space remains;
hence, Euler meant, in conclusion, that space is real, that is, concrete, independently of bodies and their qualities.

What was the meaning of Euler's conclusion that space is real,
that is, concrete, since it cannot be abstracted from a body? There
are, he held, at least two sources of conceptions, sensation and
reflection. "Genera" and "species" are examples of conceptions
arrived at by reflection, and such conceptions correspond to nothing
real: they are ideal, that is, abstract. It is a mistake, however, to
conclude that the conception of space corresponds similarly to
nothing real, that is, concrete. For it is arrived at in a different way

[5] *Ibid.*, § XV.   [6] *Ibid.*

from the way that "genera" and "species" are arrived at. If space is real, that is, concrete, in a way that "genera" and "species" are not, is it real as an object of sense or a quality of such an object? In either case, it would be apprehended by sensation. But it is neither a quality of an object, which may be abstracted from the object, nor the object itself, from which a quality may be abstracted; hence, it is not apprehended by sensation at all. Euler's theory of space is, then, twofold: (1) space is neither derived from sensation (as "extension" is) nor from reflection (as "man" is) ; (2) space is not unreal, that is, abstract (as "man" is) yet its reality is different both from that of an object of sensation and from a quality of such an object.

Kant's theories of space, as he originally worked them out in 1769, are identical with these conclusions of Euler's. Kant merely expressed them in more precise form, by means of a different and wider terminology. Since the conception of space is not derived from sensation, it is ideal, that is, pure; since it is not derived from reflection, it is an intuition, in opposition to those conceptions which are so derived. Kant narrowed the term "conception" to include only those terms which are derived by reflection, using the wider term "representation" to stand for both conceptions and intuitions. The usual general representations are arrived at by reflection: these are conceptions; singular representations are arrived at in some other way: these are intuitions. Again, Euler had concluded that space is not ideal, that is, abstract, as "man" is ideal; yet its reality, that is, concreteness, is different from that of an object of sense or a quality of such an object. Space, Kant concluded, is not ideal, that is, abstract, as "man" is ideal; but, not being empirical in its origin, it is ideal, that is, pure, in opposition to objects of sensation and their qualities. These doctrines are identical. Euler distinguished between the concreteness of space and that of empirical objects (and their qualities). Kant merely explicitly called the first type of concreteness pure, and the second empirical. But Euler had made the same distinction. Both men contended that space is real in the sense of being concrete, in opposition to general conceptions, yet ideal in comparison with empirical objects.

Euler meant by "nonempirical" and "real," that is, concrete, respectively, what Kant meant by "pure" and "intuitive." The first term refers, in each case, to the source of the representation of space; the second, in each case, to its logical status in opposition to general terms. For both men, space is nonempirical or pure because of its difference in origin from the objects of sense and their qualities. For both men it is concrete, that is, real or intuitive, because of its difference from general terms arrived at by reflection. Both men imply that space is given directly to the contemplative gaze of the mind, unlike general terms, which are inferred. Both men imply, however, that such immediate apprehension yields an object which is concrete in a different way from the empirical objects occupying it. Their views seem at first glance divergent because Euler used the term "real" ambiguously, sometimes as referring to the concreteness of space, and sometimes as referring to the empirical nature of objects and their qualities. Yet upon closer examination, it is clear that he was contending for the ideal, that is, pure or nonempirical nature of space, no less than for its reality, that is, concreteness. Kant denied the reality of space in the sense of its having an empirical nature and was in complete agreement with Euler in so doing. In what sense is space real, Kant asked, if it is neither an object nor a quality of an object? It is real in the sense of being concrete, in opposition to the abstractness of general conceptions. Such concreteness he called intuitive. But it is ideal in the sense of being pure, remaining after a body and its qualities have been abstracted. If Kant had broadened his conception of experience to include such immediate, intuitive apprehension, he would have stated a view that is roughly the same as that of S. Alexander today.[7]

Kant worked out his view that the conception of space is a singular representation and a pure intuition by contrasting it with general conceptions. What is the nature of this contrast? First, there is "space in general." What is the nature of this general conception? Is it like other general conceptions or is it different? Secondly, there is "this particular space." Is it like other logical particulars? Thirdly, there is "this particular thing in this par-

[7] Cf. below, pp. 137–38, 165–66, 239–40.

ticular space." What is the significance of the term "in"? What sort of relation does it indicate?

Consider the general conception "man." It contains less than any individual conception contains. Each individual man is more than the common denominator called "man." Peter is not meant every time a man is referred to. On the other hand, "space" is not qualitatively less than "this space." The latter contains no more space quality than the former. There are no characteristics of particular spaces which must be abstracted from them in order to obtain the general conception "space." The entire connotation of space is immediately displayed before the mind. The only way that "this space" differs from "that" is that "this" is here, and "that" there. That this space is here, means, however, no more than that this space is space. "Here" and "there" are not qualities of space; they are space itself. Space is a singular representation because of this identity of its so-called particulars with its so-called general term.[8] Peter and Paul are both men; but they do not contain the same amount of "man"; "this space" and "that," however, have exactly the same amount of the character of space. The "necessity" with which the nature of space forces itself upon our attention as precisely what it is and not otherwise constrained Kant to consider space as nonempirical.[9] The immediacy with which this necessary character displays itself is evidence of its singularity or intuitiveness.[10] Space is a pure intuition.

If this account of Kant's original formulation of his leading doctrine of space is correct, there are certain teachings usually considered intrinsic to his views which were in 1769 completely lacking. In the first place, he had so far made no reference to the well-known Kantian "subjectivity" of space; in the second place, he had made no reference to any unique significance of mathematics. Space is given to the mind whether or not special geometrical constructions and analyses are involved. In the third place, there was nothing in this earlier teaching to suggest that space is prior to experience either temporally or logically. Space does not lie in the mind, nor is it prior to sensation. It is merely not given in sensation, and, unlike the objects of sensation, it has

[8] Kant, *Inaugural Dissertation*, § 15, B.   [9] *Ibid.*, § 15, A.   [10] *Ibid.*, § 15, B, C.

a necessary nature. I do not claim that these other doctrines were not later worked out by Kant but merely that, in proceeding this far under the influence of Euler, he had not formulated them. The first addition that he made was the theory of the priority of space to experience. Since space (having a necessary nature) is not yielded in experience, hence it must be given before experience. In 1770 and in the *Aesthetic* he construed this priority to be temporal,[11] while in the *Analytic* he considered it merely as logical. In the first instance, his doctrine of a pure intuition meant, however, neither type. It could have been as readily expanded into the view that space is a necessary, empirical intuition, if he had considered experience as more inclusive.

In this earliest doctrine, the example of a right hand and a corresponding left is no more significant than the case of any logical particulars, except in one way. In every case, when usual particulars are compared with particular spaces, space is found to be a pure intuition. In every case, such a comparison shows that "space in general" is given with the so-called particulars, whereas "hand," "man," etc. are derived. In every case, it is clear that knowledge of space is immediate, in contrast to knowledge of "hand," "man," etc. The example of a pair of hands is, however, in one way different. Whereas the contrast between two men and two particular spaces shows that space is an intuition, the example of a "right hand" and its partner, a "left hand," shows this to be so, and also forces the mind *to make or construct* space in its attempt to clarify the difference between the two hands. In attempting to take away the object (hand) and all its determinations, the determinations of right- and left-handedness are left unaccounted for except by actively constructing space. Unless space remains (as Euler held that it did), the account of the nature of the two hands is incomplete. For this reason, Kant used[12] the example of incongruent counterparts to show specifically that space is a pure intuition and formulated a more general argu-

[11] *Ibid.*, § 15, A: ". . . the possibility of outer perceptions, as such, presupposes . . . the concept of space." Cf. § 15, E: ". . . space [is] given originally through the nature of the mind. . . ." Cf. § 14, 3: ". . . the idea [of time] is conceived prior to all sensation. . . ."

[12] *Ibid.*, § 15, C.

ment[13] to show that space is a singular representation. Yet the consideration of space in contrast to any general conception is evidence that it is a pure intuition. Hence, the example of incongruent counterparts has an advantage only because in it the mind is forced actively to construct space. Because of this advantage, and because he had come to realize that truth in geometry is *a priori* and synthetic, Kant stressed the nature of mathematical truth in 1770 in his main proof that space is an intuition. His own earliest formulation of that doctrine—after which he gained a more adequate insight into the nature of truth in geometry—was the much wider procedure of contrasting the conception of space with the usual general conceptions.

His selection of the example of incongruent counterparts left him, however, open to one danger. If, in proving that space is a pure intuition, he required an example which forces the mind *to construct* space psychologically, he raised thereby the question whether the doctrine of pure intuition is based upon the logical contrast of space as given, with general conceptions as derived, or whether it is an account of an *activity* of the mind (excited perhaps by sensation) in the construction of space. The doctrine, as Kant first developed it, is a denial of an activity of the mind either as abstracting from sensation or as a reflective process.[14] But Euler had stated that the conception of space is reached in a way different from that in which general conceptions are reached. And in the midst of his formulation of the doctrine that space is a pure intuition, Kant was already enough occupied with the question of how space is reached or constructed to base his proof upon the example of incongruent counterparts, which forces such a construction upon the mind. Kant made this departure from his doctrine of contemplation in an even more significant way by raising the question[15] whether the conception of space is innate or is acquired. He went on to hold that it is acquired and stated that an act of mind constructs it. Obviously, the example of incongruent counterparts is of unique importance in this connection, since it forces the mind to make precisely such a construction. From Kant's stricter point of view, space is not constructed but

---

[13] *Ibid.*, § 15, B.   [14] *Ibid.*, § 15, A, B.   [15] *Ibid.*, § 15 corollary (end).

contemplated.[16] It was to this view that his thinking led about 1769, in the first phase of his thinking, and he stated this view in his second phase, supported by the fact that truth in geometry is *a priori* and synthetic.

The first of Kant's logical problems had been solved. He had found that the relation between space and a so-called particular space is a singular one. Space is, hence, a pure intuition. Truth about space is given immediately with any particular space. It is not truth gained by abstracting qualities from a particular space, as truth about "man" is gained by abstracting qualities from Peter. The unique nature of this truth is its *apriority*. There remained for him the problem of the relation of a particular space to a particular object in it. His explanation of this second relation came also directly from Euler. What is the nature of the relation expressed by the preposition "in"? It is not the relation of a quality, such as extension, to a body, such as an extended body. An extended object is not in extension. Extension is a quality abstracted from an extended object. A planet has a certain length or extension, just as it has certain other qualities. The "in" relation is not the relation of logical, but of physical, inclusion. If it were the former, space would be derived from the object by abstraction. The relation of space to an object in it is such that no comparison of similar marks or qualities in two objects yields space. All such marks or characteristics of objects are derived from the objects. Space cannot be so derived. After a body and all of its qualities have been taken away, space is left. The space occupied by an object is quite different from the extension which is possessed by it. The body carries its extension with it when it moves; but it moves from one part of space to another. It remains in space, but it does not carry space with it.[17] Qualities or determinations are possessed by objects. A planet possesses heat, size, or extension. Peter possesses color, height, etc. Neither a planet nor

---

[16] In *ibid.*, § 15, C, he spoke of the contemplation of the pure intuition. More exactly, it would be the contemplation of space.

[17] Euler, *Reflexions sur l'espace et le temps*, § XV: ". . . l'étendue apartient au corps, & passe avec lui par le mouvement d'un lieu à l'autre; au lieu que le lieu & l'espace ne sont susceptibles d'aucun mouvement." Cf. Leibniz, Paper V, § 37; cf. above, p. 40.

Peter possesses space as a quality or determination. The relation expressed by the preposition "in" is the form-content relation. The form of an object is not capable of being abstracted from the object, but the object is in the form. Space is a form of empirical intuition.

§ 3

As WE TURN to Kant's discovery of the synthetic, *a priori* nature of the truths of geometry and mechanics (in the second phase of his thinking about 1769), we should remember that this discovery meant his explicit adoption of what was implicit in his paper of 1768, namely, the necessary, noninductive (although also non-analytic) nature of the laws of Newtonian mechanics. About 1769 he may or may not have been aware of Newton's own cautious inductive procedure. However that may be, Kant's new doctrine represented a claim which Newton himself did not make, though it might seem to follow *a fortiori* from the theory of absolute space.[18] Holding a doctrine of absolute space, Newton had held no corresponding doctrine of absolute laws of motion. Absolute motions, unlike apparent motions, are as they are; but it does not follow that they cannot be otherwise, for the laws governing them are established inductively. Kant proceeded to develop in support of his theory of the necessary nature of space as a pure intuition, a theory of the nature of the truths in mechanics involving precisely the sort of necessary laws for which Newton did not contend. Speaking technically in terms which we must proceed to clarify, Kant realized, in formulating his theory of space, that truth in geometry and mechanics is *a priori* and synthetic. This point marked the beginning of the second phase of his thinking about 1769. He concluded that the fact that there is such truth is further evidence of the nature of space. Space is a pure intuition, he concluded, because of its differences from general conceptions, and also because of the nature of truth in pure geometry. Space is a form of empirical intuition because of its relation to objects in it, and also because of the nature of truth in applied geometry

---

[18] Cf. above, pp. 14–16; 101.

(mechanics). The fact of *a priori*,[19] synthetic truth in geometry is proof of the nature of space; the nature of space is an explanation of the nature of truth in geometry. Cognizant of the nature of the relation between the fact that truth in geometry is of a certain special sort and his theory that space is a pure intuition and a form of empirical intuition, Kant developed these theories in the *Dissertation* of 1770.

This distinction between the doctrines of space as stated in the *Dissertation* and the way in which Kant first formulated them about 1769 is overlooked by Vaihinger.[20] Though accurate in his account of the problems of the nature of the truths of pure and applied mathematics, Vaihinger fails to realize that Kant did not first formulate his doctrines of space in answer to those problems. Vaihinger's analysis of the doctrines of the *Dissertation* would be true of Kant's earlier thinking about 1769 only if, throughout that thinking, Kant had held that the truths of mathematics are *a priori* and synthetic. Vaihinger says:

Die synthetisch-apriorische Natur der Urtheile der *reinen* Mathematik erforderte, dass der Raum als reine Anschauung gefasst werde (Diss. § 15, C); dass derselbe auch als "blosse Form" unserer Anschauung gelte, war durch die Natur der reinen Mathematik als solcher noch nicht nahe gelegt, sondern wurde erst durch die durchgängige Gültigkeit der *angewandten* Mathematik für alle Objecte gefordert (Diss. § 15, E).[21]

This was true of the doctrines of space as a pure intuition and as a form of empirical intuition only after Kant realized that truth in geometry (pure and applied) is synthetic and *a priori*. Before he knew this, he found in the nature of geometry no more evidence that space is a pure intuition than he did in the general contrast between the conception of space and the usual general conceptions. As I have shown, it was the contrast between space and general terms which led Kant to formulate the doctrine that space is a pure intuition. This contrast contains just as great evidence for that doctrine as does the nature of truth in mathematics. Either Kant discovered that truth in geometry is *a priori* and syn-

---

[19] This line of thought must not be confused with the later, critical problem of *a priori*, synthetic judgments with which Kant was first concerned after 1770.

[20] Vaihinger, *Kommentar*, I, 327–34.   [21] *Ibid.*, II, 434.

thetic before he knew that space is a pure intuition, or he made this discovery afterwards. If before, his development would have proceeded quite differently from the way which I have described above. For the fact that truth in mathematics is synthetic and *a priori* was of revolutionary significance.

In the *Inaugural Dissertation* §15, A and B, he ignored the problem of the nature of truth in geometry. In part of §15, C, he treated examples in nature as well as in pure geometry. In §15, D, he used the nature of truth in geometry to refute the Leibnizians, but otherwise he did not consider that truth. In §15, E, he did not treat space as more specifically related to such truth than to all sense perception. Space, he there held, is a form of all sense experience and not merely of the sense experience involved in applied science. If Kant had begun in 1769 with the insight that truths in geometry are *a priori* and synthetic, why did he use that fact only to re-enforce doctrines of space which he formulated, in every case, in answer to more general problems? Why did he use the problem of *a priori,* synthetic truth in mathematics only as strong re-enforcing evidence for doctrines which exist without that problem? It was because Kant was concerned in 1769 with the question of the nature of the conception of space, and not with the nature of truth in mathematics. In 1764 he had identified the methods of mathematics and experience, and there is no evidence that he questioned this identification until after he had completed his new doctrines of space about 1769. The specific problem concerning the synthetic, *a priori* nature of mathematical truth could not have occurred to him while he persisted in identifying these methods. In his investigation of the nature of the conception of space about 1769, he reached the doctrine of a pure intuition and a pure form of empirical intuition. Then for the first time, he realized the specific nature of truth in mathematics.

Vaihinger's view can, therefore, be accepted only with qualifications. He says: "Dass also das Problem der angewandten Mathematik bei der Wendung von 1770 mitwirkte, kann keine Frage mehr sein. . . ."[22] If by the "change of 1770," Vaihinger means here the entire development of the doctrines of space, as carried

[22] *Ibid.,* II, 435.

out in 1768-70, he is correct in holding that the problem of applied[23] mathematics assisted in that change. For it did, after Kant had formulated the doctrines of space as a pure intuition and a pure form of empirical intuition. If by the "change of 1770," Vaihinger means the change made by Kant in his doctrines of space upon his discovery that truth in geometry and mechanics is *a priori* and synthetic, he is correct. For upon that discovery, Kant developed the already formulated doctrines of space in explanation of the nature of truth in pure and applied mathematics. But if by the "change of 1770," Vaihinger means the change from the doctrine of space as absolute and real to the doctrines of space as a pure intuition and a pure form of empirical intuition, he is quite wrong. For Kant developed these doctrines, as I have shown, apart from specific problems concerning the nature of mathematics. After his development of the doctrines of space independently of the problems of the nature of truth in mathematics, Kant realized for the first time that such truth is *a priori* and synthetic, and used his doctrines of space to explain this fact. With the nature of truth in geometry and mechanics as supporting evidence, he developed the doctrines of space in the *Inaugural Dissertation* along the lines mentioned by Vaihinger. But he did not arrive at them first in answer to the problem of *a priori,* synthetic truth in those sciences. I have directed my criticism, on this question, against Vaihinger, because I follow him in regard to the nature of the doctrines of space in the *Inaugural Dissertation* after Kant knew that they are established not only in their own right but also with the support of the fact that truth in mathematics is of a special sort.

Let us turn now to Kant's second phase in 1769, namely, his development of his doctrines of space as a pure intuition and as a form of intuition, by offering as supporting evidence the fact that the nature of truth in mathematics is synthetic and *a priori*. As early as 1764, as we have found, he distinguished between the synthetic or empirical truth of mathematics and the analytic truth of metaphysics. Truths of mathematics, he held, are synthetic, since in that science conceptions are treated at random and not

---

[23] Vaihinger's view of the problem of pure mathematics requires a parallel line of criticism.

by an analysis into qualities. Those truths are likewise empirical, since the symbols of that science are singular and sensuous. He had proceeded to maintain that space is dealt with in that science, and that space is intuitively known (*anschauend erkannt*). In 1768, he had maintained that space is known clearly when intuited by inner sense. About 1769, as I have shown, he held for the first time that space is a pure intuition, that is, a nonempirical intuition. Since mathematics deals with space, and since space is a nonempirical intuition, it follows, as he almost immediately concluded, that the source of mathematical truths is nonempirical. But those truths, as he had never specifically denied, involve demonstrative certainty. The fact that their source is nonempirical would seem to account for this certainty. They are nonempirical since they deal with a nonsensuous datum, space. Consequently, they are exempt from the conditions limiting the nature of empirical truth; that is, they are necessary truths. They are nonempirical not merely in the sense that their objects are not objects of experience, but in the sense that their truth is not merely relative—as truths of experience must be—but necessary.

He continued to maintain that the procedure of mathematics is synthetic, since it is not an analysis of qualities, but he added specifically that mathematical truth is *a priori* or necessary, involving universal validity. He did not realize that the synthetic truths of mathematics are *a priori* or necessary until after he had distinguished between the truths of mathematics and experience. He did not distinguish between these truths until he had rejected the theory that the symbols of mathematics are sensuous. He did not reject this theory until he had realized that space is not sensuous, but a pure intuition. Consequently, his discovery that the truth of mathematics is synthetic and *a priori* depended upon, and followed, his formulation of the theory that space is a pure intuition. This is precisely the opposite of Vaihinger's account.[24] Since the

---

[24] Vaihinger, *Kommentar*, I, 274: "In den Grundsätzen der Geometrie, in der Construction der Postulate, in allen Beweisen ist es *Anschauung*, welche die Mathem. Sätze vermittelt, nicht *begriffliche* Analyse. Nun war es aber andererseits für K. feststehend, dass die Mathem. a priori verfahre. Wenn sie aber auf Anschauung beruht, so ist sie—empirisch. Somit wird die Entdeckung ergänzt durch den Nachweis, dass die Anschauung, welche der Mathem. zu Grunde liegt, eine *reine*, d. h. *apriorische* sei."

symbols of mathematics are not sensuous, as Kant had claimed in 1764, since space is not an empirical datum, but a pure intuition, therefore, the synthetic procedure of mathematics is not empirical but *a priori*. In this way he came to the conclusion that there are *a priori,* synthetic truths in mathematics. He did not recognize at the outset that truth in geometry is either synthetic or analytic, *a priori* or *a posteriori,* and consequently he could not even raise these questions until his doctrine of space as a pure intuition was complete.

Kant no longer held that the distinction between analytic and synthetic coincides with that between *a priori* and empirical. The former concerns solely the manner of dealing with conceptions; the latter concerns solely the validity of truths. Analysis is the breaking-up of a conception into a subject and qualities. The qualities must be implicit in the conception, and analysis can be carried on with exactitude only if the conception is kept before the mind. "Gold is a yellow metal." In analyzing the conception of gold, the quality "yellow" is found adhering to the metal and is abstracted from it. But the analysis has nothing to do with the validity of the statement, for if, in experience, a piece of white gold is presented, the statement is false. Synthesis is a different kind of consideration of conceptions. It involves relating them to each other according to principles lying in none of them. It is a random (*willkürlicher*) process only in the negative sense of not conforming to the rules of analysis. But in mathematics, it conforms to strict conditions, and is quite as apt to be *a priori* as analysis is. "A straight line is the shortest distance between two points." This truth is synthetic, since there is nothing in the conception of a straight line which involves the notion of shortness. Shortness is a quantitative conception which has meaning, in this case, only in reference to the space in which the line is assumed to be drawn. Such a truth is synthetic, since the conception of shortness does not lie in the conception of line, but not because of the validity of the proposition. In opposition to the distinction between synthetic and analytic, there is that between *a priori* and empirical. This distinction concerns only the nature of the validity of the analysis or the synthesis. The truths of geometry are *a priori,* since the synthesis of conceptions in that science carries with it necessity and universal validity[25] flowing from the nature of space. "A straight line is the shortest distance between two points." This truth is not only synthetic but *a priori*, since what is concluded about any one straight line is *ipso facto* true about all straight lines because of the nature of space in which all straight lines are assumed to be drawn.

Kant's discovery in 1769 that mathematical truth is synthetic and *a priori*, in opposition to the truths of experience, had an important effect on his theory of the nature of the truth of applied mathematics and mechanics. As I have suggested,[26] it is possible that in the very year (1768) in which he adopted the Newtonian theory of an "absolute" space, he departed from Newton's theory that the findings of mechanics can never carry demonstrative certainty. If in that year in his identification of the sensuous space of experience with the space of the geometer he had argued not merely that the space of the latter shares the reality of empirical space but that the truths of experience (including mechanics) share the validity of those in mathematics about geometrical space, we could conclude definitely that he had parted with Newton at that time. Since he took no precise stand on this matter, no definite conclusion can be drawn. In 1770, the situation was different. Synthetic, *a priori* truths, he then held, are not merely found in pure geometry; they are also found in applied science. Thus either of two possibilities were open to him. Either he could conclude that, like the truths of pure mathematics, the truths of applied geometry and mechanics are *a priori* and synthetic, since applied science, in dealing with space as a form of intuition, deals with the same pure space that is dealt with in pure mathematics; or he could make the much more radical claim that since space is the form of intuition not merely in applied science but in all sensuous experiences, therefore, there is *a priori* (necessary) synthetic truth in sense experience. In either case, he was disagreeing with Newton's view that in science there can never be demonstrative certainty, but only inductive generalization. The second, more radical conclusion would mean that there is *a priori*, synthetic

---

[25] Kant, *Kritik der reinen Vernunft*, B 4.   [26] Cf. above, pp. 111, 118.

truth not merely in applied mathematics and mechanics, but also in sense experience.

There is some evidence that Kant held this second view in 1770. Space, he held, is not merely a form of intuition in applied science but it is a form of all sensuous intuition.[27] Nothing can appear to the senses except as conditioned by space. Nothing can appear to the senses except in conformity with the nature of space as expounded in geometry. All sense experience is dependent upon the exact nature of space as described in geometry. From these statements, the conclusion might seem to follow that, since the same space conditions all sense experience that conditions pure and applied mathematics, hence sense experience yields necessary conclusions, and a science of experience is possible.

However harmonious such a view would be with a metaphysics of experience, it is clear that Kant, because of his narrow conception of experience as bound up solely with sense perception, was holding the less radical view. In the first place, if he meant that there are synthetic, a priori truths not only in pure and applied science, but also in sense experience, then in both cases necessary conclusions would result. If the truths of mechanics are a priori (necessary), and if the truths of experience are a priori (necessary), is there any distinction between these two kinds of a priori synthesis? In brief, experience and applied science would melt into one, and there would be no contingency in either. Kant confused the nonempirical source of space with its necessary nature, and hence with the necessary validity of the truths flowing from it. A representation may have an a priori (nonempirical) source, without thereby having an a priori (necessary) nature; or it may have an empirical source (defining experience in a non-Kantian sense) and yet have an a priori (necessary) nature. Kant confused the a priori origin of the conception of space and its a priori, necessary nature and considered only the second. Such

[27] Kant, *Inaugural Dissertation*, translated by Handyside, pp. 62–63; § 15, E: "[Space is] the foundation of all truth in outer sensibility. For things cannot appear to the senses in any manner except by the mediating power of the mind, co-ordinating all sensations according to a constant law inborn in it. Nothing whatsoever, then, can be given to the senses save in conformity with the primary axioms of space and the other consequences of its nature, as expounded by geometry."

a priority, involving necessity and universality of reference, could obviously never be made compatible with the highly arbitrary conditions of "experience" as Kant conceived it, namely, sense perception. Consequently, granting that the truths of mathematics apply validly to the objects of experience, and granting that space is the form of those same objects, it does not, however, follow that a science of experience is possible. Those truths whose *source* is sense experience can never be universally valid, even though those truths whose *source* is space (as a form of that same experience) are universally valid when applied even to sense objects in space. In spite of the fact that the same space conditions an object of sense perception that conditions the objects dealt with *a priori* in pure and applied science, the results of sense perception do not carry universal validity and necessity. The truths of experience are synthetic, but they are not *a priori,* in spite of the fact that space conditions the objects of these truths no less than it forms the immediate, intuitive basis of those more specifically accurate (necessary) ones of pure and applied science. Kant avoided the narrow view of experience as solely the procedures of mathematics and physics and the equally narrow view of space as a sort of function of those procedures, by making space the form of all sense objects; but he did not go to the other extreme and attempt to show that the truths of sense experience—because of the relation of their objects to space—can claim the same sort of necessary validity found only in pure and applied science. It did not occur to him that possibly this relation of space to sense objects, along with its intuitive nature, might provide a clue to a kind of empirical metaphysics, yielding necessary results.

Persisting in his equation of "experience" and "perception," he distinguished between the truths of geometry, applied science, and experience. The truths of pure geometry *arise from* the nature of space as a pure intuition and have that nature as the source of their necessity. It is to nonempirical objects (figures) in this same pure space that those truths *refer.* The truths of applied geometry *arise from* the nature of space as a pure intuition and have that nature as the source of their necessity. But it is to empirical objects in space as a form of empirical intuition that those truths *refer.* Both sorts of truths are *a priori* and synthetic, in spite of the fact that the latter sort *refers to* (although it does not *arise from*) the objects of sense experience. In opposition to the truths of pure and applied geometry, the truths of experience, *arise from* the objects of sense, lying admittedly in the same space which is dealt with necessarily in applied geometry, in fact being, perhaps, the same objects which are dealt with in that applied science. But the truths of experience, *arising from* the objects of sense, as well as *referring to* them as the truths of applied science do, carry no necessity or general validity. The truths of pure geometry *arise from* a nonempirical source and *refer* universally *to* the same source; the truths of applied geometry and mechanics *arise from* a nonempirical source and *refer* universally *to* the objects of sense experience; but the truths of experience, both *arising from* and *referring to* the objects of sense, never carry universal or necessary validity.

§ 4

In the third phase of his thinking in 1769, Kant formulated the doctrine of the metaphysical unreality of space. He superimposed this doctrine upon the quite different doctrines of space as a pure intuition and a pure form of empirical intuition, both as formulated, in the first phase of his thinking, with no special reference to scientific truth and as formulated, in the second phase, with the re-enforcing evidence from the nature of truths in geometry and mechanics.

Space is not something objective and real, neither substance, nor accident, nor relation, *but subjective and ideal.* . . .[28]

To understand this doctrine, we must remember that his results so far in 1769 were: space is real, that is, concrete or intuitive, in opposition to general terms which are ideal, that is, abstract or conceptual; space is ideal, that is, nonempirical or pure, in opposition to sensible objects (and their qualities), which are empirical. Neither of these views would have been incompatible with the further contention that sensible objects (and their qualities) are genuine (metaphysically real) substances in a real world, in which case, space, as a form of that world, would also be real, that is,

[28] *Ibid.*, p. 61, § 15, D.

metaphysically real. But Kant was constrained to avoid this conclusion. In 1770 the fact of the synthetic, *a priori* nature of truth in geometry and mechanics overshadowed in his mind the importance of the different facets of his analysis of space which had led to that discovery. Instead of using the nature of truth in those sciences as grounds for the metaphysical reality of their objects, he formulated a metaphysical dualism between sensible objects, which he called appearances, and real, intelligible objects, which, he held, are the only real substances. He did not contend that because synthetic, *a priori* truth is found only in geometry and mechanics and concerns only the world of appearances, hence analytic truth is reserved exclusively for a science of metaphysics dealing with a real world. Such a contention would have meant a return (at least in regard to metaphysics) to the position of Leibniz. Nor did Kant, as in his later, critical position contend that because synthetic, *a priori* truth is found only in geometry and mechanics and concerns only the world of appearances, hence it is equally unjustifiable to claim that such a world is unreal as to claim that it is real. Instead, he proceeded on the assumption that there is *a priori,* synthetic truth (in an as-yet-unformulated science of metaphysics) concerning an intelligible, real, nonsensuous world in precisely the same way that such truth (in geometry and mechanics) concerns the world of space and time. The basis of such truth was to be certain intellectual intuitions as the forms of that real world, just as space and time are forms of the world of appearances.

The subjectivity and ideality of space refer to the metaphysically unreal nature of the objects of sense (and their qualities) in opposition to real (nonsensuous), intelligible substances, including their qualities and relations. Space, although real, that is, concrete or intuitive (as Kant held later: empirically real),[29] and ideal, that is, pure or necessary, is, in addition, metaphysically ideal. It is neither a real substance, nor an accident, nor a relation, but merely the form of an unreal world of appearances. Such ideality (or, as he misleadingly called it, subjectivity) has nothing to do with its concrete, intuitive nature, for space is not abstract, and (what is even more important for an understanding of Kant)

[29] Kant, *Kritik der reinen Vernunft*, A 27–8 = B 44.

it has nothing to do with its necessary nature. Whatever Kant may in 1770 have meant by the "ideality" of space, he certainly did not mean that it has an arbitrary nature. The nature of space is independent of any contingent conditions of experience and also independent of any distorting, relative (in the usual sense of the term, subjective) factors in the mind. His failure to clarify his theory of the "subjectivity" of space only can lead to confusion unless we bear in mind the already completed theories of space of the first and second phases of 1769. Before we turn to a more thorough investigation of his theory of intellectual intuitions which was at the basis of his dualism of 1770, we must turn to his refutation of the theories of space held by the Newtonians and the Leibnizians and complete our examination of his specific views of space in 1770 in the *Inaugural Dissertation.*

In elaboration of his theory of the "subjectivity" and "ideality" of space in § 15 D of the *Dissertation,* Kant proceeded to criticize the doctrines of space of "the English" and "the Germans." These doctrines, he contended, are both "realistic." In the light of our study of the Newtonian and Leibnizian theories of space, it may seem surprising that Kant could have lumped them together as "realistic," in opposition to his own views. In regard to the significance and validity of his criticisms of his predecessors, we must consider two different problems: (1) The psychological-biographical: to what extent was Kant, in formulating his views, directly influenced by, and consciously considering, those of his predecessors? (2) The logical: to what extent do his views show agreement or disagreement with those of his main predecessors, apart from the question of the source of his ideas? My answer to the first question with reference to 1769 may now be summarized.

As I have tried to indicate,[30] it seems impossible to establish categorically the contention that Kant arrived at his theory of space as a pure intuition from a study of the writings of Clarke, yet in the latter's analyses of space, problems were raised which, if thoughtfully considered, could not fail to yield the very doctrines which Kant himself set up. In reference to Euler, as I have tried to show, the situation is different. Kant's theories of space about 1769 are so similar to the teachings of Euler that it seems definitely

[30] Cf. above, Chapter II, §§ 2–3.

to follow that Kant was directly influenced by, and consciously indebted to, him in that year.

In reference to Leibniz, the problem is again different. Leibniz's *Nouveaux essais* appeared in 1765, and it may possibly have suggested to Kant the general distinction between realities and appearances. That distinction appears in Kant's formulation of his dualism between the worlds of sense and of intelligence in the third phase of his thinking about 1769. Vaihinger[31] considers this possibility; while Erdmann[32] rejects it, in view of the wide divergence between Leibniz's account of our confused knowledge of phenomena and Kant's quite opposite account of our knowledge of the world of space and time. Years later Kant made two references to the Leibnizian theory of space which indicate that it is at least possible that he was indebted to Leibniz for the famous shift of his views in the direction of subjectivism or phenomenalism. In the *Metaphysische Anfangsgründe der Naturwissenschaft*[33] in 1786, he referred to a "great man" whose influence had beer supreme in mathematics in Germany, who formulated a doctrine of space which really meant that space is the form of outer appearances. This man, he went on to say, had been misunderstood; but concerning his view of space, once the distortions made by others have been removed, the following may be said:

Daher war Leibniz's Meinung, soviel ich einsehe, nicht, den Raum durch die Ordnung einfacher Wesen neben einander zu erklären, sondern ihm vielmehr diese als correspondirend, aber zu einer blos intelligiblen (für uns unbekannten) Welt gehörig zur Seite zu setzen, und nichts Anderes zu behaupten, als was anderwärts gezeigt worden, nämlich dass der Raum sammt der Materie, davon er die Form ist, nicht die Welt von Dingen an sich selbst, sondern nur die Erscheinung derselben enthalte, und selbst nur die Form unserer äusseren sinnlichen Anschauung sei.[34]

As we have found, there were two different views of space in Leibniz's *Nouveaux essais:* first, that it is an abstraction from extension, a sort of ideal order, existing only in reference to concrete, particular, extended things; secondly, that it is the relation of coexistence of phenomena. Fundamental to both of these specific, divergent theories of space was, as we have found, his

[31] Vaihinger, *Kommentar*, I, 47–8, 157; II, 428–31.
[32] Erdmann, *Reflexionen Kants*, Vorrede, p. XXIII, p. XLVIII.
[33] Kant, *Werke* (Hartenstein edition), VIII, 491–93.   [34] *Ibid.*, VIII, 492–93.

wider view that space is metaphysically ideal with reference to monads. It seems to be possible, and not improbable, that Kant discovered in the *Nouveaux essais* about 1769 the general distinction between realities and appearances, and, in the third phase of his thinking at that time, superimposed the theory of the metaphysical unreality of space (its "subjectivity" and "ideality") upon his already formulated views, as a result of the influence of Leibniz. His general criticism in 1770 of the "Leibnizians"[35] cannot be considered conclusive; for—at least in 1786—he considered the view of Leibniz not to have reduced mathematics to an empirical status. He may have realized, even in 1770, that Leibniz's general theory of the ideality of space in reference to monads, in no way prevented it from having an essential role in reference to phenomena. Furthermore, it is not impossible that Kant discovered in the *Nouveaux essais* the more specific view that space, even in reference to phenomena, is an order rather than a relation. In this event, he may have construed this teaching to mean that it is a form somewhat like the cardinal numbers, in opposition to the relational, ordinal numbers. This possibility seems, however, to be much less likely than the former, both because of the fact that Leibniz also put the other, different, relational theory of space in the *Nouveaux essais* and because of the much greater likeness between Kant's own treatments of space and those of Euler.

As regards Erdmann's claim that Kant did not derive his dualism of 1770 from Leibniz's dualism in the *Nouveaux essais* because of their utterly different views of the "clarity" of our knowledge of appearances, Kant provides us with another suggestive, although probably not decisive, clue. In 1790, replying to Eberhard, he asked:

Is it to be believed that so great a mathematician as Leibniz held that bodies are composed of Monads (and consequently that space is made up of simple parts)?[36]

Here again we find a tribute to the significance of Leibniz as a mathematician hardly compatible with the contention that Leib-

---

[35] Kant, *Inaugural Dissertation*, translated by Handyside, p. 62, § 15, D: The Leibnizians "dash down geometry from the supreme height of certainty, reducing it to the rank of those sciences whose principles are empirical."

[36] *Über eine Entdeckung, nach der alle neue Kritik der reinen Vernunft durch eine ältere entbehrlich gemacht werden soll*, in Kant, *Werke* (Hartenstein edition), III, 391–92. Quotations translated by Latta, *Leibniz's Monadology*, p. 209.

niz himself committed the serious error of reducing geometry to
an empirical status. Kant repeated that Leibniz had had in mind a
realm of supersensuous realities of a Platonic sort, grasped in
intellectual intuition, in opposition to appearances. He then
proceeded to deal expressly with Leibniz's theory of the lack of
"clarity" of our knowledge of appearances:

With regard to this we must not allow ourselves to be perplexed by
[Leibniz's] explanation of sensation as a confused kind of perception,
but must rather substitute for it another explanation more in harmony
with his main purpose; for otherwise his system would be inconsistent
with itself.[37]

At this much later date, Kant doubtless considered Leibniz's
account of our knowledge of appearances to be not incompatible
with his own. This fact, of course, proves nothing about the source
of his own theory of appearances. It does show, however, that he
may have first formulated that theory about 1769 with Leibniz's
view of 1765 in mind, deliberately rejecting the theory of confused
thought as extrinsic to Leibniz's more considered position.

Whatever Kant's indebtedness to Leibniz may have been in
regard to the dualism of sense and intellect, Kant's original formulation of his more basic views of space as a pure intuition and a
pure form of intuition would seem to have proceeded upon the
very different lines which we have sketched, without reference to
Leibniz or Clarke and probably only under the influence of
Euler. Nevertheless, once these views had been formulated, it is
quite possible that he was influenced by Leibniz in superimposing
the doctrine of the metaphysical unreality (the "subjectivity" and
"ideality") of space upon them. In looking back over a period of
some twenty-five or thirty years (in which he had grappled much
more intensively with the problem of the precise status of appearances than with his views of space), he was much more apt to have
noticed the likeness between his general doctrines and those of
Leibniz, purged and shaped into his own terms, than the vast
differences between his own views of space as he originally worked
them out and those of his predecessor.

In regard to the question of the likeness between his views and
those of his predecessors apart from the matter of influence, many
more significant facts can be established. Quite apart from the

[37] *Ibid.*

problem of how Kant arrived at his theories of space about 1769, there is the identity between Euler's views of space and Kant's theory of a pure intuition as completed in the first phase of his thinking in that year. This identity we have already established. Of equal importance is the problem of a comparison of the views of Clarke and of Kant, to which we must now turn. If we set Clarke's summary[38] of his views of space alongside a summary of the various views of space of Kant in 1770, certain striking likenesses as well as certain obvious differences are apparent.

Clarke	*Kant*
	Dissertation § 15, A. The conception of space is not abstracted from outer sensation.
	B. The conception of space is a singular representation, with the parts *in* and not *under* the whole.
	C. It is thus a pure intuition.
Space is not nothing.	D. Space is not something objective and real, neither substance, nor accident, nor relation, but subjective and ideal. It is not a boundless receptacle of possible things because: (a) such a theory would involve an infinity of real relations without things related; (b) such a theory would place a stumbling block in the way of such rational conceptions as a spiritual world, omnipresence, etc.
Space is not a mere idea.	
It is not a relation.	
It is not body.	
It is not any kind of substance.	
It is, by elimination, a property: immensity or omnipresence.	E. Space is a pure form of intuition. §§ 14–15 corollary: The infinite whole of space is given.
We have a partial apprehension of infinite space.	
Space is infinite because it is contradictory for it to be otherwise.	§§ 14–15 corollary. The parts of space do not prescribe the possibility of the whole, but are limits within the whole.
There are no actual, but only figurative, parts of space. Space is indivisible.	Hence, space is indivisible.

[38] Clarke, Paper V, § 46 note.

In the first place, Kant held that space is different in its origin from the objects (and qualities) of sense, and that it is a singular representation with its parts *in* it. These doctrines seem to be linked only with the views of Euler and to have no counterparts in the views of Clarke. Merely to point to this apparent difference and leave the matter there is, however, to ignore a fundamental likeness in the doctrines of the two men, which Kant's highly specialized terminology obscures. In his doctrine of the fictitious nature of the parts of space, Clarke asked us to perform a crucial experiment, which, if properly interpreted, yields both the non-empirical origin of space and what Kant called its singularity.[39] Whether by abstraction we try to get objects of sense out of space, or to get the parts of space out of the whole, we find that space must remain: in the first case, where the object had been; in the second, between the two supposedly separated spaces. Consequently, Clarke's experiment not only establishes the fictitiousness of the parts, but a unique relation, in the first case, between space and the sense objects in it, and, in the second, between the whole of space and its parts. These differences, properly interpreted, mean nothing more or less than that space is nonempirical and singular and, in the specific Kantian terminology, a pure intuition.

What is even more important, Clarke's argument that space is not an idea, raises the possibility of precisely the distinction involved in Kant's theory of intuitions and conceptions. Our ideas of space, Clarke held, yield characteristics which we know that space does not have.[40] Our ideas of space are of finite spaces, but we know that space is infinite. Ideas of space yield properties different from, and in contradiction to, the ones which it actually possesses (infinitude and indivisibility). Clarke did not proceed to explain satisfactorily the type of apprehension by means of which we correct our ideas, implying that it is done by rational analysis, but his account of the indivisibility of space and the fictitiousness of the parts is in flat contradiction even with such an implied teaching. Consequently, Clarke's views imply—and require by way of amplification—precisely such a type of apprehension as the one that Kant called intuition. Such apprehension would be different from the process of framing ideas, that is, different, in Kant's terminology, from conception in the abstract. And what is of even greater significance, there is nothing in Clarke's statements to preclude the possibility that space (or time) would be only one example of such a new kind of "conception." In the face of such likenesses, it is difficult to conclude categorically, in answer to our psychological-biographical question, that Kant was not directly influenced by Clarke; and in reference to our logical question, it seems to follow necessarily that Kant's views on these matters are similar to those of Clarke.

There are, furthermore, obvious likenesses between the views of the two men, such as their common rejection of the theories that space is a relation or a substance and their theories of the infinitude of space. On the latter point, it is true, Clarke held that we have a partial apprehension of the infinite whole of space, whereas Kant went farther and held that the infinite whole is given. But, as I have hinted above[41] and shall further show below,[42] Kant's more detailed accounts in 1781 and 1787 of the infinite given whole of space differ widely among themselves, and he nowhere came so close to what seems to be the correct version of spatial infinitude as did Clarke.

In regard to the differences between the theories of the two men, the problem is further complicated because Kant professed definitely in 1770 to be differing from the Newtonians. We have, therefore, the dual problem of disentangling the grounds which Kant himself gave as the basis of this difference and those differences which we know to exist in the light of our study of Clarke. The grounds which Kant himself gave are found in the argument that space is "subjective" and "ideal." In that argument, he was not working out the theory of space as a pure intuition, with the emphasis upon the concreteness (reality) or the necessary nature (ideality) of space, but the theory that space and all the bodies of sense (their qualities and relations) are metaphysically unreal (ideal) in opposition to intellectual intuitions, real substances, properties, and relations. His condemnation of the English was not, therefore, of their account of the relation of space to the

<hr />

[41] Cf. above, pp. 25–26.

[42] Cf. below, pp. 191–97.

objects of sense nor of their account of the necessary nature of space. On these points, he was a Newtonian, if such views are considered to be Newtonian. His criticism was based upon his own belief in an intelligible, real world, nonspatial in nature, involving in our knowledge of it intellectual intuitions as its forms. Such a view, he could validly hold, would be precluded by the Newtonian theory that space is a form (container) of the real world. If omnipresence is omnipresence in an intelligible, nonspatial world, then the Newtonian doctrine of the reality, that is, metaphysical reality, of space would place a stumbling block in the way of such omnipresence.[43] This criticism is, from his own metaphysical view, a valid criticism of the Newtonian theory that space is a property of God. Clarke considered that his theory of space, far from placing a stumbling block in the way of a conception of omnipresence, was the very cornerstone of such a doctrine, space itself being God's omnipresence. Yet Kant could validly conclude that if the spatial world is not the real world, then any attempt to base divine omnipresence upon space would be to link God not with reality but with appearances. This was the conclusion that he reached.

His other criticism of the English, however, miscarried. An absolute, real space is, he held,[44] an empty fancy of the mind since it involves an infinite number of real relations without things related. Whatever is the validity of his criticism of Newton's theory of space as metaphysically real and a property of God, Kant's argument here involves a mistaken conception of the Newtonian view, and, in fact, is equally out of harmony with his own doctrine that space is nonempirical and pure. Such a criticism could be made only from the very Leibnizian point of view which Kant was exposing in the same sentences in which he was attacking the Newtonians, from the point of view that space is a relation. The infinitude of space along with the assumptions of vacuums in nature and empty space outside of the universe (if the universe is finite) does not mean that there are real relations in such empty spaces. Space, according to Newton and Clarke, is a container prior to, and different from, the qualities and relations of bodies in it. It exists where there are no bodies, not as a relation but as an

---

[43] Kant, *Inaugural Dissertation*, § 15, D.   [44] *Ibid.*

empty receptacle. There would be real relations without things related only if space is a relation and if parts of it are empty. By assuming the truth of the Leibnizian theory that space is relational and uniting this assumption with the Newtonian conception of empty space, Kant arrived at the weird conclusion that the latter conception would involve real relations without things related. This assumption is not only unwarranted with reference to the Newtonian position, but is equally incompatible with Kant's own theory that space is nonempirical and pure. If space is relational and if it is prior to the objects of sense, it would involve real relations without things related. If it is relational and if it remains after the objects of sense have been abstracted, it would involve real relations without things related. If this criticism offers grounds for Kant's rejection of the Newtonian theory of space, it offers also, for the same reason, grounds for the rejection of the theory that space is a pure intuition.

The fact that Kant used this argument in 1770 against the Newtonians shows a relative lack of familiarity on his part with their views, and would seem to justify our hesitancy in ascribing to Clarke any direct influence upon Kant at that time in spite of the close resemblance between the views of the two men. It re-enforces our contention, also, that Kant worked out his theory of the "subjectivity," that is, metaphysical unreality, of space in a different phase of his thinking from those two in which he arrived at his own more specific doctrines. It is possible, although not probable, that he worked out his refutations of the Newtonians and Leibnizians in the very first portion of his thinking between 1768 and 1770. It seems more probable that he worked them out hastily in 1770, after he had completed his other doctrines of space. Both refutations are based upon his dualism between nonsensuous realities and appearances; both are extrinsic to his main theories of space.

The general question of the validity of Kant's criticisms in 1770 of the Leibnizian theory that space is a relation raises many problems both within and beyond the framework of the Kantian philosophy of space. In brief, his criticisms were two.[45] (1) The

[45] *Ibid.*

Leibnizian view involves circular reasoning. (2) It deprives the truths of geometry of their necessary quality and reduces them to the status of empirical generalizations. Both of these criticisms are so important in the light of present-day developments in philosophy and mathematical physics that I shall defer a more complete discussion of them until we turn to the problem of Kant's relation to certain present-day theories. We should notice here, however, that only the second involves an appeal to the nature of mathematical truth. The first means that space cannot be derived from empirical objects not merely because they lie *in* it and hence it is *outside* them, but also because it determines their nature. This view assumes great significance in the teachings of Mr. S. Alexander, and I shall merely defer our discussion of these matters. The second criticism, involving, as it does, the problem of the dimensionality of space and the significance of Euclidian geometry, can also be more profitably considered below in reference to the views of Alexander, Whitehead, and Broad.

§ 5

IN THE first paragraph of the Corollary to §§ 14–15 of the *Inaugural Dissertation,* Kant returned to the problem of the relation of space to various spaces. In § 15 A, he had merely described that relation as one of inclusion *in* rather than *under* space and had referred to the many spaces as being parts of the same boundless space. He proceeded to work out this relation more specifically. In the cases of space and time

it is not true that the parts, and in especial the simple parts, contain, as the laws of reason prescribe, the ground of the possibility of the composite; but instead . . . the infinite contains the ground of every thinkable part, and finally of the simple, or rather of the limit. For only if infinite space and time be given, can any definite space or time be marked out by limitation of it; neither a point nor a moment can be thought by itself; they are conceived only as limits in an already given space or time.[46]

Did Kant mean that infinite space, finite parts of space, and limits of those parts are all three given to the mind as equally intrinsic aspects of the intuition? This view would seem to be hardly what

[46] Kant, *Inaugural Dissertation,* translated by Handyside, p. 64, § 15 corollary.

he meant, for limits are not space at all, since they lack three-dimensional extension. Did he mean that infinite space and its finite parts are given to the mind, but that the limits are simply thought of as in what is given? Professor Paton holds that "Kant is always clear that a line is made up of parts, and that points are not parts, but limits, of a line."[47] While it is clear that Kant distinguished between space and such limits in it as points, lines, and surfaces, it is by no means clear that he held that lines are "made up" of parts. If, in marking out a definite space by limitation of the given infinite whole, the mind confers upon the particular space the status of a part, then space has parts. The test of a part in this case is, however, not the fact that such space is given, but the fact that it is marked out by the mind. If, however, Kant meant, as would seem to be the case, that the marking out or limitation of infinite space confers no special qualities upon a definite space, then space either has no parts, or at best, only in a figurative sense. If "here" and "there" are not qualities of space, but merely space itself, then space has no actual parts. Such is precisely what Kant meant in 1770 and in the *Aesthetic*. Infinite space is given to the mind; finite spaces as well as the limits of these are merely thought of, or conceived, as in what is given. That this space is here and that there means nothing more or less than that this space is space. A foot is "space" no less than an ell. We completely misunderstand Kant if we take him to mean that a line, a surface, or a solid is made up of parts. Similarly, we misunderstand him if we hold him to mean that space is made up of spaces or parts. The whole of space contains the ground for the determination of every particular. We may, in Clarke's language, treat space in our imagination as composed of parts, but these parts are fictitious. We may, in Kant's words, think or conceive of infinite space as limited and definite spaces as marked out in it. In fact there is nothing of this sort in the intuition. In reference to space as it is, all thinkable parts, including the simple or limit, are limitations of the given whole.

Kant's position in 1770 was, therefore, that the infinite whole of space is given as a pure intuition as well as the form of all empirical intuitions. Its nonempirical nature, its singularity, its differences from general conceptions, its relation to *a priori,* synthetic truth in geometry and mechanics and to sense experience are features of this position. Space is given and not constructed; the only activity of the mind is a delimitation of the already given. In spite of these contentions, Kant was concerned possibly in the example of incongruent counterparts with the problem of an activity of the mind which constructs or generates space. To this question he turned again in the last paragraph of the corollary to §§ 14–15 of the *Dissertation.* There he raised a question that is independent of his doctrine of space as a pure intuition and in partial contradiction to it.

Finally, the question naturally arises whether [space and time] are connate or acquired. The latter alternative, it is true, seems already refuted by our demonstrations, but the former is not to be rashly admitted, since, in appealing to a first cause, it opens a path for that lazy philosophy which declares all further research to be vain. Both concepts are without doubt acquired, as abstracted, not indeed from the sensing of objects (for sensation gives the matter, not the form, of human apprehension), but from the action of the mind in co-ordinating its sensa according to unchanging laws—each being, as it were, an immutable type, and therefore to be known intuitively. For, though sensations excite this act of the mind, they do not determine the intuition.[48]

According to the rest of the *Dissertation* (with the possible exception of the example of incongruent counterparts), space is given and not derived or generated. In this passage, however, Kant held that it is generated on the occasion of sense experience by a synthesis which does not begin with the materials of sensation. It is gained neither by reflection nor from sensation, yet a synthesis generates it. We shall find that these two views of space become even more sharply divergent in the *Critique of Pure Reason.* Let us postpone, therefore, the problem of whether or not they are compatible with each other.

§ 6

KANT'S THEORY of knowledge in the *Dissertation* will remain an enigma unless his theory of *intuitus intellectualis* is carefully con-

[48] Kant, *Inaugural Dissertation,* translated by Handyside, pp. 65–66.

sidered. In portions[49] of that writing he assumed that there are certain intellectual intuitions available to the human mind, differing from general conceptions in the same way that space and time do, and playing the same fundamental role in the science of metaphysics that space and time do in the sciences of geometry and mechanics. The investigation of these intellectual intuitions was for him a study preliminary to the science of metaphysics itself and involved the consideration of two worlds, the sensible and the intelligible, and the forms and contents of each. In other portions[50] of the same writing, Kant contended explicitly that there are no intellectual intuitions available to man. The *Dissertation* can be understood only if these two contradictory positions are noted in it. Two clear and self-consistent, but contradictory theories of knowledge flow from the assumptions (1) that man has intellectual intuitions, and (2) that he lacks them. Confusion results from Kant's attempt to combine the second contention with conclusions flowing from its contradictory, the first.

Kant's position in the *Dissertation* based upon the assumption that human beings have intellectual intuitions is briefly as follows:

We rightly suppose that what cannot be known through any intuition whatever is not thinkable at all, and so is impossible.[51]

Everything that is thinkable and possible can be known only through intuition. Objects of sense are thinkable and possible, and they are apprehended through intuition. They are, however, appearances. Real objects are, likewise, thinkable and possible. They are, likewise, apprehended through intuition. They are, however, nonsensuous. They are not apprehended, consequently, through sensuous intuition or its forms (space and time). Hence they must be apprehended through intellectual intuitions. But they are apprehended by human beings. Hence human beings have intellectual intuitions.

This view is fundamental to the *Dissertation,* so fundamental that three of Kant's leading distinctions rest upon it: (1) his distinction between a real and a logical use of the intellect (understanding); (2) his distinction between a qualitative and a quan-

---

[49] *Ibid.,* §§ 1, 2, 16, 17, 25 (in part).
[50] *Ibid.,* §§ 10, 25 (in part).   [51] *Ibid.,* § 25, Handyside's translation, p. 75.

titative synthesis; (3) his distinction between a whole of representation and a representation of a whole. Let us examine Kant's contention that intellectual intuitions are given to man, by tracing these three distinctions in turn.

A logical use of the intellect is common to all sciences[52] (geometry, mechanics, and metaphysics), involving solely the subordination of conceptions to one another by a comparison of common marks and by reference to the principle of contradiction. Its real use is different not merely from the logical one, but also from sensuous intuition. Its real use is not merely a logical ordering of material already given to the mind, but a manner of apprehending material. Yet it is not a manner of apprehending the materials of sense. Hence it cannot involve any sensuous intuition or its forms. But all apprehension is based upon intuition. Hence the real use of the intellect must be based upon intuition. Since it is not based upon sensuous intuition or its forms, it must be based upon intellectual intuition. The logical use of the intellect, not concerning the apprehension of any type of material but merely involving the ordering of materials already given, proceeds identically with the materials of sense and of reality. In human knowledge of the world of sense, there is the act of apprehension by means of sensuous intuition, followed by the logical use of the intellect, clarifying and ordering the materials of sense. In human knowledge of the real world, there is the real use of the intellect (involving intellectual intuition) followed by its logical use, clarifying and ordering the materials of reality. In both cases, the logical use of the intellect operates in a minor role subsequent to the act of apprehension.

The difference between the real and the logical uses of the intellect is the difference between the intellectual apprehension of a special type of object (the real, intelligible object), and the process of ordering objects once apprehended, whatever be their nature. The difference between the real use of the intellect and the act of sensuous apprehension is, however, the difference between two methods of apprehending objects (or relations), and involves a difference in kind between two types of apprehended

[52] *Ibid.*, § 5.

entities, the real and the sensuous. There are two types of apprehended material, one sensuous and the other real; but neither case involves an activity of the mind merely of a clarifying, logical sort. On the contrary, both types, once apprehended, are ordered and clarified by the same logical use of the intellect. The logical use orders appearances, giving them greater universality but never freeing them from their sensitive source.[53] It likewise orders realities. What has happened to appearances prior to the logical activity of the intellect? Kant's answer to this question is ambiguous. What has happened to realities prior to that logical activity? He seems to be clear concerning this question, holding that the real use of the intellect is involved. In spite of his ambiguity in regard to sensuous apprehension and his apparent clarity in regard to the real use of the intellect, it is, however, in regard to the latter that his view is on shaky foundations; for he did not give a single example of an intellectual intuition of a real object, whereas he had already formulated his doctrines of space and time as the forms of sensuous intuition. He contradicted himself in regard to the nature of sensuous apprehension, saying in some places[54] that the intellect passively receives the contents of the world of appearances, and also in one place[55] that there is an activity of the mind from which even space and time, the forms of that world, are abstracted. But in both of these accounts of sensibility, he assumed that a set of materials is given to, and is dealt with by, the mind. Similarly, in the real use of the intellect, another set of materials is given to, and being dealt with by, the mind. In both cases, logical abstraction and analysis are subsequent to the process of apprehension. But the materials dealt with by the intellect in its real use are not sensuous appearances given in sensuous intuition. The materials of reality are nonsensuous, and consequently, if apprehended at all, they involve intellectual intuitions. But in the real use of the intellect, they are apprehended. Hence human beings have intellectual intuitions.

A second distinction in the *Dissertation* flowing from Kant's

[53] *Ibid.*, § 5, end.
[54] *Ibid.*, § 10, towards the end; § 15, A, B, C (except the example of incongruent counterparts), and §§ 14–15 corollary (beginning).
[55] *Ibid.*, §§ 14–15 corollary (end).

view that human beings have intellectual intuitions is the distinction between a qualitative and a quantitative synthesis.

Synthesis is either qualitative, *i.e.*, progress in series whose members are subordinate to each other, in each case as consequent to ground, or quantitative, *i.e.*, progress in series of co-ordinated members from a given part through its complements to the whole.[56]

In one sense, there is a qualitative synthesis from ground to all possible consequents. In the act of knowledge, this type of synthesis follows upon the process of quantitative synthesis, doing nothing besides ordering and clarifying the material that the latter has yielded. It involves the relation of completely determining ground and completely determined consequent. On the other hand, of chief importance is the quantitative synthesis, involving progress along a series of co-ordinated members to a whole. This process, depending upon conditions of time, can never be completed. Kant realized that the inability of the mind to reach a whole in this fashion is not an argument against the objective reality of the co-ordinated parts (and of the whole) but indicates merely the subjective limitations of our minds. Had he pushed this consideration to its logical conclusion, he would have realized that the co-ordinated members dealt with in this quantitative synthesis are necessarily the parts of the sensuous world of space and time, and that the "infinite whole" which the mind is subjectively incapable of reaching is the whole of such a world. Instead of doing so, he held that the mind is incapable, on the one hand, of completing in the given sensuous intuition, the quantitative synthesis of the "whole" of the world of sense; and, on the other, of completing, in the likewise given intellectual intuition, the quantitative synthesis of a "whole" of the real world.

Kant's third distinction based upon the assumption that human beings have intellectual intuitions is the distinction between a whole of representation and a representation of a whole. There is, he held, "form, which consists in the co-ordination, not in the subordination, of substances. . . . This co-ordination is conceived as real and objective. . . . For by embracing a plurality you may without difficulty make a *whole of representation*, but not,

[56] *Ibid.*, § 1 *n.*, Handyside's translation, p. 36.

thereby, the *representation of a whole*."[57] He distinguished not merely between co-ordination and subordination, but also between two types of co-ordination. Subordination of substances as ground and consequent involves, he meant, an activity of the mind common to all the sciences, never in itself yielding more than a whole of representation. However accurate such an activity of the mind may be, the resulting whole is merely ideal. A whole of representation involves only the accurate application of analytical principles. Co-ordination, on the other hand, involves the representation of an object, but in two sharply different fashions. In the first case, there are sensuous objects presented or intuited according to spatial and temporal conditions. This presentation involves a co-ordination, rather than a subordination, of substances sensuous in nature. In the second case, there are, however, real, intelligible objects, likewise presented or intuited according to certain conditions, the nature of which Kant was trying to determine. This presentation is also a co-ordination, rather than a subordination of substances nonsensuous in nature.[58] Both types of co-ordination yield a representation of a whole, different from a mere whole of representation. Both types involve a quantitative synthesis different from the merely qualitative synthesis which follows upon the heels of each for the purpose of clarification. A representation of a whole conforms, in some cases, to the conditions of intellectual intuition; in others, to the conditions of space and time. A whole of representation conforms, in every case, merely to the conditions of conception. Objects presented or intuited intellectually are real objects. Objects presented or intuited sensuously are the objects in space and time.

The theory that human beings have intellectual intuitions is, consequently, fundamental to Kant's views in the *Dissertation*. He came, however, to the conclusion that human beings have no intellectual intuitions, and tried to superimpose this conclusion upon the doctrines traced above. Since those doctrines rest upon the contradictory theory, the result was quite unsatisfactory. Let us sketch this change in Kant's views.

---

[57] *Ibid.*, § 2; Handyside's translation, pp. 39–40.   [58] *Ibid.*, §§ 16–17.

No intuition of things intellectual, but only a symbolic knowledge of them, is given to man. Intellection is possible to us only through universal concepts in the abstract, not through a singular concept in the concrete.[59]

Here Kant departed from his view that human beings have intellectual intuitions. There were two alternatives open to him with reference to intelligible, real objects. First, such objects are known solely through intuition, which cannot be sensuous; human beings, having no such nonsensuous, intellectual intuitions, do not know such objects, which are hence known only by God.[60] This is the view to which Kant would have been driven if he had retained his contention that all knowledge is based upon intuition and that human beings have no intellectual intuitions. Secondly, such objects are known in either of two ways: either immediately by intuition, which cannot be sensuous, or mediately by conception. In this view, human beings, lacking such nonsensuous, intellectual intuitions, know these objects only in the second way, while God knows them in the first. Rejecting his own contention that all objects are known through intuition, sensuous objects through sensuous intuition and real objects through intellectual intuition, Kant adopted this second alternative, and held that some knowledge is solely conceptual. He distinguished between God's knowledge of realities and human knowledge of them. All divine knowledge is based upon intuitions. Like human knowledge of appearances, God's knowledge of realities is intuitive. Human beings know the world of appearances by means of sensuous intuitions (including their forms, space and time). God knows the real world by means of intellectual intuition. Human knowledge of realities is different. Such knowledge, Kant held, is not based upon intuition, but solely upon conception. It is symbolic knowledge through universal conceptions in the abstract instead of immediate knowledge through a singular conception (intuition) in the concrete.

[59] *Ibid.*, p. 50, § 10.

[60] *Ibid.*, p. 75, § 25: "But since by no effort of the mind can we attain even in imagination another kind of intuition than that which takes place according to the form of space and time . . . we regard as impossible all intuition whatever which is not bound by these laws (neglecting the pure intellectual intuition which is exempt from the laws of the senses, such as the divine intuition which Plato calls an idea) , and so subject all possible things to the sensitive axioms of space and time."

Such was Kant's compromise view flowing from his conclusion that human beings have no intellectual intuitions. It left him open to three dangers. In the first place, to avoid the conclusion that human beings have no knowledge of realities, he would be forced to justify his view that some knowledge can be entirely symbolic, abstract, and conceptual, in opposition to his own specific contention to the contrary. In the second place, to the extent that he might be successful in justifying his claim that some knowledge is purely conceptual, he would be forced immediately to answer the charge that all knowledge is purely conceptual, and that sense perception and intuition are merely modified, blurred, and weakened forms of conception. If, in proving that some knowledge is conceptual, he could not, at the same time, show that some knowledge is nonconceptual or intuitive, he would be forced to reject his doctrines of space, time, and sensibility, in favor of the very Leibnizian view that he so rigidly criticized.[61] In the third place, even if he should be successful in maintaining his contentions that some human knowledge (namely, of realities) is conceptual and other human knowledge (namely, of appearances) is intuitive, he would be forced to answer the charge that God's knowledge is the prototype of the latter rather than the former, and hence even God does not have intellectual intuitions. If some human knowledge is conceptual, what is the justification for claiming that God's knowledge is the prototype of human intuitive knowledge of appearances rather than of such conceptual knowledge?

In spite of these difficulties, Kant proceeded to elaborate the view that some knowledge of realities is purely conceptual.

Since, then, no empirical principles are to be found in metaphysics, the concepts there met with are not to be looked for in the senses, but in the very nature of pure intellect, not as concepts *connate* to it, but as abstracted (by attention to its actions on the occasion of experience) from laws inborn in the mind, and so to this extent as *acquired*. Concepts of this sort are: possibility, existence, necessity, substance, cause, etc. . . .[62]

The real use of the intellect is its operation upon such conceptions and does not involve any intellectual intuition. It yields knowl-

[61] *Ibid.*, §§ 7, 11, 15, C, D.   [62] *Ibid.*, pp. 48–49, § 8.

edge of real objects, but such knowledge, because of its conceptual nature, is entirely symbolic and abstract. Primarily by means of the categories of substance, causality, and reciprocity, the mind reaches knowledge of the real world.

If Kant had retained his view that whatever is knowable is knowable through intuition, his theory of the nature of the categories would not be evidence that human beings know nonsensuous realities. The categories, however similar their mode of derivation may be to that of space and time, are conceptions or forms of conception, whereas space and time are intuitions or forms of intuition. Consequently, even if the mind is in possession of the categories independent of, yet on the occasion of, experience, such possession is no evidence that they yield knowledge unless they may be referred to intuition. Unless nonsensuous substances are apprehended by means of intuition, their reciprocal interaction and their dependence on one cause are in no way guaranteed by the possession of these categories by the mind. Only if the categories are supplemented by intellectual intuitions can they yield knowledge of a nonsensuous, intelligible world.

Kant attempted to avoid this conclusion by his theory that they yield a symbolic knowledge of such a world and, hence, that human knowledge of that world is possible without intellectual intuitions. Aside from the fact that this contention exposed him to the three dangers mentioned above, it represents a complete reformulation, if not a destruction, of his theory of the real use of the intellect, his distinction between quantitative and qualitative syntheses, and his distinction between a whole of representation and a representation of a whole. If the real use of the intellect yields knowledge, there must be a set of materials given to the mind to which that knowledge refers. If such materials are the intelligible, real world, then there must be intellectual, nonsensuous intuitions involved. If such intuitions are lacking, the difference between the real use of the intellect and its logical use vanishes, and both uses involve merely logical clarification. The fact that the one use is clarification according to one set of principles (for example, causality) and the other, clarification according to the principle of contradiction is no evidence that there is knowledge in either case, if no materials are given. If there is a quantitative synthesis by the mind of the nonsensuous materials of reality, then such materials must be given to the mind in intellectual intuition. If the mind has a representation of any whole other than the world of sense, such a representation must involve a set of materials presented in intuition, other than the materials of sense, or else merely a whole of representation results. These distinctions all rest upon the assumption that two sets of materials (the sensuous and the real) are given to the mind and, hence, that human beings have intellectual, no less than sensuous, intuitions. By holding that human beings have conceptual knowledge of the real world, Kant cut the ground from under his theories of a real use of the intellect, a quantitative synthesis of the materials of reality, and a representation of the whole of the real, intelligible world. He could not successfully combine these doctrines with the theory that human beings have no intellectual intuitions.

Kant's distinction of 1770 between the world of sense and the world of reality formed the basis for his answer to the problem of the spatial finitude or infinitude of the world. He held that the sensuous world is infinite in regard to space. He did so, partly because of his conviction that the materials of quantitative synthesis are inexhaustible, and partly because of his belief that his reduction of the world of sense to a world of appearances had saved the nature of the real world from the ethical and religious consequences of such a theory. He was thus in a position to treat the question of the spatial infinitude of the world. There are different answers to this highly ambiguous question: is the world infinite in respect to space?[63] If the real world is meant, the answer is that the real world, not being in space, is neither spatially finite nor infinite. If the sensible world is meant, the answer is that the sensible world is infinite in space because in the quantitative synthesis the mind is presented with an infinite amount of material to be traversed. If the whole yielded by a qualitative synthesis is meant, then such a whole, being subjective and ideal, is apprehended neither as the intelligible world nor as the sensible world. Such a whole, not apprehended by any sort of

[63] Kant, *Kritik der reinen Vernunft*, A 427 = B 455.

intuition, is, therefore, not a world, or at least only an imaginary one. Dismissing the third possibility, the other two are fairly clear. The only meaningful question is the first: is the sensible world infinite in respect to space? No antinomy arises from this question, for the answer is unequivocably "yes." The second question is also clear. The intelligible world is, by definition, not in space. Hence the answer to the second question is: the intelligible world is neither finite nor infinite in respect to space, for it is not in space. How then does an antinomy arise? It arises by sensuous conceptions crossing their boundaries and meddling with the intelligible ones.[64] There arises, Kant claimed, an antinomy only when the sensible world, admittedly infinite in space, is confused with the intelligible world, and the latter is falsely held to be in space and finite or infinite in respect to it. The defenders of the infinity of the sensible world in respect to space, not satisfied with having established their position, go further and claim that it is the real world. This arrogance provokes the defenders of the finitude of the world to take up arms equally arrogantly in defense of a position which they had been willing to abandon, namely, the view that the sensible world is finite in respect to space. By trying to prove too much about the world of sense, the empiricists force their opponents, the dogmatists, to try to do the same. The former try to prove that the spatially infinite sensible world is the real world; the latter, that the sensible world is spatially finite. This sham conflict is an antinomy. It is easily avoided, Kant held, by formulating rules to prevent the sensitive conceptions from meddling with the intelligible.[65] These rules formulated, the sensible world could peacefully be granted to be infinite in respect to space, and the real world held to be neither spatially finite nor infinite.

Alas for poor Kant! The collapse of his theory of intellectual intuition removes the very distinction between the world of sense and the world of intellect upon which the solution of the antinomy rests. If the inability of the mind to complete the quantitative synthesis is taken not as evidence that the world of

---

[64] Kant, *Inaugural Dissertation*, § 24.   [65] *Ibid.*, §§ 24–25.

sense is a world of appearances, but that it is the real world, the conclusion is unavoidable that the real world is infinite in respect to space and time. The solution of the first antinomy in the *Critique of Pure Reason* rests upon an assumption that Kant had undermined even in 1770.

CHAPTER VII

THE CRITIQUE OF PURE REASON: THE SPACE OF THE *AESTHETIC*

§ 1

WE ARE NOW in a position to consider Kant's philosophy of space in the *Critique of Pure Reason,* 1781 and 1787, especially in the light of the results of our investigation of his earlier views. Let us first consider the five formal space arguments in the *Aesthetic,* the third of which he broke off from the others in the second edition and called a Transcendental Exposition in opposition to the other four, which he called a Metaphysical Exposition.[1] The significance of this splitting of his arguments into two parts in the later edition is briefly as follows. The third argument of the first edition differs radically from the other four in that it is based solely upon the nature of mathematical truth. Kant inserted the five arguments in the first edition almost in the form worked out in the *Dissertation,* and he probably did not analyze them very carefully in 1781 in the light of his whole position. In 1787, however, he had completed his *Prolegomena,* in which he had dealt with his general position almost exclusively from the point of view of the nature of truths in geometry and mechanics. Such an approach to his philosophy of space is much more limited than his doctrine that space is the form of the objects of sense experience, no less than of mathematical figures and mechanical bodies. However significant the doctrine of *a priori,* synthetic truth in geometry and mechanics was as a re-enforcing argument for his theories of space, that doctrine was not the chief basis for those theories. The separation of the direct, or so-called assumptionless, space arguments in 1787 under the title of a Metaphysical Exposition, from the re-enforcing argument from the nature of mathe-

[1] I shall refer to the arguments of the Metaphysical Exposition as the first, second, third, and fourth space arguments respectively.

matical truth under the title of a Transcendental Exposition was highly desirable since it brought out precisely the distinction between the two types of arguments. Furthermore, if our account of Kant's original formulation of his views of space about 1769 is correct, this division accords with his own mental biography in that much earlier year. The difference between his views of 1769 and those of 1787 in regard to the two different types of exposition lies in the fact that in the earlier year he first worked out his theory of space not only independently of the theory of synthetic, *a priori* mathematical truth, but even without being aware of that theory. In the *Critique,* on the other hand, he designed each exposition to yield his views of space in their entirety.

Let us turn to the first two space arguments of the *Aesthetic.* In spite of their close similarity to the corresponding sections of the *Dissertation,* one striking difference is apparent. In 1770, Kant's argument ran roughly as follows: since space is nonempirical and different from general conceptions, therefore it is a pure intuition —which conclusion is supported by the nature of mathematical truth.[2] A silent assumption underlies this entire body of argument: a nonempirical representation is a necessary representation, and a necessary representation is nonempirical. Unlike the intuitive nature of space, which depends upon a different argument, its "pure," necessary nature is assumed to be the outcome of its nonempirical character. The doctrine that space is nonempirical in its source is, however, quite different from the view that it has a necessary nature.[3] As S. Alexander[4] has pointed out, the latter may be held without the former, if a sufficiently broad view of experience is taken. But Kant was committed both in 1770 and in 1781 to the view that experience refers only to the contents of sense perception, conditioned admittedly by such elements as space, time, and the categories. Now all such contents are relative and contingent whereas space has a necessary nature. Hence to establish its necessary nature meant to establish its nonempirical nature, and vice versa. Kant was in 1770 so far from considering

[2] Kant, *Inaugural Dissertation,* § 15, A, B, C.
[3] Cf. above, pp. 125, 137–38.
[4] Alexander, *Space, Time and Deity,* I, 4–5; cf. below, pp. 239–40.

the possibility that a "pure," that is, nonempirical, space might be different from a "pure," that is, necessary, space that he mentioned its necessary nature chiefly in relation to the nature of mathematical truth. In the *Aesthetic* he improved this situation considerably by separating the theory of the nonempirical nature of space from the theory of its necessity and dealt at length with the second.

In analyzing the first two arguments in the *Aesthetic*, therefore, we must remember that none of the difficulties and contradictions into which Kant ran in regard to the nonempirical nature of space are necessarily involved in the quite different theory that space has a necessary nature. Nor need the fact that Kant nowhere considered the possibility of broadening his conception of experience to include such necessary elements as space prevent us from realizing that if such a broader view of experience is taken, an essential portion of the Kantian position[5] would remain, while one part[6] involving a contradiction between his views in the *Aesthetic* and his views in the *Analytic* would drop out. Let us turn then to Kant's first space argument in the *Aesthetic*, in which he held that space is nonempirical.

Space is not an empirical conception which can be abstracted from external experiences. For in order that certain sensations [*Empfindungen*] may be related to something external to me (that is, to something in a part of space different from that in which I am), and similarly, in order that I may represent them as outside of and next to each other, and consequently as not merely different from each other but also as in different places, the representation of space must already be there as a basis [*schon zum Grunde liegen*]. Consequently, the representation of space cannot be borrowed from external appearances through experience; but, on the contrary, that external experience is itself first of all [*alleerst*] possible solely through the said representation.[7]

The chief point at issue is the meaning of the expression *schon zum Grunde liegen*. It would seem to have a temporal emphasis because of the word *schon;* but this word need not be taken literally, in which case the phrase might have a nontemporal, logical

---

[5] The theory that space has a necessary nature.
[6] The theory that space is nonempirical.
[7] Kant, *Kritik der reinen Vernunft*, A 23 = B 38.

emphasis. In either case, the priority means priority to what? Again there are two different meanings which suggest themselves in Kant's words. He may mean that space is prior to all sensations, or that it is merely prior to any attempt on my part to give already existing sensations *a reference to* external things. In the former case, no sensing at all occurs prior to the representation of space. In the latter, sensing comes first, but it cannot refer to anything as outside me, or to one thing as outside another, except by means of a representation of space that is prior to such an act or process of reference. The pairs of answers to these two questions overlap. First, Kant may mean that space is temporally prior to all actual sensation and *a fortiori* temporally prior to the act or process of external reference; or he may mean that it is contemporary with, or subsequent to, sensation but temporally prior to the act or process of external reference; or he may mean that it is logically prior to sensation and to the act or process of external reference.

Let us turn next to other passages in the *Aesthetic* for aid in regard to these questions. At A 20 = B 34, we find that space, as the form of all appearances,

. . . muss zu ihnen insgesamt im Gemüte a priori bereitliegen, und daher abgesondert von aller Empfindung können betrachtet werden.

Does Kant mean here that space is temporally or logically prior to sensation and to the act of giving such sensing an outward reference? He is distinguishing between the *material* of appearances which is given *a posteriori* and their *form*. The following considerations mediate in favor of logical priority. (1) The word *betrachten* may mean merely "to consider," in which case the passage would mean that space can be considered apart from all sensation. The fact that it lies in its entirety ready in the mind *a priori* would merely mean that the principles of its nature are not deducible from its sensuous contents but are worked out from within the mind on the occasion of sensation. (2) The word *absondern* is the same one which Kant uses two paragraphs later in reference to the general procedure that he is following in the *Aesthetic*.

In der transzendentalen Ästhetik also werden wir zuerst die Sinnlichkeit *isolieren,* dadurch, dass wir alles *absondern* [italics mine], was der Verstand durch seine Begriffe dabei denkt, damit nichts als empirische Anschauung übrigbleibe.

Again in the next sentence the same meaning is conveyed by the term *abtrennen:*

Zweitens werden wir von dieser noch alles, was zur Empfindung gehört, *abtrennen* [italics mine], damit nichts als reine Anschauung und die blosse Form der Erscheinungen übrigbleibe, welches das einzige ist, das die Sinnlichkeit a priori liefern kann.

These passages would seem to indicate that Kant meant that sensibility and understanding are actually united and that the mind isolates the former by separating from it everything relating to the latter. When this is done, only empirical intuition remains. The empirical intuition is further divided into everything which belongs to the sensation and the only thing that sensibility can deliver to us *a priori,* namely, space (and time). When empirical intuition is thus broken up, sensation is considered as falling on the one side (as content), and space on the other. But both are separated out of empirical intuition and, hence, come temporally after it. From such evidence, it would seem to follow that Kant meant that space is separated out of empirical intuition in the same sense that empirical intuition is itself separated out of the wider whole of knowledge that includes understanding, and hence that space is merely logically prior to sensation.

Against these considerations, the expression *muss zu ihnen insgesamt im Gemüte a priori bereitliegen* contains in almost every word suggestions of temporal priority. (1) "In its entirety" suggests more than a mere potential disposition. Space seems to be displayed in its own person. (2) If so, *im Gemüte* means that space is given in the mind. But if this is so, how can it be considered to be separated out of what is certainly not in the mind, namely, empirical intuition? (3) Again, if it is considered merely as separated out of empirical intuition and *then* given in the mind, it does not lie ready (*bereitliegen*) in the mind, but in empirical intuition. Yet Kant says that it lies ready in the mind. (4) Again, every one of the above considerations is independent of the word "*a priori*" itself. They would suggest temporal priority, even if *a priori* is taken to mean merely the logically necessary nature which space is considered to have after it has been given. But Kant puts "*a priori*" in the midst of the other words. He does not say that space is separated out of empirical intuition and then found to be *a priori*. It lies in its entirety in the mind *a priori* ready. The meaning of this statement seems to link its *apriority* with the fact that it is in the mind, ready in the mind, and ready in the mind in its entirety. Only by distorting Kant's meaning can such *apriority* be considered as a type of logical necessity involving merely what is separated out of empirical intuition. He may be accused of careless expression. He may be accused of using words that obscure from us ideas which we know he elsewhere advocated. Such accusations are merely interesting speculations about Kant's habits of expression and prove nothing. (5) Lastly, there is another consideration which does not prove that Kant meant that space is temporally prior to sensation, but at least suggests the possibility. The word *betrachten* may mean "to gaze at." Kant may have meant merely that space is *considered as separated out of* sensation. The probability would seem to be, however, that he meant that space is *gazed at, as separate from sensation*. If this interpretation is correct, while it does not show that Kant might not have meant that space is gazed at as separate, after being separated from empirical intuition, at least what is *betrachtet* would not be an innate tendency or disposition, for one does not gaze at a tendency, but at space. This consideration is by no means on a par with the preceding ones, but it deserves, I believe, to be mentioned. For all of the various reasons given above, we may conclude that in the passage before us Kant was contending for the temporal priority of space to sensation.

Several other passages in the *Aesthetic* are important in reference to Kant's meaning in the first space argument. At B 41, Kant says:

Aber diese Anschauung muss a priori, d. i. vor aller Wahrnehmung eines Gegenstandes, in uns angetroffen werden, mithin reine, nicht empirische Anschauung sein.

Again, at A 26 = B 42:

Weil nun die Rezeptivität des Subjekts, von Gegenständen affiziert zu werden, notwendigerweise vor allen Anschauungen dieser Objekte vorhergeht, so lässt sich verstehen, wie die Form aller Erscheinungen vor allen wirklichen Wahrnehmungen, mithin a priori im Gemüte gegeben sein könne, und wie sie als eine reine Anschauung, in der alle Gegenstände bestimmt werden müssen, Prinzipien der Verhältnisse derselben vor aller Erfahrung enthalten könne.

The crux of this argument lies in the term *Wahrnehmung*. Space is both the form of appearances and a pure intuition, and here Kant held that it is encountered in us (*angetroffen in uns*) *before* all perceptions, or given (*gegeben*) in the mind *prior to* all real perceptions (*wirklichen Wahrnehmungen*). The same words are repeated at A 43 = B 60.

[Space and time] können wir allein a priori, d. i. vor aller wirklichen Wahrnehmung erkennen, und sie heisst darum reine Anschauung. . . .

In all three passages, if perception (*Wahrnehmung*) is equated with sensation (*Empfindung*), then our problem is solved. Here Kant holds that space is encountered, given, and known before (*vor*) actual perceptions. Whatever Kant may have meant by such expressions as *abgesondert von* and *abgetrennt von,* the meaning of *vor* here is temporal.

It might be contended that, for the following reasons, even here Kant means only the logical priority of space to perceptions. (1) Only as a potential disposition is the receptivity of the subject prior to its becoming "affixed" by an object. (2) In the second passage above, Kant held that space is given before all actual perceptions, only as the form of appearances. (3) The pure intuition is said merely to determine the objects, actually or potentially. (4) In the third passage above, he held that we *know* the pure intuition; all knowledge involves some mediacy; hence space is *given* only as a disposition of the mind and is known later, in and after the perceptions which it logically determines.

In spite of some plausibility in these considerations, I believe that it can be shown that Kant had in mind the theory of temporal priority. (1) Although he compared space, in some regards, with the receptivity of the subject, he nowhere said that such receptivity is *given* or encountered prior to all perception, whereas he made three such explicit statements about space. Space "can be given *a priori* in the mind prior to all perceptions"; he nowhere says that such receptivity can be so given. As a potential disposition, space—like receptivity—is logically presupposed. But space is more than such a formal condition; it is also a pure intuition. (2) While Kant says that space, as a form of all appearances, is prior to perception, there are not two different spaces. The space that is logically prior to all perceptions is also actual space. Space is given temporally prior to all perceptions as a pure intuition and, in addition, is logically prior to them as the form of the not-yet-experienced appearances. As the form of all appearances, space is logically a determinant of its contents; but space is itself given in its entirety to the mind temporally prior to perceptions. Even if Kant meant in the second passage above that space is prior to all real perceptions merely as the form of intuition, in the first and third passages he reverses this situation and contends that space is a *pure intuition* because we know or encounter it in the mind before all perceptions. (4) The fact that Kant holds in the third passage that we *know* space before all real perceptions does not prove that space is given mediately, because he refers to it there explicitly as an intuition and so known. In all of these passages, Kant's words show unmistakably that he meant the temporal priority of space to perception.

The situation is somewhat more complicated in regard to the problem of the relation of the term "sensation" of the first space argument to "perception" in these passages. Did Kant mean that space is before sensation in the same sense that it is before perception? It is a curious fact that in neither of the two sections of the *Critique*,[8] in which he was clarifying and ordering his terms did he consider *Wahrnehmung*. In both sections, sensation (*Empfindung*) is clearly treated as the effect of an empirical object upon the apprehending subject and is considered in every case to concern a sensuous content. In the latter section, he uses the Latin *perceptio* as a representation with consciousness (*Bewusstsein*). When such a perception is linked with the subject as a modification of its state, it is sensation. When it is an objective perception, it is knowledge (*Erkenntnis*). On the other hand, he either equates perception (*Wahrnehmung*) with sensation[9] or holds that

[8] *Ibid.*, A 19–22 = B 33–36; and A 319–20 = B 376–77.
[9] *Ibid.*, A 24; A 41 = B 58; B 207.

the former involves a consciousness of the latter as a content.[10] According to both views, sensation is the sole content of perception; but according to the one, that content is simultaneous in its entirety with the perception, while according to the other, sensation may be considered as prior to, as well as coextensive with, the consciousness which generates the perception. Obviously, these differences are crucial in reference to the first space argument. If sensation and perception are simultaneous in their entirety, then the temporal priority of space to the latter is *ipso facto* temporal priority to sensation, in the first space argument. On the other hand, if sensation is in part temporally prior to perception, the temporal priority of space to the latter is no indication of its temporal priority to the former. Later on, Kant[11] prides himself upon being the first to notice that imagination is an ingredient of perception. He reiterates the claim that the activity of the knowing subject contributes to perception. Do these views carry over into the first space argument?

A sensation is not the same thing as a representation of that sensation as referring to something outside of me. In external experience there are certain sensations. For these, however, to be accompanied by the representation of their externality to me or to each other, space must be there at their basis. In reference to my sensations, space need not be temporally prior; in reference to my perception of these sensa as outside of me and as the content of my representation, space is, and must be, temporally prior. Space cannot be abstracted from external experience as the completed body of perceptions of external relations; it may be abstracted from individual sensations.

This view is clear, but it does not seem to have been Kant's. In the first place, in the first space argument he did not mention perception at all; he did not hold that perception is the representation of things as outside of the subject. He did not distinguish between sensing *qua* sensation and sensing *qua* perception. In the second place, there is a marked similarity between those passages, which we have considered, in which he held that space is in the mind apart from sensation and in the mind prior to perception.

---

[10] *Ibid.*, B 68; B 147; A 120; A 167 = B 209.   [11] *Ibid.*, A 120 *n.*

With no greater specific evidence to the contrary, he would seem to have meant the same type of priority in both cases. In the third place, of the seven references to perception in the *Aesthetic,* four have nothing to do with its relation to space [12] and the other three specifically hold that space is temporally prior to it. Lastly, if sensation is the content of perception, sensation could hardly be prior to perception even in part. A green patch may be in nature prior to my perception of it; it could hardly be the content of my perception until I perceive it. For these reasons, we may conclude that in the *Aesthetic* Kant did not distinguish between sensation and perception and that his defense of the temporal priority of space to perception must be considered to carry over and include —in the first space argument—its temporal priority to sensation.

At this point it is necessary to consider briefly the views of a recent[13] opponent of the interpretation of the *Aesthetic* as involving the doctrine of the temporal priority of space to the objects of sense. Paton, in no uncertain terms, dismisses this view as (a) not found in Kant, and (b) nonsense.[14] These two charges are different and require different answers.

Paton contends that Kant could not have meant temporal priority in the *Aesthetic,* because he explicitly rejected this doctrine elsewhere.[15] Such an argument, of course, needs no answer. What Kant said in 1770 and 1790 is not necessarily what he said in the *Aesthetic.* However, Paton mentions the end of the corollary to §§ 14–15 of the *Dissertation,* as well as the corresponding part of § 14 on time, in support of this contention. It is true that Kant's original formulations of his doctrines of space about 1769 involved, as we have found,[16] neither the temporal nor the logical priority of space to sense experience, but merely a difference between the concreteness of space and objects in it. But in 1770, Kant added that the origin, as well as the logical status of space, is nonempirical. Such a doctrine could mean a nontemporal prior-

[12] *Ibid.,* A 24; A 41 = B 58; B 68.

[13] For earlier attacks upon the temporal view, see Riehl, *Der philosophische Kritizismus,* I, 347 ff.; Cohen, *Kommentar,* pp. 26–34, p. 130 ff. For defenses of it, see Vaihinger, *Kommentar,* II, 170–82; Kemp Smith, *A Commentary,* pp. 88–90, 99–103.

[14] Paton, *Kant's Metaphysic of Experience,* I, 136–37, esp., 137 note 1; 177.

[15] *Ibid.,* I, 137 note 1, 177 note 2.   [16] Cf. above, pp. 126–27.

ity only on the assumption of an activity of the understanding. Paton overlooks the fact that, throughout the *Dissertation*,[17] Kant held that space is given and not generated and departed from this view only at the end of the corollary to §§14–15 and, possibly, in the example of incongruent counterparts. In the rest of the *Dissertation* he may be considered to have held that space is temporally prior to sense experience, a conclusion which he states clearly with reference to time.[18] Interestingly enough, the example of incongruent counterparts was omitted in the *Aesthetic*. It might have served there to establish the temporal *or* the logical priority. Its very ambiguity may have constrained Kant to omit it, along with every other suggestion of an activity of the understanding *in order to stress the temporal priority* of space.

Secondly, Paton argues that since Kant meant logical priority in 1770, and since he, nevertheless, used such words as "before" and "precedes" in that year, hence he must have also meant logical priority in the *Aesthetic* when he used such terms.[19] If my analyses are correct, Kant used such terms in 1770 *because* he then meant what those terms normally mean, namely, temporal priority, and it follows *a fortiori* that he meant the same by them in the *Aesthetic* where his views are free from the doctrine of a synthetic activity of the understanding with its corollary that sensa call forth, even though they do not contribute to, the intuition. Lastly, Paton's[20] reference to the fact that space "remains over" when space is abstracted concerns more properly the second space argument and proves nothing about the manner in which space precedes sense perception.

Let us turn now to Paton's second contention, namely, that the doctrine of temporal priority is nonsense. He feels that it is more charitable "to suppose that in spite of his terminology [Kant] means nothing quite so crude"[21] and that we must, in this matter, show that we have a better understanding of the critical philosophy than Kant, by supplying what he failed in the *Aesthetic* to supply, namely, "an explicit repudiation of a temporal mean-

---

[17] Kant, *Inaugural Dissertation*, § 15, A, B, C; §§ 14–15 corollary, first paragraph.
[18] *Ibid.*, § 14, 3.
[19] Paton, *Kant's Metaphysic of Experience*, I, 177 note 2.
[20] *Ibid.*   [21] *Ibid.*, I, 137.

ing." Is the doctrine of temporal priority sheer nonsense? The meaning of that doctrine cannot be understood by attempting to reconcile it with any and every statement of Kant's from 1770 to 1790. It is bound up with problems which can be grasped only in the light of considerations which we know that he had had in mind in those crucial years about 1769. To study Kant's views in any other fashion is to assume that he had his whole philosophy in mind throughout many months and years, even if he could not display it all on any one page. The meaning of the doctrine of temporal priority is, in my opinion, to be found by considering it as the outcome of two other doctrines, both of which Kant was constrained to accept, but which remain mutually incompatible *unless* united by the doctrine of the temporal priority of space as a pure intuition. The first of these doctrines is the theory that space is not abstracted from objects of sense; the second, that it is the product of a synthetic activity of the mind. The difficulties into which Kant ran in trying to reconcile them we shall trace in detail in our consideration of the *Analytic* in the next chapter. We need only to point out here how they conflict and how the doctrine of the temporal priority of space reconciles them.

If space is yielded by a synthetic activity of the understanding, such a synthesis must proceed from some content. It comes *from* the mind, but it must begin *with* some given "material." Now, in conformity with Kant's other main tenet, it cannot begin with the materials of sense. With what, then, can it begin? It cannot begin with conceptions, for only analysis does this. It cannot begin with parts of space *qua* parts, as a sculptor begins with rough stone; for parts of space, according to the very doctrine of pure intuition which emerges, are themselves space. Therefore, the only thing with which it can begin is *space* as a whole. But if it begins with space, space is given temporally prior to it. And since it begins on the occasion of sense experience, space is temporally prior also to sense experience. Space is not generated from sensa, but from itself, and for this to be the case it must be temporally prior to the conditions of sensing which touch off the generative activity.

I do not claim that this doctrine is not full of difficulties. If space is generated from itself, is it not really given? Does not the doctrine of a synthesis become much more meaningful if it proceeds from the manifold of sense? As we shall see, Kant was driven to this conclusion in the *Analytic,* where he abandoned the theory that space is given. How, as Paton and many others have asked, can space be literally given temporally prior to sense experience? Without in any sense minimizing these difficulties, I wish to point out that the doctrine of temporal priority is the result of a number of meaningful considerations. On some matters a philosopher may feel constrained to accept a view, not because it involves no difficulties, but because other views involve, or seem to involve, even greater ones.

§ 2

KANT'S SECOND space argument concerns the necessary character of space, its necessary relation to the knowing subject and its necessary relation to outer intuitions. He held:

Space is a necessary representation a priori, which lies at the basis of all external intuitions. We can never represent the absence of space, though we can quite well think that no objects are encountered in it. Space is, therefore, considered (*angesehen*) as the condition of the possibility of appearances, and not as a determination dependent upon them, and it is an *a priori* representation which lies in a necessary fashion at the basis of outer appearances.[22]

This argument presupposes the one which precedes it. Space, which was there shown to lie at the basis of our representation of things as temporally prior to them and, in that sense of the word, *a priori* and nonempirical, is now held to stand in that relation necessarily. The necessity of space for external intuitions we shall call, following Vaihinger,[23] relative necessity. If external things are there, space is there; if they are absent, such relative necessity of space tells us nothing of the presence or absence of space. But Kant proceeded to deal with this further question and held that space cannot be thought away.

Here in even clearer terms than in the *Dissertation,* he followed through the line of thinking which he took over from Leonhard

[22] Kant, *Kritik der reinen Vernunft,* A 24 = B 38–39.
[23] Vaihinger, *Kommentar,* II, 193–95.

Euler and possibly noticed also in the views of Clarke. Euler held
that we may abstract things and their qualities from space, but
space remains. Clarke held that we may assume things in space to
be parted, but the space in which those things are parted is itself
not partible and remains between them. Kant held that we may
represent space without objects, but never objects without space.
This view is the famous *Nicht-Hinweg-Denkbarkeit* of space.
Again following Vaihinger's terminology, I shall refer to this
doctrine as the theory of absolute necessity.

Does the theory mean: (1) Space necessarily has the nature that
it has, whatever that nature may be (*i.e.*, it is homaloidal), and it
must be so represented? (2) Space is necessarily three-dimensional,
continuous, uniform, etc.—in a word, Euclidian—and must be so
represented? (3) We are under such constraint that we must represent space or we cannot think at all? (4) We are under such constraint that we must represent space whenever we do any intuitive
representing? Because Kant divided his views of space into two
expositions—the metaphysical, dealing with space itself, and the
transcendental, dealing with space in geometry and mechanics—the
first of these possibilities is apt to be too hastily dismissed. Vaihinger holds [24] that Kant could not have meant here that we cannot
think of space as other than it is because such a contention concerns
our propositions about space and not our representation of it, which
was, in this argument, his exclusive concern. We must remember,
however, that the distinction between the two expositions is one of
procedure and type of argument, but not one between two different kinds of space as objects of investigation. If this fact is remembered, it is clear that, whatever else Kant meant in addition,
he meant by this argument that space is and must be represented
as it is and not otherwise. The constraint under which the knowing subject finds itself in representing space is a constraint to
represent space as it is, not merely as without any specific connotation. The argument is not primarily a defense of the homaloidality
of space, but it bears the same relation to the whole metaphysical
exposition of space that specific geometrical examples bear to the
transcendental one. In the latter, space must be what it is (a pure

[24] Vaihinger, *Kommentar*, II, 188.

intuition) and not otherwise because, if this were not so, geo-metrical truths could not be what they are and must be. In the argument before us, space must be represented as it is and not otherwise (our *Nicht-anders-denken-können*), because of its *Nicht-Hinweg-Denkbarkeit*. It is not that some connotatively indetermin-ate space cannot be thought away, but space with its connotatively necessary, and its denotatively singular, nature cannot be thought of as absent. Such not-to-be-thought-away space bears the same rela-tion (*zum Grunde*) to the objects of empirical intuition (doctrine of relative necessity) as the same space bears (in geometry) to the objects of applied geometry and mechanics. The applied intuitions of mechanics are some of all possible empirical intuitions in the same way that the pure intuitions of space in pure geometry are some of the pure intuitions of space which human minds are con-strained necessarily to have prior to experience. In all of these cases, the space involved, whether lying at the basis of empirical (including applied geometrical) intuitions, or given in pure intui-tion (including pure geometrical cases) is necessarily what it is and not otherwise. For this reason, this argument may be said to involve, among other things, the theory that space is homaloidal.

It of course never occurred to Kant that space might be homa-loidal and non-Euclidian. His argument here may be considered a direct defense of the necessary Euclidian nature of space in pure geometry, in applied Newtonian science, and in the empirical intuitions of daily life; and, therefore, as the long-sought-for answer to his questionings years before, in 1747, concerning the basis for the necessary nature of space. Space is what it is and not otherwise and also Euclidian and Newtonian, because of the con-siderations in the metaphysical and transcendental expositions taken as a whole. An important feature of these considerations is the doctrine of absolute necessity.

It is an interesting speculation, not foreign to our wider pur-pose, to consider what Kant's second space argument, if taken by itself, would mean in the light of present-day space theory. Con-sidered alone, the theory of the necessary nature of space leaves every feature of space unspecified. Neither a nonempirical, nor an intuitive, nor an Euclidian, nature is implied in the argument.

As we shall discover below,[25] such men as Alexander, Whitehead, and Broad differ widely on the question of the homaloidal or non-homaloidal nature of space as the outcome of relativity physics. If, however, the outcome of present-day physics should be the theory of a homaloidal, non-Euclidian space, Kant's second space argument, taken alone, could provide a theoretical or epistemological justification of precisely such a stand. Abandoning the first argument, the necessary, empirical nature of space would result. Space would be yielded in experience (widely construed), and yet it would be impossible to think of space as absent. Abandoning the third and fourth arguments, the necessary, nonintuitive nature of space would remain. Space would be singular and denotatively unique, but it would not be an intuition. Thus like a four-dimensional space-time, it could not be contemplated by the mind, yet it would be necessary and homaloidal. The findings of relativity physics would supply the basis for a further, transcendental exposition of its nature. We shall return to such considerations below: they form no part of our account of Kant's views.

Of the four possible meanings of the theory of absolute necessity listed above, Kemp Smith holds the third alternative:

The ground upon which the whole argument is made to rest is the merely brute fact (asserted by Kant) of our incapacity to think except in terms of space.[26]

While it is true that Kant says that we cannot represent space as absent, we must remember that he cannot refer to the fact that space is an intuition, since this part of his theory is yet to come. He would seem to mean, however, that only in the type of representing which turns out to be intuiting is it impossible to think of the absence of space. Strictly speaking, *Nicht-Hinweg-Denkbarkeit* means *Nicht-Hinwegschaubarkeit*, if we may coin such a term. Intuitions are, it is true, necessary to knowledge, but thought may pass beyond knowledge, and hence some thinking need not involve the representation of space. Again, possibly some of the procedures of logical, conceptual analysis would be cases of thinking which would not require the representation of space. However

[25] Chapter IX.   [26] Kemp Smith, *A Commentary*, p. 103.

this may be,[27] Kant assuredly meant that there is constraint put upon a human subject to represent space whenever it does any intuiting, in geometry, applied science, or sense perception. He was maintaining the theory of Euclidian homaloidality, but he makes an addition to it. Space has a necessary nature, and, in addition, it is essential to all intuitive thinking. These two doctrines turn out to be but different ways of stating one view, but the reason for this fact cannot be worked out by Kant until he has established the intuitive nature of space itself. Any representation of space is a representation of its necessary nature. Any representation of space is a case of intuitive thinking. Therefore, some cases of intuitive thinking are representations of the necessary nature of space. These two types of necessity become identified in the next two space arguments, where space itself is shown to be intuitive. If space is an intuition, the representation of the necessary nature of space is not merely one case of intuitive thinking. All such thinking becomes a representation of the necessary nature of space. This ultimate identification[28] of space, the necessary ingredient of all intuitive thinking, with space, the pure intuition, depends upon the intuitive quality of space and not upon its *apriority*. Pending the establishment of its intuitive quality, a representation of space may be considered as only one case of intuitive thinking. The representation of space and the representation of x intuited triangles are x *plus 1* cases of intuitive thinking. In the light of the subsequent arguments, these x *plus 1* cases would remain, but the representations of the x triangles would be each of them representations of space. The homaloidal (and for Kant *ipso facto* Euclidian) nature of space becomes identical with its necessity in all intuitive thinking.

The theory of the absolute necessity of space for the intuiting subject means that the mind is under such constraint that it must represent space when it does any intuitive representing. Not

[27] Kemp Smith's mistake on this point is quite minor. On the other hand Paton completely distorts Kant's meaning. He holds (I, 112) Kant to mean that ". . . if we try to think away space and time from objects of experience, we have nothing left." Kant actually says that if we try to think space away, we fail in the attempt, for space cannot be thought away. Space and the objects of experience remain, rather than nothing. Cf. Euler, *Reflexions sur l'espace et le temps*, § XV.

[28] Cf. Kant, *Inaugural Dissertation*, § 12; *Kritik der reinen Vernunft*, A 20 = B 34–35; B 376–77.

merely did Kant mean that space has a necessary nature; he also meant that the activity or process connecting it with the self *must* occur. The intuiting subject cannot represent to itself the absence of space.

This doctrine may seem to be one that was in no way needed to complete Kant's theories of space. Even if space is temporally prior to sense experience as well as necessary in its nature, it would not from this fact seem to follow that the act or process of knowledge by means of which the knowing subject apprehends space would itself be necessary. Whether Kant was concerned to extend the necessary nature of space in this fashion to include the very nature of the knowing self is a question beyond the compass of our investigation. For our purposes one fact and one probability are important: In the first place, in the theory of absolute necessity, Kant meant both that the object (space) has a necessary nature and that the process of intuiting space is a necessary one. In the second place, it is probable that he considered the necessity of the process to be re-enforcing evidence for the necessary nature of the object. Such a contention as this would, moreover, be highly effective. If the process of apprehending space is one which the mind must carry out, then the evidence for the necessary nature of space as the object is re-enforced by the constraint imposed upon the mind in the process.

Here again Kant added to his general philosophy of space a theory which is of great significance beyond his own views. If there are necessary elements which are discoverable in experience, and if space is one of these, then space would be empirical and necessary. The necessary nature of space would be discoverable immediately as experienced. In addition, such a necessary nature might be discoverable by comparing those cases of experience which the mind is under no constraint to carry out with those which it must carry out. Not only Kant's account in 1770 of space as a pure intuition, but also his theory in 1781 of space as absolutely necessary for the intuiting subject could be turned into valuable aspects of a theory that space is empirical and necessary. Obviously, in such a case, both doctrines would have to be stripped of the theory of the apprehension of space temporally prior to sense experience.

Kant's transition from the doctrine of absolute necessity to the doctrine of relative necessity provides a neat link between the subjective conditions of apprehension and the objective conditions of the externally real. His distinction in 1770 and 1781 between the metaphysical unreality of space and its objects, and the metaphysical reality of things in themselves should not blind us to this fact. In 1770 he mentioned the following formula as one of the illusions about the scope of sensitive knowledge:

The sensitive condition, under which alone the intuition of an object is possible, is a condition of the possibility of the object itself.[29]

If our analysis of the manner in which Kant superimposed the doctrine of the metaphysical unreality of space upon his theory of a pure intuition is correct, his formulation of this theory of such an illusion was bound up with the belief that the condition of the possibility of objects themselves could and would be discovered by means of intellectual intuitions. With the collapse of this hope, Kant found himself faced with the problem of the relation of the spatially conditioned objects of experience to the things in themselves. The problem of his answer, or answers, to this question does not directly concern our study. In any case, he believed, both in 1770 and in 1781, that the nature of space is a guarantee that the sensitive condition under which the intuition of an object is possible is a condition under which we may have knowledge of the externally real. Whatever limitations his wider metaphysical theory might impose upon that reality, it could not destroy its externality and its independence of all of the contingent conditions of sense perception. We can know *that* spatial objects are external and that *what* we know of them falls on the objective side of our knowledge. What they are in themselves over and above such knowledge is a different, and a wider, problem. Newton's more realistic view of perception as stated in the *Principles* is reaffirmed.[30]

How is such a contact with the external real assured? It is assured by the fact that space is at once absolutely necessary for the

---

[29] Kant, *Inaugural Dissertation*, translated by Handyside, p. 76, § 26, 1.

[30] Newton, *Principles*, p. 506; cf. above, p. 66 *n.;* pp. 67–68. Newton's distinction in the *Optics*, pp. 344–45, between the sensible species of things, *sensibiles rerum species,* and things themselves, *res ipsae,* quoted by Clarke, Paper I, § 3 *n.*, should be recalled as a possible source of Kant's expression "things in themselves."

knowing subject and relatively necessary at the basis of objects in it. Such relative necessity flows from its absolute necessity in every case of our experience of external objects in the same way that (in the Transcendental Exposition) the truths of applied geometry flow from those of pure. There are two types of inclusion involved, a logical and an epistemological. Logically, all pure intuition in pure geometry is a special case of the pure intuition of space as encountered prior to experience. Logically, the form of intuition in applied geometry is a special case of the form of intuition lying at the basis of all sense experience and including its objects. Epistemologically, the absolute necessity of the representation of space as a pure intuition for the knowing subject (prior to experience) includes, as a special case, the representation of space as a form of empirical intuition lying at the basis of the known objects, the sensuous objects of experience.

In reference to the narrower relation of space as a pure intuition in pure geometry to space as a form of intuition in applied geometry, the epistemological inclusion would be expressed as follows and would be included logically in the broader one. The absolute necessity of the representation of space as a pure intuition for the knowing subject in pure geometry includes, as a special case, the representation of space as a form of empirical intuition in applied geometry. As we have found in reference to the *Dissertation*,[31] Kant meant that there can be *a priori* conclusions in those cases of knowledge which have as their source the pure intuition of space and which refer back to the same pure intuition: that is, such conclusions carry absolute necessity and universal validity. An example of such a procedure is found in pure geometry. Secondly, there can be *a priori* conclusions in those cases of knowledge which have as their source the pure intuition of space but which refer to the empirical contents of that same space considered as a form: that is, such conclusions carry relative necessity and validity for the spatial features of the external world. An example of such a procedure is found in applied science and mechanics. Thirdly, however, there can be no *a priori* conclusions in those cases of knowledge which have as their source, and also as their objects

---

[31] Cf. above, pp. 137–39.

of reference, the empirical contents of space considered as a form of intuition. Such knowledge is the factual knowledge of sense perception. The second and third types provide the connection between the knowing subject and the external object. Space guarantees this connection because its absolute necessity in relation to the subject includes its relative necessity in relation to the object. In the second example, there is *a priori,* synthetic knowledge of the external real (whatever its ultimate metaphysical status). In the third, there is *a posteriori* knowledge of the external real (whatever its ultimate metaphysical status). But in both examples, there is *knowledge.* The passage from the absolute necessity of space to its relative necessity is the cornerstone of Kant's theory of knowledge.

It might, of course, be argued that we are not justified in arguing from the absolute necessity of space to its relative necessity, that is, from the subjective conditions of apprehension to the objective conditions of existence. Kant could, in rebuttal, maintain that such an objection would validly hold only with reference to the possibility of objects in themselves, whereas the epistemological object with reference to which space is relatively necessary is merely an appearance. For such an object, the relation may be established both in applied geometry and in sense experience. There is but one space, which is given to the subject and must contain the object. This reply, based as it is upon the metaphysical unreality of outward objects in space, would seem to be relatively weak in comparison to the realistic position which might have been erected upon his views of space.

To complete our consideration of the second space argument, the general difference between our interpretation and those of certain major commentators should be mentioned. Adickes says that in Kant's completed theory of space there was but one main problem dealt with—namely, how is mathematics possible? In defending this contention, he states the basis of his disagreement with Paulsen, Fischer, and Vaihinger.

Man darf also weder mit Paulsen behaupten, dass Kant *nur* das Problem der *angewandten* Mathematik erörtert, noch mit Fischer, dass es *nur* das Problem der *reinen* ist, noch mit Vaihinger, dass es *beide*

sind (bald vermischt bald . . . von einander getrennt) : man muss vielmehr sagen, dass Kant nur *ein* Problem kennt, *die Möglichkeit der
Mathematik überhaupt.*[32]

All these men assume that Kant's preoccupation throughout
both expositions was primarily with the space of mathematics,
pure, applied, both, or as one. If my contentions have been correct, every one of these views is incorrect. It must be remembered
that absolute necessity involves the necessary nature not merely
of the space of pure geometry, but also of any pure space whatsoever; while relative necessity involves the necessity of space not
merely for the objects of applied geometry, but also for all empirical objects whatsoever, however random and chaotic some of their
features may be. Consequently, the relation between pure geometry and applied is merely one case of the wider problem of the
relation between space and empirical objects. The latter problem
concerns the validity of *a priori* intuiting with reference to all of
the objects of experience. It concerns the possibility not merely of
universally valid truth in science, but also of relatively valid truth
in sense perception. In the second space argument Kant implied
that the problem of the relative validity of sense experience was
a problem independent of, although in applied mathematics over-
lapping with, the problem of absolute, intuitive necessity. Pure
mathematics is one, but only one, example of truths of which the
origin and the object of reference are both pure; applied science
is an example of truth of which the origin is pure, but the objects
of reference empirical; all cases of experience, as such, are examples of truths of which the origin as well as the objects of
reference are empirical.[33] The absolute necessity of the first kind
of truth may in some cases (for example, the second kind) include
a relative necessity for objects; but, in other cases (the third kind) ,
the origin of the truth as well as the nature of its necessity is different.

Consequently, it is a mistake to hold, with Fischer, Vaihinger,

---

[32] Adickes, *Kant Studien*, p. 128 *n.;* cf. Cohen, *Kommentar zu Kants Kritik der
reinen Vernunft*, p. 27: "Nicht um die Vorstellung aber handelt es sich hier,
sondern um die Erkenntnis. Man kann sich 'denken,' dass keine Gegenstände im
Raume seien; dieses Denken nennt man Geometrie."

[33] Cf. above, pp. 137–39.

Adickes, or Cohen that in the second space argument Kant was solely concerned with mathematics, pure, or applied, or both. He was considering all cases in which space is presented to the mind: in pure geometry, in applied science, and prior to any experience whatsoever. The fact that some of these cases are in pure and applied mathematics in no way singles them out as Kant's exclusive concern. The experience prior to which, and at the necessary basis of which, space lies, according to Kant, is no more specifically the highly sophisticated "experience" of the mathematician and Newtonian physicist, than any man's ordinary experience of an object is the more exact and elaborate description of that object by the mathematician. This fact is of great significance in appraising Kant's views with reference to present-day mathematical physics.[34]

§ 3

WE COME NOW to Kant's third space argument in the *Aesthetic*. In addition to being nonempirical and necessary, space is an intuition and not a conception. Repeating his conclusions of the *Dissertation*,[35] he contended that space is not a general conception with particulars *under* it, but a pure intuition. For we represent only one space, and when we talk about many spaces, we mean only parts of this one, single space. No reference is made in this argument to the boundlessness or infinity of space, for these matters are reserved for the next argument. The parts of space cannot precede the one, all-inclusive space as the constituent parts or ingredients out of which it is compounded but are merely thought of as in it (*in ihm gedacht*). As in the corresponding view in the *Dissertation,* the parts are not given features of the intuition: only the whole is given. Thinking of spaces as in space is the process of delimitation by the mind of the wider given whole of space. The conceptions of the parts and the general conception of all parts refer to nothing in the intuition. "This" space and "that" space are merely space. There is nothing in space corresponding to the "thisness" which our minds read into it. The conception of "this-

---

[34] Cf. below, pp. 210-11.
[35] Kant, *Inaugural Dissertation*, § 15, B; §§ 14-15, corollary, first paragraph.

ness in general" lacks *a fortiori* all reference to space. When by a process of delimitation the mind thinks of parts of space as in space, what really lies back of each such conceived part is the one space. The same situation obtains in reference to geometrical figures and propositions. If the mind attempts to deal with particular triangles, lines, etc. as conceptions, true geometrical propositions never flow from them, and *a fortiori* never from the general conceptions "line," "triangle," etc., but rather from the intuition back of these. The introduction of geometrical truths in this argument anticipates the Transcendental Exposition. The entire argument is designed to show that the method of conceptual analysis fails to yield any of the qualities of space. The so-called parts of space are merely the result of a process of delimitation *by the mind* of what is entirely unlimited and a subsequent empty generalization from the limited "parts" in a way wholly unjustified by what is given.

In spite of the straightforward nature of this exposition, in spite of the fact that it is Kant's reaffirmation of his doctrine of space in the *Dissertation,* Paton contends that both in this and in the succeeding argument, Kant means that we have a conception of spatiality as well as the intuition, space.

Kant is not denying that we have a concept of spatiality, a concept of the characteristics or "marks" common to all different spaces, or, as he calls it, "a *universal* concept of spaces in general." His argument seems to be (1) that one common mark of the many different spaces is that they are necessarily limited; and (2) that consequently our concept of spatiality is derived from our immediate intuition of spaces as necessarily limited. The intuition of spaces as necessarily limited presupposes a pure intuition of one all-embracing space. Hence our concept of spatiality presupposes a pure intuition of one all-embracing space. In other words, one pure intuition of space must underlie all our concepts of spatiality.[36]

This is an interesting argument, but is it Kant's? Unfortunately for his purposes, Paton admits that Kant used the same word "space" for space and spatiality. Even if Kant's argument did not convey a quite clear meaning, it seems highly improbable that he would have persisted in conveying two quite different meanings

---

[36] Paton, *Kant's Metaphysic of Experience,* I, 116.

by the same term. He did not mean that space is both a conception (*Begriff*) and an intuition (*Anschauung*). Apart from the sharp distinctions between the two types of representation (*Vorstellung*) in the *Dissertation* and in the *Aesthetic*, he tells us at A 320 = B 377, that knowledge is either an intuition or a conception (*intuitus vel conceptus*), the former relating directly to the object and the latter indirectly in terms of various characteristics common to several things. These facts would hardly seem to be offset by a quotation from Kant's *Nachgelassene Werk*[37] to the effect that

Der Raum ist Anschauung (*intuitus*), noch nicht Begriff (*conceptus*), d. ist die Vorstellung des Einzelnen, noch nicht die, welche vielen gemein ist; er ist *intuitus, quem sequitur conceptus.*

Kant would seem in this fragment to mean merely that the mind persists in mistakenly thinking of parts of space and in generalizing from "this space" and "that" in a wholly unwarranted fashion. In forming a conception of space, the mind considers space to have aspects that it really does not possess.

Kant nowhere denied that we have a conception of spatiality, but he also nowhere affirmed it, because he did not mention spatiality at all. If we have a conception of the characteristics or "marks" of different spaces, how are these related to the characteristics or "marks" of space itself (for it has qualities too)? If any particular space has the characteristic of being limited, then spatiality, in general, would have that quality. But space is unlimited. Did Kant mean that space is unlimited, but spatiality is limited? He held:

[Der Raum] ist wesentlich einig, das Mannigfaltige in ihm, mithin auch der allgemeine Begriff von Räumen überhaupt, beruht lediglich auf Einschränkungen.[38]

The many spaces in the one, as well as the general conception of these many, rest entirely upon limitation. Particular spaces *qua* particulars, far from revealing any such notions as spatiality or limitedness, indicate a tampering by the mind with the given

---

[37] Quoted by Vaihinger, *Kommentar*, II, 233; cf. Paton, *Kant's Metaphysic of Experience*, I, 122; cf. Kant, *Opus postumum*, II, 9, 12, 15, 19, 42.
[38] Kant, *Kritik der reinen Vernunft*, A 25 = B 39.

THE CRITIQUE OF PURE REASON 189

space, and tell us nothing about the latter. The continuity of "this" space is the continuity of space, not of spatiality. The three-dimensionality of "this" space is the three-dimensionality of space, not of spatiality. Far from indicating that there is a general conception of spatiality, the limited nature of spaces shows that they are not features of space at all, for their limitedness contradicts its limitlessness. Therefore, Kant did not mean that the one pure intuition of space underlies our conceptions of spatiality but that such conceptions tell us nothing about space, since they are merely conceptions of what in itself is not a conception at all and cannot be treated as such. It is as impossible to conclude anything about space from this space considered *qua* particular, or from space considered *qua* general conception, as it is to arrive at the proposition that two sides of a triangle are together greater than the third from "triangle" or "side" treated *qua* conceptions. The nature of space is as incapable of derivation from "this space" or "space in general" as such a proposition of geometry is from "this side" or "side in general." Paton confuses the fact that we attempt to subject any and every representation to the conditions of conceptual analysis, with the fact that some representations conform, and others fail to conform, to those conditions. He confuses our conceiving with a *conceptus*. If every representation became a conception because of the fact that we effectually or ineffectually submit it to conceptual tests by seeking particulars with common marks in order to subsume them under a general term, then, indeed, space or Peter or any singular term would be a conception, in spite of the fact that its nature is totally different from such conceptions as "man."

If we abandon this unhappy distinction between space and spatiality and return to Kant, we find a clear reaffirmation of his views of 1770. In the second space argument he has shown that space is connotatively homaloidal. That argument alone, however, in no way shows that it is denotatively one or singular. Space might have a necessary nature (which he, of course, supposed to be Euclidian) which must be, in addition, necessarily represented by the knowing subject, and yet such nature might lie in many individual objects, as man lies in Peter, Paul, and John, which are

hence subsumed under it logically. The third argument is designed to show that this situation cannot obtain in the case of
space. The reason for this fact lies not in its homaloidality, but in
its intuitive nature. It is displayed to our minds (necessarily, to
be sure) in its own proper nature and not as abstracted from particulars. Socrates is similarly displayed, although empirically. Any
singular presentation contains the parts in it and not under it.
Since the parts of space are limitations of the wider whole, space
is denotatively one as well as homaloidal. Hence space is a pure
intuition. Its infinity and its more specifically Euclidian connotation in geometry, while presupposed in this argument as well as
in the preceding one, are not elaborated. The exposition of the
former quality is reserved for the last Metaphysical Argument,
and the exposition of the latter is the concern of the Transcendental Exposition.

Vaihinger's account of this third space argument,[39] while on the
whole quite accurate, involves one important error. He contends[40]
that if we consider Kant's meaning closely, we cannot escape the
thought that the infinity of space is involved (*mitgesetzt*) in the
argument. For if all parts of space are limitations of a still greater
space, then the principle of the boundlessness in the progression,
dealt with in the subsequent argument, is already involved. As
further evidence of this view, Vaihinger appeals to the beginning
of the corollary of §§ 14–15 of the *Dissertation*, which we have
considered above,[41] where Kant explicitly used the infinity of space
as a part of this argument. While it is, of course, true that this
third space argument implies the boundlessness in the progression if the question of infinitude is raised; and while it is true,
furthermore, that Kant had before him in the development of all
four arguments, as well as the Transcendental Exposition, the
completed theory of space as homaloidal, singular, infinite, and
Euclidian; yet it in no way follows that the infinity of space is definitely meant (*mitgesetzt*) in the third argument. Kant's omission
of an explicit reference to its infinity is significant and is clearly
explained by the fact that he intended to deal with this particular

[39] Vaihinger, *Kommentar*, II, 204–36.

[40] *Ibid.*, II, 221.   [41] Cf. above, pp. 150–52.

problem in the following argument. In the third argument he was anxious to show that the intuitive nature of space and its denotative unity can be established first, independently of the question of its infinity, in the same way that the entire Metaphysical Exposition can be worked out independently of the problem of synthetic, *a priori* truth in geometry and mechanics. While, therefore, Vaihinger is correct in regard to what the third argument implies, both by itself and in relation to Kant's wider theory, it does not follow that it is explicitly a treatment of the infinitude of space as well as its denotative oneness.

§ 4

KANT'S FOURTH space argument in the Metaphysical Exposition involves, except for the first sentence, two entirely different variations in the first and second editions. In A, it runs:

Space is represented as an infinite magnitude given. A general conception of space (which is common to a foot as well as an ell) can determine nothing in reference to quantity. If there were not a boundlessness in the progression of the intuition, no conception of relations would ever yield a principle of infinity.[42]

There are four problems which arise with reference to this argument: (1) What did Kant mean in the first sentence? (2) In what relation do the other two sentences stand to it? (3) In what relation does the argument stand to the whole Metaphysical Exposition? (4) Can we detect in the argument any suggestion of the reason for Kant's revision of it in the second edition? Let us turn to these questions successively.

Space is represented (*vorgestellt*) as an infinite magnitude given. As we remember, representations, for Kant, were of two sorts, mediate, that is, conceptions, and immediate, that is, intuitions. If there were no indication in this sentence to the contrary, the word *vorgestellt* would imply either type of apprehension. But there is such an indication. Space is represented as *given*. Therefore, Kant meant undoubtedly that space is represented immediately as contemplated or gazed at. He reaffirms his position in ·

---

[42] Kant, *Kritik der reinen Vernunft*, A 25.

the other three arguments that space is given in its own person and not derived. The addition to those other arguments which he makes here lies in the words "infinite magnitude." Space is given to the mind; it is given necessarily to the mind; it is given as denotatively one to the mind; in addition, it is given as an infinite magnitude. Kant is here defending the contemplated infinity of space. Another distinction is important, however, in reference to the first sentence. If we represent space as an infinite given magnitude, does the infinitude refer to the object or to the process of knowledge? In other words, did Kant mean that space is infinite, or that our representation of it is total or complete? In my opinion, he meant the former but confused it with the latter. He meant that space is an infinite given whole and also that our representation of it is complete or total. It is infinite, and we have it displayed in its entirety in such a way that our act of apprehension is complete. Such an argument involves obvious difficulties. If he were contending merely that we apprehend all its qualities immediately, that our act of apprehension is able to exhaust its connotation, there would be no difficulty. For all of the connotation of space is given directly to the mind, and its infinitude as one of its qualities is so given. But he could not have meant merely this. We have displayed to us not simply all of the connotation of space, but space itself. Its infinitude is given to us as a quality, and also completely given as a quantity or magnitude. We have a total apprehension of infinite space. It is obvious that this contention involves a striking addition to the theory that space is itself infinite and given. Infinite space might be immediately yet partially given; but Kant is holding that it is infinite and totally displayed.

In his defense of this wider contention, he considered the nature of finite quantities. Every finite length such as a foot or an ell tells us nothing about quantity. One size, such as a foot, is no less "space" than another larger size, such as an ell, and vice versa. No particular space is "space" any more than any other particular space. There is always a larger space which with equal justification may be considered to be "space." This boundlessness in the progression is essential to the attainment of a principle of infinity. But we have such a boundlessness in the space that is immediately displayed to our minds. Therefore, space is an infinite given quantity and is represented by us in its entirety.

If this analysis of the meaning of Kant's argument is correct, the first sentence contains the idea for which the rest of the argument is advanced as support. Space is represented as an infinite magnitude because of the considerations which Kant elaborates in the later sentences. Aside from the difficulties in the argument, there is one consideration which causes Vaihinger[43] to invert it. The above analysis does not allow this argument to prove that space is an intuition; though the Metaphysical Exposition, as a whole, is designed to show this. Therefore, Vaihinger claims that what Kant meant is the following: space is an intuition and not a conception *because* space is represented as an infinite magnitude, while no general conception including what is common to all particular spaces would determine anything with reference to magnitude and *a fortiori* nothing with reference to infinite magnitude. For this reason, space cannot be a conception and must be an intuition.

This interpretation of Vaihinger's is certainly possible in the light of the Metaphysical Exposition considered as a whole. It is doubtless true that the infinitude of space forms the fourth element in Kant's proof that space is a pure intuition. It would seem, however, quite arbitrary to invert Kant's sentences in this particular argument in the fashion Vaihinger suggests. To do so is to assume that Kant hardly realized what he was about when he worked out the argument. If Kant meant merely that space is intuitive because no conceptions of it tell us anything with reference to size, and least of all with reference to infinite size, why did he not say so? If the fact that space is represented as an infinite given quantity were intended merely to serve as the minor premise, why did not Kant put it there? Vaihinger confuses the role that the infinitude of space (along with its singularity) plays in the Metaphysical Exposition considered as a whole with the fact that Kant was trying to demonstrate such infinitude in this argument in order that it might then play that wider role. Therefore, we may conclude that the infinitude of space is the thesis

[43] Vaihinger, *Kommentar*, II, 237–39.

which the argument is intended to demonstrate; while the thesis along with the considerations of the preceding argument, as well as those of the Transcendental Exposition, is designed to culminate in showing that space is an intuition.

Does the argument following the first sentence establish the thesis successfully? In my opinion, it fails to do so, and the reasons for this failure are the reasons for Kant's reformulation of the argument in the second edition. As we have suggested, Kant silently assumed that an infinite space given implies the total or complete representation of it by the subject. His defense of the former view passes over into a defense of the latter. Therefore, when he holds that the nature of the apprehension of infinite space by the subject involves merely "a boundlessness in the progression of the intuition," the nature of the given space becomes stripped of its infinity. If the representing or intuiting mind begins with feet, yards, ells, and the like and progresses outward, it never finds an infinite magnitude of space given immediately but represents it mediately, if at all. Such a progression is contemplated as far as it is actually continued by the mind, and its parts are immediately viewed, but a principle of infinity is not a contemplated or presented infinite magnitude. If we arrive at a principle of infinity, we merely conceive the whole of space. Therefore, if this account of the infinitude of space is adopted, not only do the subjective conditions of apprehension limit the act or process of representation by making it partial rather than total, but they likewise restrict the given space to finite lengths, and space becomes a conception. If the infinite whole of space is conceived, then "space" and "man" are similar rather than different. In other words, the very argument which Kant used in the first edition to show that space is an infinite given magnitude, turned out (as he realized after 1781) to show that it is conceived as infinite. It seemed to show that space is, after all, conceptual, with the parts prior to, and in a sense determining, at least one characteristic of the whole, namely its infinitude. Although this conclusion is somewhat in harmony with his position in the *Analytic*,[44] it works havoc upon the preceding space arguments in the

[44] Cf. Kant, *Kritik der reinen Vernunft*, B 202-4, cf. below, pp. 220-24.

Aesthetic, as well as with the general theory of pure intuition. The difficulty involved, as I hope to show below,[45] does not concern the intuitive nature of space, or even its infinitude, but merely the subjective conditions of our apprehension. By persisting in confusing the nature of space with our apprehension of it, Kant worked out an argument here that threatened not only the view that space is infinite, but also his wider theory of its intuitive nature. The same mistake is found in one of his *Reflexionen:*

Es kann uns kein Quantum als infinitum gegeben sein, denn es wird nicht an sich selbst gegeben, sondern nur durch den Progressus, der niemals als infinitus gegeben ist. Aber ein Progressus in infinitum kann gegeben sein; indefinitum, dessen Grenze wir unbestimmt lassen.[46]

Here at least Kant recognized that the theory of a progression is incompatible with the view that space is represented as an infinite magnitude *given.* If from the given progression, the mind infers the possibility of continuing indefinitely, the infinitude of space is conceived, and, at least as regards this feature of its nature, space is conceptual. The implications in the last space argument in the first edition threaten the edifice of thought of which it was designed to be the completion.

For these reasons, Kant recast his fourth argument on space in 1787.

Space is represented as an infinite *given* magnitude. Now we must think of every conception as a representation which is contained in an infinite number of various possible representations (as their common identifying mark) and therefore as containing them *under itself;* but no conception as such can be thought of as containing an infinite number of representations *in itself.* Nevertheless, space is thought of in this fashion (for the parts of space are all at once [*zugleich*] into infinity) . Therefore the original representation of space is an intuition *a priori* and not a conception.[47]

He italicized the word "given" in the leading sentence to stress the fact that he was not referring to a conceived infinity, and he formulated a new argument designed primarily to show (parallel to the third space argument) that space is not conceptual. To this extent he was successful. The new argument is an additional basis

[45] Cf. below, pp. 197–200.   [46] Erdmann, *Reflexionen Kants,* No. 360.
[47] Kant, *Kritik der reinen Vernunft,* B 39–40.

for the intuitive nature of space. Space is an infinite given whole, he argued, in the sense that an infinite number of representations are in it and not under it. The parts of space are in the whole all at once (*zugleich*) into infinity. Every remnant of the fatal theory of a progression is eliminated. Space is represented as an infinite given quantity since the parts are all at once given into infinity. The infinite space is given equally with a foot and with an ell, not because the mind may progress from the one to the other and so on, but because all such parts are simultaneously in the given space. In the same way that the parts in space were held in the third space argument to be mere limitations of the one, singular, given space, apart from the finitude or infinitude of the latter; so in this argument the infinite number of parts are mere limitations of the one, infinite, given space. In both arguments, the difference between parts ordered under general conceptions and parts in the intuitive whole is evidence for the intuitive nature of the latter. This argument may be considered as re-enforcing evidence for the intuitive nature of space.

In addition, however, Kant designed this argument as evidence that the mind has a total or complete apprehension of the infinite given magnitude of space. As in the corresponding argument in the first edition, he assumed that the infinity of the object of knowledge as given implies a complete perspective in the act of apprehension. In this attempt he again failed. The parts *in* space are infinite in number, but this fact is known about them mediately. The mind is just as incapable of viewing an infinite number of parts immediately as actually displayed before it as it is of continuing in the progression far enough to reach the infinite whole of space and viewing it directly. The principle of infinity which is the outcome of a boundless progression is a conceived principle. Similarly, the facts that the parts of space are all together into infinity and that each of them is *in* the infinite magnitude of space rather than *under* it show not that the infinite whole is directly given, but that it is indirectly inferred from this characteristic of the parts. Hence, in this argument as in the other, space turns out to be conceptual as far as its infinity is concerned. In neither case does the proof of the main thesis turn out to be effectual. In neither case is the whole of infinite space shown to be immediately given. If the fact that a progression in space is possible indefinitely is the only basis for Kant's claim that the infinite magnitude of space is directly given, then actually it is not given, but derived from that fact. If the fact that an infinite number of representations of space are *in* it rather than *under* it is the sole basis for his claim that the infinite whole of space is directly given, then actually it is not given, but derived from that fact. Space is immediately given to the mind as an infinite quantity only if any representation of space which the mind has is an immediate (although partial) representation of such infinitude. Such a contention is probably what Kant had in mind in the first sentence of both arguments, but in both cases the proof used was insufficient to establish it.

A more adequate statement of the theory of the infinitude of space would seem to be Clarke's view[48] that we apprehend infinite space but that such apprehension is only partial. We have noted difficulties in Clarke's statement of this view, but in one regard he avoided some of the difficulties into which Kant fell. Clarke mistakenly held that a partial apprehension of space involves treating it *as if* it had parts, but, nevertheless, he referred to the partial nature, not of space, but of our apprehension. Stripped of his theory of the fictitious parts of space—which, after all, is a different problem from its infinitude—Clarke's view suggests certain important distinctions. The object of knowledge is different from the act or process of knowledge. Questions concerning the nature of the object are different ones from those concerning the process. Is space, as the object of apprehension, finite or infinite? Is the nature of the process of apprehension partial or total? These questions, although related, are different, and the answer to one of them does not commit us to the corresponding answer to the other. In brief, space, as the object of knowledge, may be infinite, but the process of apprehending it may be partial rather than total. Such partial apprehension may be, nonetheless, direct or immediate. Hence there would be direct, partial apprehension of infinite space.

[48] Clarke, Paper IV, §§ 11–12; cf. above, pp. 24–25.

Such a solution of the problem of the infinitude of space as this one was nowhere stated by Kant, and even Clarke merely hinted at it in holding that we have a partial apprehension of infinite space. Kant was prevented from realizing its possibility, probably for two reasons. In the first place, his concern in the fourth space argument both in 1781 and 1787 was not solely the immediate apprehension of the infinite whole of space, but also the additional evidence that such an argument would yield for the intuitive, nonconceptual nature of space, as worked out on independent grounds in the preceding argument. In the second place, Kant fell into that unhappy confusion with reference to the term "representation" that G. E. Moore so successfully pointed out concerning the use of the term "sensation" by the idealists.[49] Like "sensation," "representation" in the Kantian arguments is used ambiguously to refer to the object and to the process. Sensa, Moore showed, are not mind-conditioned merely because the process of sensation is necessarily so. It is unjustifiable to argue from the fact that the texture of the process of sensation is of a certain sort to the quite different conclusion that the object is likewise of that sort. Similarly, from the fact that the nature of the process of representing space is of a certain sort, it does not follow that space is likewise of that same sort. Kant began both of his arguments for the infinitude of space in the *Aesthetic* by stating that the "representation" of space is of an infinite given whole. He then proceeded in both cases to attempt to establish both the infinitude of space as the object and the totality or completeness of the act of apprehension as the process. But the second contention is very different from the first. Space may be infinite whether or not it is completely apprehended. Furthermore, it may be infinite whether it is apprehended immediately as given or mediately as thought of. Again, its apprehension as total or partial is not the same as its apprehension as mediate or immediate, but both sets of distinctions refer to the process rather than to the object. For the purposes of his view that it is an intuition, he needed only to show that it is apprehended immediately—which he had done in the preceding argument. Yet since he confused the infinitude of the object with the totality of

[49] Moore, *Philosophical Studies*, pp. 18–26.

the process, he proceeded to attempt to establish the latter as an aspect of the former. This attempt could, however, succeed only at the expense of his theory that it is given immediately and that, hence, it is an intuition. If the infinitude of the object means the totality of the process, the former can be established only if the mind has a total apprehension of space. Such apprehension would be either immediate or mediate. It is, however, not immediate, since the mind never reaches the whole in the progression (A 5) and since the infinite number of its parts are not presented (B 4). Hence it is mediate. Hence space is not given directly to the mind, and, as far as its infinitude is concerned, it is conceptual and not intuitive. Kant's confusion of the conditions of the process of apprehension (partial or total) with the nature of the object (finite or infinite) necessarily cuts the ground from under his theory that infinite space is immediately given in intuition.

This entire difficulty is avoided if the two meanings of "representation" of space are remembered. As an object, the representation of space is infinite, and immediately given as such. As a process, the representation of space is always partial rather than total, at least for man. Since space is directly given in such partial apprehension, and since it is given as it is and not as distorted by the mind, it is given immediately as infinite, and not merely thought of mediately as such. Unlike Kant's two arguments concerning the infinitude of space, there would be, in this view, an infinite whole of space, given directly to the mind, admittedly partially, but nevertheless immediately given.

Perhaps the objection will be raised against this view that the infinitude of space cannot be given both partially and immediately, any such alleged limitation in the process precluding any apprehension of infinitude except mediately. In the story of the blind men and the elephant, one of the men had a partial apprehension of the elephant, apprehending immediately the flat surface of his side, and inferring (mediately and falsely) that it was a wall. Similarly, it might be claimed, if the apprehension of space is partial, a finite portion is directly apprehended and its infinitude is necessarily inferred, truly or falsely, but in any case, mediately. Can apprehension be partial and immediate and yet have as its object infinite space? To this question, it seems that both Clarke and Kant provide the basis for an answer. The blind man made his true or false inference from the given datum (the flat side) because the connotation of that datum did not exhaust the connotation of the object (elephant). On the other hand, the whole purport of Kant's preceding arguments has been that the entire connotation of space is given immediately to the mind. The process of apprehension is partial rather than total not because the infinitude of space (as well as its other qualities) is not given immediately, but because other apprehensions of the same object (space) are possible. If the datum given to the blind man (to suppose the impossible) exhausted the nature of the elephant, he would know that an elephant was given without any inference whatsoever, and so it is with our apprehension of infinite space. We apprehend it immediately *qua* infinite because this characteristic is as directly displayed to our contemplative gaze as any of its other qualities. The fact that there are several ways of gazing at it would involve a limitation of the qualities presented each time only if the connotation varied with each. Since there is no such variation, each partial apprehension yields the entire nature of the object. Infinite space is immediately and partially apprehended. This fact is a guarantee of our contact with the external real.

§ 5

KANT'S TRANSCENDENTAL EXPOSITION of space in 1787, as well as his corresponding argument in 1781, adds little to his formal position of 1770. In all three years he was holding that the synthetic, *a priori* character of truth in geometry and mechanics is evidence —separate from, yet re-enforcing, his other analyses—that space is a pure intuition. In one regard, however, his argument is of importance in throwing light upon his general philosophy of space. As I have pointed out, he equated throughout his expositions the terms "experience" and "perception," thereby giving a somewhat narrow meaning to the former. In this connection it is significant that only in the Transcendental Exposition (and in A 3) did he use the term *Wahrnehmung*. In 1781 he stated quite generally that if space were not *a priori,* the first principles of mathematics would be merely perceptions and would hence be merely contingent, but in 1787 he was more specific:

Aber diese Anschauung muss a priori, d. i. vor aller Wahrnehmung eines Gegenstandes, in uns angetroffen werden, mithin reine, nicht empirische Anschauung sein.[50]

He was arguing, admittedly, from the nature of mathematical truth to the nature of space, but he sums up quite clearly the conclusion to which his other four arguments had been also designed to lead, and in so doing, he states the core of his theory of perception. The priority of space to experience meant for him the temporal priority of space to every perception of an object. What is the significance of this theory for the problems of perception with which we dealt above?[51] As we have found, the issue between the subjectivists and the realists is briefly whether the objects of perception are ideas or images in the mind or in some special place of perception such as a sensorium, or whether they are portions of an external order of reality in a public space. Which of these views did Kant hold in the *Aesthetic?*

To attempt a straightforward answer to this question concerning Kant's views is a perilous procedure for a number of reasons. First, his distinction between things in themselves and appearances, which he never abandoned, although he stated it in at least two forms, would seem either to be out-and-out subjectivism, or, at least incompatible with a strict realism. Secondly, his account of the secondary qualities both in the conclusion to the section on space in the *Aesthetic* and in his general conclusion to that part of the *Critique* seems beyond doubt to involve a subjective account of those qualities; in the *Prolegomena* he would seem in at least one place[52] to extend this conclusion to the primary qualities. On the other hand, his doctrines of space in the *Aesthetic,* as well as his reiterated distinction between appearances and illusion in the conclusion to the *Aesthetic* (particularly in the edition of 1787) seem to provide the basis for a realistic theory of perception and to show his concern lest the reader consider his view to be

---

[50] Kant, *Kritik der reinen Vernunft,* B 41.   [51] Cf. above, Chapter IV, §§ 1–2.
[52] Kant, *Prolegomena zu einer jeden künftigen Metaphysik . . .* § 13, Remark II.

subjectivistic in the Berkeleyan sense. Because of this unhappy situation, the student of Kant is forced either to point to the quantitatively larger sections of the *Critique* as evidence that Kant was a subjectivist, whatever the nature of the realistic conclusions involved in his doctrines of space and whatever the extent that Kant could have developed such realism, or to ignore his distinction between realities and appearances in its various forms and work out the realistic theory of perception involved in the doctrine of space as it remains stripped of that distinction, stressing the phases of the first and second space arguments which guarantee the externality of objects in space.

Since our study does not enter the field of controversy concerning the wider implications of Kant's critical philosophy (as well as its precritical and semicritical phases) we shall take no definite stand on these more general matters. In his philosophy of space, and notably in such a later section of the *Critique* as the "Refutation of Idealism" in the 1787 edition, a certain type of epistemological realism is, however, quite obvious. In that particular section he mentioned his distinction between things in themselves and appearances as a doctrine which refutes the dogmatic idealism of Berkeley, "who declares space and all things to which it belongs as an inseparable condition, as something impossible in itself, and, therefore, things in space as mere imaginations."[53] He went on to hold that such a view is inevitable, if space is considered as a property of things in themselves, and to hold that his views in the *Aesthetic* sufficiently answer Berkeley's subjectivism. In the rest of the "Refutation of Idealism," he took issue with Descartes's view that the external world is an inference from the inner self, and held that external objects in space and time are the basis for all inward imagination. We can recognize the products of mere imagination only by distinguishing them from our preceding experience of the external world. There is no evidence in this particular section that he was not ascribing a kind of metaphysical reality to the external objects in space. Our immediate consciousness of external objects is a guarantee of their independent existence. The distinction between things in themselves and appear-

---

[53] Kant, *Kritik der reinen Vernunft*, B 274, translated by Müller, p. 778.

ances is either held in complete abeyance or referred to only as the antidote for the dogmatic idealism of Berkeley. It is, then, safe to conclude that this position involves an epistemological realism with reference to the objects in space, accompanied at least by a complete neutrality on the matter of the ultimate metaphysical status of those objects as real or unreal. Such a position is the antithesis of Newton's subjectivistic theory of images in a sensorium set over in opposition to things themselves in public space. It is not unlike Newton's realistic tendency in the *Principles,* stripped, of course, of the theory of space as an attribute of God. In both views, we know qualities of objects as aspects of things themselves, without knowing *what* the essential nature of those things are.

On the other hand, it would seem to be nearer the truth to say that, in general, Kant did not follow out the realistic implication of his theories of space. In general, the external objects with which we are in cognitive contact, as guaranteed by his theories of space, are appearances. Objects in space—whether obscuring from us things in themselves of an intrinsically different nature from their own or whether constituting that portion of things in themselves which we are able to know, or whether so neutral in their nature that neither metaphysical reality or unreality may be predicated of them—are in any case appearances. If our account of Kant's views of space about 1769 and 1770 is correct, the doctrine of the metaphysical unreality of space and time was extrinsic to his development and based upon his hope of discovering intellectual intuitions, yielding a face-to-face knowledge of some reality other than the world of appearances. With the collapse of that hope, the doctrines of space remain on their original basis apart from the theory of appearances.[54] Let us consider the realistic theory of knowledge which may be reared upon them.

The *a priori* nature of space means, he held in the *Aesthetic,* that space is temporally prior to "all perception of an object." Doubtless in the light of his wider theory, he meant that it is

[54] Possibly ethical considerations influenced Kant in his retention of the theory of appearances after the collapse of the doctrine which had been designed to render that theory tenable. This is a psychological-biographical problem and not our concern.

prior to all perception of appearances; but in this particular passage he said "object." Stripped of his theory of things in themselves, this doctrine would mean that space is prior to the real objects encountered in perception. Even in terms of his phenomenalistic interpretation of appearances, it would mean that space is prior to one portion of reality, namely, that portion called appearances. In either case, his assumption would seem to be that the object of perception is real and not an image or idea. His theory of space as a pure intuition provides the basis for such realism. Since space is prior to the perception of an object, the nature of the object, once encountered in space, is dependent upon conditions different from the conditions of perception, namely, the conditions of space itself. Space is independent of the self and the conditions of the act of perception, and thus by its very nature guarantees that in perception the mind is in contact with an order of things external to, and independent of, itself and whatever subjective conditions the act of perception may involve. The priority of space to sense perception provides an answer to the question of how the mind can, in perception, know the independently real. The transcendental ideality of space means that it is the gauge by means of which the independent reality of empirical objects in it may be experienced and confirmed. Space guarantees to objects in it a concreteness of independent existence which it lacks itself when judged by the same standards which it imposes upon them. Space is transcendentally nonempirical because empirical objects, including their qualities and relations, are dependent upon it for their very nature. Such dependence, far from meaning mind-dependence, is the guarantee of the very opposite. Even in his most subjective account of appearances, Kant contended that the dependence of space upon the mind is unlike the dependence of such qualities as the smell of a rose. Space has its own necessary nature, linked with the mind though it may be, whereas the smell is not only linked with the mind but has a nature dependent solely upon the mind and its sensory equipment and variable as the latter varies. Thus, space and the secondary qualities are related to the mind, but only the former has a necessary nature. Again, in his phenomenalism, appearances, though different from things in themselves, are a subspecies of the latter and, as such, are not merely related to the mind, but are also, in part, external to it and independent of it. Space, in this view, would continue to provide a necessary type of contact for the mind with appearances, but those appearances would no longer be, in their nature, solely mind-dependent. Hence space would be, to a certain degree, a factor enabling the mind to be in contact with the external, independently real. Up to a point, then, such phenomenalism would be realistic, and it is tempting to conclude that Kant's theory of perception is, in this phase, realistic. For reasons which I have mentioned, however, it would seem best not to draw this conclusion.

Summarizing: Even in his more subjectivistic account of the objects of perception as appearances, Kant stressed the difference between the relation of the mind to space and to objects in space. In his phenomenalistic account of appearances, he held the nature of space to be a guarantee that the mind is in contact with certain features of things in themselves. In addition, outside the framework of the conclusions which Kant himself drew, it would seem to provide the realist with the basis for contending that the mind is, in perception, in contact with the independently real and that all the features of the objects of perception (even the secondary qualities) which are dependent upon space are non-mental in their nature and exist apart from any relation to the mind.

Another significant feature of Kant's Transcendental Exposition is his claim that space is prior to "perception." If "experience" is given the wider significance ascribed to it by Alexander,[55] and if Kant's contention here is considered to involve not the temporal priority of space to experience, but only the temporal priority of space to perception, an interesting variant of Kant's views results. Space has a necessary nature, yet it is empirical in its origin. Those features of experience which lack such a necessary nature are the parts of experience involved in perception. Therefore, space, although encountered only in experience, is encountered temporally prior to sense perception and prescribes conditions determining the latter. Kant might have recast his arguments in

[55] Cf. below, pp. 238–39.

the *Aesthetic* along these lines, retaining the temporal priority of space to the object of sense perception, yet making it empirical. While more satisfactory than Kant's position, this view would still involve the troublesome problem of the manner of temporal priority of space to the objects and processes of perception. This difficulty might be partly solved, without departing too far from Kant's position in the *Aesthetic,* by distinguishing more sharply between the object of perception and the process. Space might be considered empirical in its origin, yet necessary in its nature. Space might be temporally prior to the objects of perception, yet not temporally prior to the process or act of perception. Even this view would involve the difficult problem of the nature of the temporal priority of space to sense objects. To eliminate this difficulty completely, it would be necessary to make a shift to Kant's views in the *Analytic,* and to abandon the doctrine of the temporal priority of space to objects of sense in favor of the theory of a mere logical priority.

Retaining the non-Kantian feature of the empirical nature of space, such a position would be briefly the following: Space would be empirical in its source but necessary in its nature; yet it would be nonperceptual in reference to both its source and its nature. It would not be temporally prior to experience or to perception, but its origin would lie solely in nonsensuous portions of experience. Its necessary nature, although derived from experience, would be independent of the objects and processes of sense perception. Space would formally or logically determine the materials of sense in such a fashion that in the process of perception the mind could come into contact with the independently real object. The dependence of perceptual conditions upon space would involve logical but not temporal priority. Those features of experience which are necessary (for example, space) would prescribe conditions limiting those features (perceptual) which in themselves would be merely contingent, and such limitation would enable even those latter features to yield parts of the independently real world and not merely mind-conditioned images or ideas. With these modifications, far-reaching though they may seem, the Kantian theories of space would provide a cornerstone for a realistic theory of perception.

CHAPTER VIII

THE *AESTHETIC* vs. THE *ANALYTIC*

§ 1

To COMPLETE our study of Kant's philosophy of space, we must now turn to his views of space in the *Analytic* and consider especially the question of the relation of those views to the *Aesthetic*. We have shown[1] that he put two different views of space in the *Dissertation* of 1770. According to the first of these, space is a pure intuition, immediately contemplated in its entirety, prior to sense experience; of such contemplation one set of examples is found in geometry. This view received its fullest elaboration in the *Aesthetic*. On the other hand, as we have found, Kant raised in addition quite a different problem in 1770, namely, the problem of an activity of the intellect (understanding) which generates space. He raised it implicitly in the example of incongruent counterparts, explicitly at the end of his treatment of time and space.[2] To explain the difference between two similar but incongruent objects, the mind does not merely refer them to an already given spatial framework but is forced to construct such a space. Space is not presented to the contemplative gaze of the mind but is constructed. In this example, an activity of the mind is implied. The mind is constrained to carry out an activity, and space is the result of this activity. This theory he stated explicitly at the end of his treatment of space. Space is not abstracted from the objects of sensation, nor is it innate. It is gained from an activity of the mind. Sensation excites this activity, but it does not contribute to the resulting intuition, which is the product of such constructive mental activity.

In this doctrine, and in the example of incongruent counterparts, Kant's view was at variance with the rest of § 15 of the *Dissertation*. In § 15, A, he stated that space is prior to me and to two

---

[1] Cf. above, pp. 151–52.
[2] Kant, *Inaugural Dissertations*, § 15, C, §§ 14–15, corollary.

objects which I arrange outside me and outside each other. There is an activity of the mind, but space is not abstracted from it. Space is prior to that activity. Also space remains when the elements of a sensation are abstracted. The conception of space is not acquired from an activity of the mind. In § 15, B, he contrasted space with the usual general conceptions, such as "man," or "extension." He was concerned, not with the manner in which the conception of space is gained, or arrived at, by the mind, but with the nature of space, whatever is the way in which it is represented. He contrasted "space" and "man," not two types of activity of the mind. In § 15, C, he said that space is contemplated. There is no activity of the mind. In the first paragraph of the corollary to §§ 14–15, he said that space is an infinite given whole, with the parts determined by the whole. In spite of these doctrines in other paragraphs of § 15 of the *Dissertation,* Kant turned around and held in the last paragraph of the corollary, that the conception of space is abstracted from an action of the mind.

Can his other doctrines of space in *Dissertation* § 15 and in the *Aesthetic* be reconciled with this view? What is the nature of such mental activity? As I have tried to show,[3] Kant's general philosophy in 1770 can be understood only if it is borne in mind that he hoped in that year to discover certain intellectual intuitions which would form the basis for an intelligible, real world in the same way that space and time are the forms of what he called, as a result of this hope, the sensible world of appearances. Such intellectual intuitions would yield synthetic, *a priori* truths in an as-yet-unformulated science of metaphysics in the same way that space and time yield such truths in geometry and mechanics.

This hope not only had a marked effect upon Kant's general views, but also directly affected his theories of space by causing him to formulate the theory in § 15, D, of the *Dissertation,* that space is "subjective" and "ideal." The fact that such "ideality" of space is, if my contentions are correct,[4] out of harmony with Kant's more specific views of space, does not alter the fact that it played an important role in Kant's thinking both in 1770 and afterwards

---

[3] Cf. above, pp. 152–61.   [4] Cf. above, pp. 119–21, 126, 139–41.

in the *Analytic*. With reference to the nature of the synthetic activity of the intellect, this effect was quite prominent.

How did this happen? In his hope for the successful development of the theory of intellectual intuitions, Kant developed three sets of correlated distinctions: (a) a real use of the intellect in opposition to its logical use; (b) a qualitative synthesis in opposition to a quantitative one; (c) a whole of representation in opposition to a representation of a whole. A logical use of the intellect is one which clarifies already given materials. It proceeds by qualitative synthesis or analysis. It yields only a whole of representation, ideal and not real. A real use of the intellect involves the apprehension of the materials of sense or of intelligence by sensuous intuition or by intellectual intuition, respectively. It proceeds by a quantitative synthesis of the materials of sense or of intelligence. It yields a representation of a whole, either of the world of appearances or of the real, intelligible world. The nature of the synthetic activity of the intellect which generates space can be understood in reference to these distinctions. Did Kant mean that space is generated by the real or by the logical use of the intellect? Did he mean that it is yielded by a qualitative synthesis or by a quantitative synthesis? Did he mean that it is merely a whole of representation or that it is a representation of a whole? According to his main view of space in the *Dissertation,* space is, of course, not generated at all, but given. It is, in both views, a representation of a whole of the world of sense, rather than a mere whole of representation.

In shifting to the view that space is generated, Kant could not, however, have meant that it is the result of a merely logical use of the intellect (a merely qualitative synthesis). Such activity of the intellect is only a conceptual clarification of the already given materials of intuition; therefore, if space were the result of such an activity of the mind, then space would be conceptual rather than intuitive. Consequently, Kant could have meant only that it is generated by a real use of the intellect, that is, by a quantitative synthesis. Whatever difficulties may turn out to be involved in this view (and those difficulties led to his reformulation of his theories

of space in the *Analytic*[5]), it was to this view that he came in
1770 as a result of his theory of intellectual intuitions.

Two sets of materials are given to the mind, the materials of
sense (appearances) and the materials of reality (things in themselves). Any real use of the intellect (quantitative synthesis) yielding space must begin with the one or the other of these sets of
materials. But if such an activity begins with the materials of
sense and yields space, then space is not prior to, and a determinant of, those materials, but posterior to, and determined by,
them. Consequently, in 1770 Kant meant that space is yielded by
an activity of the intellect (quantitative synthesis) that begins
with the only other possible source, namely, the materials of reality. From the nature of the real world, the intellect by a synthetic
activity extracts space, the form of the world of appearances;
hence, space is dependent upon an activity of the intellect, yet
prior to, and determinant of, the materials of sense. Such a doctrine is, briefly, the second theory of space which Kant put in § 15
of the *Dissertation*.

This view is self-consistent. It allows the theories of space as a
pure intuition and a pure form of empirical intuition to retain
their full significance *once space has been generated* and yet allows a real use of the intellect (a synthesis of a quantitative sort)
to yield it. There is, however, a difficulty with this view which is
basic enough to cause its complete collapse in the *Analytic*. This
doctrine rests, as I have shown,[6] upon the contention that there is
a set of nonsensuous, real materials in an intelligible, real world,
given to the intellect, with which the synthetic activity yielding
space may begin. This contention, in turn, rests upon Kant's hope
that certain intellectual intuitions could be found at the basis of
such materials. In fact, Kant's entire dichotomy of the real, intelligible world and the sensuous appearances rests upon the theory
of such intellectual intuitions. Now, as I have shown above, even
in 1770 Kant came to realize that such intuitions are not given to
man, and he worked out his position in the *Dissertation* upon the
two contradictory theories that man has and has not intellectual
intuitions. It was after 1770 in the *Analytic* that he faced the con-

[5] Cf. below, § 3.   [6] Cf. above, pp. 154–56.

sequences of this contradiction. Realizing that there are no intellectual intuitions, he realized further that there is no non-sensuous, intelligible set of materials given to the mind with which a synthetic activity designed to yield space could begin. What alternatives remained open to him? He could abandon entirely the theory that space is generated and stand squarely upon the main teaching of § 15 of the *Dissertation* and of the *Aesthetic,* that space is given temporally prior to experience in its complete necessary nature, or he could turn to the one alternative theory of a real use of the intellect (synthesis of a quantitative sort) yielding space, namely, the theory of such a synthetic activity beginning with the only other set of materials, the materials of sense. As I hope to show, it was to this latter view that he came, not realizing as he did so that he was thereby contradicting the central contentions of the *Aesthetic,* or perhaps realizing it, yet believing that the alterations required in the *Aesthetic* were too great to be undertaken.

Other possible compromise views were closed to him. He could not claim that such a synthetic activity of the intellect could begin with the materials of reality, for, with the collapse of the theory of intellectual intuitions, the existence of those materials was itself called into question. He could not claim that a mere qualitative synthesis, a mere logical use of the intellect, generates space, for, by definition, such a synthesis (such a use of the intellect) is conceptual only, designed merely to clarify what is already given in sensuous intuitions or intellectual ones (if such there be) . Finally, he could not claim that a quantitative synthesis (a real use of the intellect) could begin with something other than the materials of sense or the materials of reality (which had now been discarded from Kant's theory) . Such a claim would be tautologous; if space is not derived from the contents of the world of sense or of the real world, nor from the forms of the real world, then it must be derived from the forms of the world of sense. Such forms of the sensuous world of appearances Kant had, in 1770, called "sensitive."[7] They are two in number: space and time. But if space itself is that with which such a synthesis begins, then space pre-

[7] Kant, *Inaugural Dissertation,* § 5.

cedes and determines such synthesis and is not itself generated
by it. It is tautologous to claim that space is generated by a synthetic activity which itself begins with the sensitive (space) .[8] All of
these other alternatives being precluded, the retention of the
doctrine of a synthetic activity meant for Kant in the *Analytic* that
the synthetic activity begins with the manifold of sense. Only by a
return to the abandoned theory of intellectual intuitions as forms
of a nonsensuous, intelligible world could another account of such
an activity be retained.

§ 2

To sketch Kant's theory of knowledge in the *Analytic* is beyond
the scope of this investigation. His doctrine of categories involves
complications which are sufficiently great to require treatment
independently of any discussion of his philosophy of space. Consequently, it also lies beyond our province here to try to work out
an account of the various alterations in his views which he carried
out after 1770 and before 1781. His reflections give us clues to
these alterations, and such men as Vaihinger, Erdmann, and Kemp
Smith have added to our knowledge of them. Yet those phases of
his theory of knowledge which bear directly on his theories of
space need to be sketched briefly. For our purposes, his theory of
knowledge as treated in the transcendental deduction of the categories in the second (1787) edition provides the necessary clue.
To think an object, he there held,[9] and to know an object are not
the same. There are two ingredients of knowledge: the conception
in terms of which an object must be thought (the category) , and
the intuition in terms of which it is given. If there can be no
intuition corresponding to the conception, such a conception is a

<hr/>

[8] It is an interesting fact that S. Alexander, while not following such a tautologous
procedure to establish the qualities of space or time, reasons deliberately in a circular fashion from the nature of time to the nature of space, and vice versa. Assuming
the nature of the one to be given in experience, widely construed, he establishes the
nature of the other by a process not unlike Kant's synthetic activity and then reverses the procedure to establish the nature of the first. This device results in a
unique combination of the doctrine that time is given and space constructed, with
the doctrine that space is given and time constructed. Kant, of course, had no such
solution in mind. Alexander, *Space, Time and Deity*, I, 50–58. Cf. below, p. 239.

[9] Kant, *Kritik der reinen Vernunft*, B·146–47.

thought only in form; it is without an object; and by means of it no knowledge of any object at all is possible.

This rather straightforward argument involves a restatement of his distinction of 1770 between a whole of representation and a representation of a whole. The former, he had then held, is merely a conceptual unity, referring to nothing real, and serviceable only in the conceptual clarification of the materials of sense or of reality. The latter is the whole either of the world of sense or of the intelligible, real world. In 1787, he less presumptuously referred the distinction to an object rather than to a world. Knowledge of an object rather than a world requires both an intuition and a conception. Conceptions without intuitions refer, he held, only to a thought in form, through which no knowledge is possible, rather than to a whole of representation.

So far in his account there are no limitations imposed upon knowledge other than those imposed in 1770, with the exception of the metaphysical implications of his references to objects rather than to worlds and to thoughts rather than to wholes. He continued,[10] however, as follows: intuition is either pure (of space and time) or empirical (of that which is represented through sensation immediately in space and time). By the determinations or modifications (*Bestimmungen*) of a pure intuition we get knowledge *a priori* of objects (in mathematics), but only according to their form. The question of whether or not there are things (even appearances) that must be intuited in this form is quite a different matter. Consequently, mathematical conceptions are in themselves not knowledge.

This teaching has two features that are important for our purposes. In the first place, Kant imposes two limitations upon knowledge of space and time as pure intuitions: first, such knowledge is only of the form of objects; secondly, it is knowledge only of appearances. Could he have meant the same thing by these two limitations? Could he have meant that knowledge of appearances is knowledge of the form of real objects? Such an equation is impossible in the light of his continued contention that appearances are the sensuous contents of experience. More important

[10] *Ibid.*

for our purposes is, however, the fact that he referred to mathematics as a case of knowledge only of the form of objects (appearances), and held that the conceptions in that science are not themselves knowledge. It may be asked whether this teaching represents any advance over his theory of 1770 that mathematical truth is synthetic. If he merely meant that the conceptions in mathematics, like any other conceptions without intuitions, are not knowledge, but that, with the addition of the pure intuitions of space and time, there is (synthetic) knowledge in that science, such a view would involve no change from his earlier position. In this case, it would be surprising, however, that with the transcendental exposition of space in the *Aesthetic* intact, he should merely repeat in the *Analytic* that mathematical truths are synthetic.

In fact, he was not merely repeating this conclusion. He meant that the conceptions of mathematics, even when referred to space and time as pure intuitions, are not yet knowledge. Even in mathematics, the reference of conceptions to the pure intuition of space is no guarantee of knowledge.

Kant held furthermore[11] that things in space and time are given only in so far as they are perceptions (that is, representations accompanied by sensation) and hence empirical representations. Hence, the pure conceptions of the understanding (intellect) even when applied *a priori* to intuitions (as in mathematics) yield knowledge only in so far as these (pure) intuitions—and along with, and by means of, them, the pure conceptions of the understanding—can be applied to *empirical* intuitions.

Kant referred to three different kinds of application. There is, first, the straightforward application of a conception to an empirical intuition. This means that the object is thought and intuited and that the conception and intuition are correlated in knowledge. There is, secondly, the application *a priori* of a conception to a pure intuition. This occurs, for example, in pure mathematics. In this type of application, the object is not necessarily existent. There is an object which is thought and intuited, but since this object is not intuited empirically, there is no assurance that it exists. This is knowledge in form only. In both of these cases, the

[11] *Ibid.*

application depends upon a correlation between a conception and an intuition. The third kind of application is quite different. It is the application of a pure intuition (space or time) to an empirical intuition. It is based upon the relation of a form to an empirical content. The pure intuition (space) is a form of every possible empirical intuition. If a conception has been applied to a pure intuition which is at once a form of every empirical intuition, the conception could be applied to any empirical intuition. If conception A has been applied to pure intuition B, and if pure intuition B could be applied to empirical intuition C (since pure intuition B is a form of empirical intuition), then it follows that conception A could be applied (along with B) to C. Kant's statement of this doctrine is obscure, due to its inclusion in a clause (*mithin auch die Verstandesbegriffe vermittelst ihrer*) [12] which breaks his train of thought. Yet it is vital to his argument. For only in the application of a conception to an empirical intuition does knowledge occur. The significance of the doctrine is that it shows how we may, without gaining any knowledge (that is, by means of knowledge in form), ascertain the conditions of knowledge.

Kant would seem, in a broad way, to argue thus: I am going to state a doctrine which, at first glance, will seem only to limit all knowledge to experience and to deny that pure mathematics belongs to experience and, therefore, to deny that in pure mathematics there is knowledge. If you follow me closely, however, you will see that in this doctrine something more important emerges than this negative conclusion. In pure mathematics, without turning to experience, I find a way of accurately limiting knowledge and of setting up conditions to which knowledge must conform. I do, in fact, deny that in pure mathematics there is knowledge; but I hold that there is knowledge in form in that science. This is no merely negative conclusion, for by means of knowledge in form, we can determine the possibility (limiting conditions) of knowledge. The application of a conception to an empirical intuition gives knowledge. The application of a conception to a pure intuition (which may be applied to an empirical intuition) de-

[12] *Ibid.*

termines the conditions under which knowledge occurs and to which knowledge must conform. Space is a pure intuition and a pure form of empirical intuition. The application of a conception to the pure intuition of space yields knowledge in form, but not knowledge. Knowledge in form determines the conditions of knowledge. This fact does not mean that any nonempirical intuition whatsoever can determine the conditions of knowledge. There may be some intuition (intellectual) which is not given to man. Unless such an intuition were also a form of empirical intuitions, it would not determine the possibility of knowledge. The pure intuitions of space and time are not the source of knowledge, but they bear an important relation to it. They are intuitions to which conceptions are applied and which are the forms of all empirical intuitions.[13] The knowledge in form resulting from that application is a determination of the limits of knowledge.

In this doctrine Kant had broken with his earlier views of space. Intuitions and conceptions are not to be considered as separated from each other, but as conditioning each other in the knowing situation. Both are determinants of knowledge and must be considered as operating always together rather than in isolation. Furthermore, knowledge is possible only if its intuitive features are first and last empirical. Consequently, however legitimate the consideration of space as a pure intuition may be and however fruitful (for example in mathematics) the application of the categories to such a pure intuition may be, in neither case is there knowledge. Only if there is an empirical intuition with contents consisting of sensuous objects would an analysis of "pure" space with or without categories yield knowledge. This marked change in his views is involved in most of the *Analytic*.

§ 3

IN ADDITION TO this more general shift in Kant's views of space, we must consider the extent to which he departed from the con-

---

[13] This significance of the pure intuition of space in pure geometry lies in its being at the same time the form of any possible empirical intuition. This makes geometry a science which determines the limitations of knowledge and makes the pure intuition of space significant in spite of the fact that it is an *ens imaginarium;* cf. below, pp. 219–20.

clusions of the individual space arguments of the *Aesthetic*. (1) Did he abandon the view that space is given to the mind temporally prior to experience? If so, did he abandon that view in favor of the view that space is given to the mind on the occasion of, or after, experience, or did he deny that it is given to the mind at all? (2) Did he abandon the view that space has a necessary nature and is necessarily represented by the mind? (3) Did he abandon the view that the parts of space are merely thought of in it as limitations of one wider, singular space? (4) Did he abandon the view that space is represented as an infinite given magnitude? In general, did he abandon—or to any extent alter—the theory that space is a pure intuition and a pure form of sensuous intuition?

In reference to the first question, there are two different views in the *Analytic*. In the one, space is given but given after a synthetic activity of the understanding which begins on the occasion of sense experience. For general reasons which we have mentioned,[14] Kant would seem to have meant that this activity begins with the materials of sense, although he was not always clear on this point. In the other view, space is not given at all but is merely a formal condition involved in the apprehension of the materials of sense.

In reference to the second question, these same two points of view appear. In the one, space is given after a synthesis and is represented as necessarily what it is and not otherwise. The mind is compelled to represent it whether with or without objects in it. In the other, the nature of space is determined by a synthesis beginning with the materials of sense. While not clearly worked out, the implication of this view is that there is no guarantee that space has a necessary nature, while Kant explicitly repudiates the view that space exists as an object with a nonsensuous content of its own. This repudiation has significance in reference to present-day theories of space.[15]

In regard to the third question, and therefore also in regard to the fourth, Kant takes two stands. According to the one, while the parts of space determine the whole in the process of our representation, nevertheless the whole determines the parts in the resulting intuition. According to the other, space is a composite constructed out of the parts, which thereby determine its nature as a whole. While not clearly worked out, the implication of this view is that space is conceptual. In general, the theory that a synthetic activity of the understanding generates space upsets the entire structure of Kant's argument in the *Aesthetic,* although in certain passages in the *Analytic* he tries ineffectually to avert this result. Let us turn to the specific arguments in which he worked out these alterations.

In regard to the first space argument, the following passages are decisive.

Wenn das Licht nicht den Sinnen gegeben worden, so kann man sich auch keine Finsternis, und, wenn nicht ausgedehnte Wesen wahrgenommen worden, keinen Raum vorstellen.[16]

Again:

Die Zeit geht zwar als formale Bedingung der Möglichkeit der Veränderungen vor dieser objektiv vorher, allein subjektiv, und in der Wirklichkeit des Bewusstseins, ist, diese Vorstellung doch nur, so wie jede andere, durch Veranlassung der Wahrnehmungen gegeben.[17]

In these passages, Kant clearly abandons the theory of the temporal priority of space to sense perception. Space is given on the occasion of, or after, sense perception, but certainly not before. It is an object which may be viewed immediately, but it is so given only by means of our experience of its contents. While Kant is not specific concerning this matter, he would seem to mean, for reasons which I have already mentioned,[18] that it is yielded as a given manifold by a synthesis which not only begins upon the occasion of experience but which begins *with* the materials of sense. With the collapse of his belief that there is a pure nonsensuous manifold given in intellectual intuition with which such a synthesis could begin, the materials of sense remain as the sole source from which space can be extracted or generated.

But Kant also developed another view of the nature of space involving the abandonment of the contention that it is *given* at all.

---

[16] Kant, *Kritik der reinen Vernunft,* A 292 = B 349.
[17] *Ibid.,* A 153 *n* = B 481 *n.*
[18] Cf. above, § 1 esp. p. 212; cf. below, pp. 229–32.

Die blosse Form der Anschauung, ohne Substanz, ist an sich kein Gegenstand, sondern die bloss formale Bedingung desselben (als Erscheinung), wie der reine Raum, und die reine Zeit, die zwar Etwas sind, als Formen anzuschauen, aber selbst keine Gegenstände sind, die angeschaut werden (*ens imaginarium*).[19]

This doctrine marks the collapse of the theory of a pure intuition contemplated by the mind either prior to, during, or after, experience, in the science of geometry or in any other case. Space is the mere (*blosse*) form of empirical intuition. It is neither pure (*rein*) in the sense of being given to the mind apart from objects nor pure (*rein*) in the sense of being given to the mind as the form of empirical intuition. It is such a form only as a formal condition (*Bedingung*) of appearances. As such, it is something when there is something in it; but with nothing in it, it is an *ens imaginarium*. The theory that space remains when objects have been abstracted is repudiated. In addition, Kant made no reference here to a synthetic activity of the mind. Space is not given as a pure intuition either before or after any activity of the mind, for it is not directly given at all. In this passage, Kant did not call space an aggregate, nor did he hold that it is generated out of the materials of sense.

The same position is worked out in several crucial *Reflexionen,* which Erdmann dates late enough to fall in the period in which Kant was formulating the views of the *Analytic.*

Raum und Zeit sind selbst nichts anderes als Formen der Zusammensetzung der Objecte der Empfindung; daher auch, wenn man alle Zusammensetzung da aufhebt, nichts übrig bleibt.[20]

Or again:

Raum und Zeit sind beide nichts als Zusammensetzungen sinnlicher Eindrücke.[21]

Whatever is the manner in which space is generated or arrived at by the mind, it is not something subsequently presented or given, with or without things in it, but merely a form according to which objects are ordered or set together. In the second passage, Kant does not refer to it even as a form, but merely as the arrangement

---

[19] Kant, *Kritik der reinen Vernunft,* A 291 = B 347.
[20] Erdmann, *Reflexionen Kants,* No. 985.   [21] *Ibid.,* No. 410.

of impressions as set together. The problem of whether space as
an object is generated merely on the occasion of sense experience
or actually extracted from the contents of such experience drops
out, because such space is nonexistent. To the extent that there is
any space at all, there is merely the manifold of sense which is
ordered in a fashion called spatial.

These considerations are important not merely in reference to
Kant's first space argument in the *Aesthetic,* but also in regard to
the second and third. If space is generated from the materials of
sense but is subsequently immediately given to the mind, the
possibility that it has a necessary nature (once given) is considerably greater than if it is an *ens imaginarium,* or the mere arrangement of objects as set together. In the first case, the mind might
still be compelled to represent space as necessarily what it is and
not otherwise, once the generative activity had yielded it as an
object. But there are difficulties even in such a view. In the second
case, there would be no assurance that space would have a necessary nature, and the possibility of its being given apart from objects (its *Nicht-Hinweg-Denkbarkeit*) is eliminated. In the second
space argument in the *Aesthetic,* the necessary nature of space was
bound up with its given nature and presupposed its intuitiveness
which was to be developed in the succeeding argument. But the
basis of such intuitiveness turned out to be a special type of relation between the whole and the parts, which was discoverable only
on the assumption that the whole is given and the parts carved
out of it. Therefore, the necessary nature of space presupposed the
theory that it is given first as a whole. With the introduction of
a synthesis, this situation is reversed. Whatever is the nature of the
materials with which a synthesis begins, it yields first the parts, and
only later, if at all, does it generate the whole. In any case, the
necessary nature of space is jeopardized, while if the whole of
space is not generated, its very intuitive nature is threatened, and
the resulting doctrine would be that space is a conception.

Now Kant fought to avoid both conclusions. He tried to retain
both the necessary nature of space and its intuitive nature as compatible, both of them, with the theory of a generative activity of
the mind. He held that space and time are continuous quan-

tities (*quanta continua*).[22] A synthesis of such quantities through the parts may yield, he held, both the necessary nature (as the basis for *a priori,* synthetic truth in geometry) and the whole of space, which may then be considered to determine the parts and, hence, to establish the intuitive, nonconceptual nature of space. Both of these conclusions are, however, dubious; particularly the second. If a synthesis begins with the parts, what is the guarantee that it yields any continuity in them, and hence any necessary nature? And if the continuity and necessary nature of space are called into question, its intuitiveness is *a fortiori* to be doubted. For even if some kind of basis could be discovered for *a* necessary nature of the parts of space, it would still be far from certain that such necessity would involve the inclusion of the parts in the whole as mere limitations of it. Some conceptions refer to necessary uniformities in objects without the parts of such conceptions being *in* rather than *under* the whole.

Kant's justification of the necessary and intuitive nature of space as yielded by a synthesis of the parts is as follows:

Raum und Zeit sind *quanta continua,* weil kein Teil derselben gegeben werden kann, ohne ihn zwischen Grenzen (Punkten und Augenblicken) einzuschliessen, mithin nur so, dass dieser Teil selbst wiederum ein Raum, oder eine Zeit ist. Der Raum besteht also nur aus Räumen, die Zeit aus Zeiten. Punkte und Augenblicke sind nur Grenzen, d.i. blosse Stellen ihrer Einschränkung; Stellen aber setzen jederzeit jene Anschauungen, die sie beschränken oder bestimmen sollen, voraus, und aus blossen Stellen, als aus Bestandteilen, die noch vor dem Raume oder der Zeit gegeben werden könnten, kann weder Raum noch Zeit zusammengesetzt werden.[23]

His argument hinges upon the distinction between parts (*Teile*) and constituent parts (*Bestandteile*). Formally, the parts (*Teile*) of which space consists (*besteht*) are mere limitations of space between boundaries (*Stellen*). Formally, the whole precedes and determines the parts. However, in the order of our construction of space, the parts are given first, and out of them the whole is constructed by the synthesis.[24] The parts (*Teile*) and their limits (*Stellen*) presuppose the necessary, intuitive nature of the whole

[22] Kant, *Kritik der reinen Vernunft,* A 169–70 = B 211.
[23] *Ibid.*   [24] Cf. Kemp Smith, *A Commentary,* p. 96.

of space in which they are found. Hence out of the parts, space may be constructed in a way that would be impossible if the synthesis were to begin with the constituent or determining parts (*Bestandteile*) of a general conception. Space has a necessary, intuitive nature which is presupposed in a synthesis of the parts.

This attempted reconciliation of the views of the second and third arguments in the *Aesthetic* with the doctrine of a synthesis is quite neat, but is it successful? The question may be quite fairly asked: How are the parts (*Teile*) of space with which the synthesis is about to begin known to be merely between limits (*Stellen*) in a continuous quantity (*quantum continuum*). How do we know prior to and during the synthesis that such quantities will "flow" in such a fashion as to justify our contention that space has a necessary nature? If we are merely beginning with parts, what is the justification for saying that all of the parts will flow in their homaloidal, Euclidian simplicity? Or after the synthesis has proceeded a certain distance and yielded only Euclidian continuity, what is the justification for holding that it will continue to do so? Might not a sudden shift in the nature of space occur in such a way that two different kinds would emerge, each contingent upon the particular synthesis yielding it? Furthermore, even if the necessary nature of space could be established, does such a synthesis through the parts reach the whole? If it does not, how would we know that the parts are being generated, all along, in a whole of space of which they are actually limitations? In other words, if the synthesis begins with the parts, what assurance have we that those parts (*Teile*) are not constituent parts (*Bestandteile*)? Even if space has a necessary nature, how would we know that it is an intuition rather than a conception, if the synthesis does not reach the whole?

Kant's answer to these questions is merely that the parts are not constituent parts but are limitations of the whole. But this contention presupposes the very doctrine which is called into question, namely, that the whole is given and the parts are carved out of it. The contention that the parts are limitations of the whole cannot be established if the synthesis does not reach the whole. The only assurance that the parts of space are not constituent parts must lie in the fact that they are so *given,* and for this to be the case the whole must be given, out of which they may be carved. If we begin with a synthesis of the parts, the contention that they are not constituent parts can never be established; while if that contention is established, the whole is given and we do not begin with the parts. The doctrine of the third space argument is threatened by the theory of the synthesis. As long as the possibility remains open that the parts of space are constituent parts, the intuitiveness of the whole is in jeopardy.

While, therefore, Kant's doctrine of a synthesis does not require us to deny the necessary and the intuitive nature of space, it quite definitely prevents us from affirming these qualities. This difficulty seems to have been recognized by Kant in the very sections where he tries to reconcile his different views. In the first edition, he worked out the following argument in support of the contention that all appearances are, as such, extensive magnitudes.

Eine extensive Grösse nenne ich diejenige, in welcher die Vorstellung der Teile die Vorstellung des Ganzen möglich macht, (und also notwendig vor dieser vorhergeht). Ich kann mir keine Linie, so klein sie auch sei, vorstellen, ohne sie in Gedanken zu ziehen, d. i. von einem Punkte alle Teile nach und nach zu erzeugen, und dadurch allererst diese Anschauung zu verzeichnen. Ebenso ist es auch mit jeder auch der kleinsten Zeit bewandt.[25]

He went on to hold that appearances, as bound up with space and time and determined by the same synthesis which yields them, are aggregates of previously given parts and, hence, extensive quantities. This argument is of great significance in indicating Kant's departure from his views in the *Aesthetic.* The new doctrine of space and time is used in the first edition to prove that appearances are aggregates, constructed out of parts which determine them. But the basis of that proof is that space and time are themselves constructed by a synthesis of the parts, which precede and determine the whole. In working out the second edition,[26] Kant seems to have realized that the proof itself involves the contention that space and time are also extensive magnitudes. In any case, in the later edition, he substituted a new main thesis: *Alle Anschauungen*

[25] *Kritik der reinen Vernunft,* A 162–63 = B 203.   [26] *Ibid.,* B 202–4.

sind extensive Grössen. Between that thesis and the above-quoted proof of the first edition he inserted a paragraph in which the burden of his contention was that the same synthesis which constructs appearances in space also constructs space. All intuitions are constructed. But space is an intuition. Therefore, space is constructed; it is an extensive magnitude and, hence, an aggregate. If the same synthesis yields space that yields the aggregates in it, upon what basis could Kant turn around and hold that the continuity of space indicates that their parts are merely *in* it as between limits rather than *under* it as constituent parts (*Bestandteile*)? He continued to make this latter claim only because he assumed that the results of his third space argument could hold formally, even after their basis in fact had been removed. If he had faced the consequences of his new view, the result would have been somewhat as follows: A necessary nature of space *may* flow from the synthesis of the parts. The synthesis of these parts *may* reach the whole, which would then be known to have contained them in it from the outset as limitations of itself. Space would then turn out to be an intuition. Yet equally possibly there may be no necessary nature of space further than such has been found in a synthesis already carried out; while *a fortiori* the failure of the synthesis to reach the whole of space would leave open the possibility that the parts with which the synthesis begins are merely constituent parts (*Bestandteile*) out of which a composite or aggregate is constructed. There is no assurance that any already constructed aggregate is really the whole of space, since with further synthesis a new and connotatively different aggregate might emerge. There is no assurance, therefore, that space is not conceptual rather than intuitive. Both the second and third (and with them the fourth) arguments of the *Aesthetic* are threatened by his doctrine of a synthesis beginning with the parts.

§ 4

How SUCCESSFULLY can Kant's general points of view in the *Aesthetic* and in the *Analytic* be combined? His narrow conception of experience might be retained, and space might be considered to be logically prior to, and a determinant of, experience, yet neither temporally prior to, nor actually detachable from, the objects of sense. Cassirer points out such a unity in Kant's doctrines. Intuitions and conceptions, he says,[27] are inseparable, but they may be treated as separated. In the synthetic construction of knowledge, the intuition conditioning an object can in no way be separated from the functions of thought. On the other hand, there is no logical contradiction involved, no violation of the highest principle of analytical judgments, in treating them as separated. The diversity in the *Critique* lies, Cassirer holds, in the fact that in the *Aesthetic* Kant treats intuitions and conceptions as separated, while in the *Analytic* he treats them as joined.

Cassirer realizes that in the *Aesthetic* Kant said one thing and in the *Analytic,* another. The genuine separation of conceptions and intuitions in the *Aesthetic* becomes the logical correlation in the *Analytic.*

So löst sich die anfängliche Trennung von Anschauung und Begriff immer deutlicher in eine reine logische Korrelation auf. Die Unterscheidung, die die transzendentale Ästhetik an die Spitze stellt, betrifft zunächst nur die Absonderung von den gewöhnlichen Gattungsbegriffen.[28]

If we could overlook the wording in the *Aesthetic* and in § 15 of the *Dissertation,* and interpret Kant's teaching solely in the light of his conclusions in the *Analytic,* we might readily claim that from the time of his original contrast of space and general conceptions in 1769 until the publication of the *Critique,* he was concerned only with the logical nature of space. Such an interpretation would ignore the manner in which he discovered in 1769–70 that truth in geometry and mechanics is *a priori* and synthetic. It would also ignore the arguments in § 15 of the *Dissertation* and the *Aesthetic.* There is a lack of unity in the doctrines of space in the *Critique,* whatever significance the teachings of the *Aesthetic*

[27] Cassirer, *Das Erkenntnisproblem,* II, 700: "Die Anschauung kann im synthetischen Aufbau der Erkenntnis, sofern also durch sie ein Gegenstand gegeben und bestimmt werden soll, die Denkfunktion freilich in keiner Weise entbehren; dagegen bedeutet es zum mindesten keinen logischen Widerspruch, bedeutet es keinen Verstoss gegen den obersten Grundsatz aller analytischen Urteile, sie von ihr losgelöst zu denken."

[28] *Ibid.,* II, 698.

retain if viewed from the point of view of the *Analytic*. In denying this unity to the *Critique,* I wish in no way to undervalue the interpretation which Cassirer gives to the *Analytic*. I wish merely to emphasize that, after all, it is only the point of view of the *Analytic* of which he speaks. From the point of view of the *Analytic,* the conditions of conception are dependent upon the intuitions of space and time and the conditions of sensibility are dependent upon the categories. In the act of knowledge, the categories are bound to intuition. We may abstract from the conditions of knowledge and arrive at the conditions of sensibility apart from the conditions of knowledge. This doctrine is important whether or not the conditions of sensibility referred to here are the conditions described in the *Aesthetic*. To make such an abstraction, laying bare the conditions of sensibility, is a valid procedure logically. In this way, we discover certain formal conditions to which knowledge must conform, but we do not discover the conditions of knowledge. Knowledge is dependent both upon space and time and also upon the categories. The limiting conditions imposed in both cases upon all knowledge may be discovered by abstraction from the very knowledge that they limit. The results of such abstraction must not, however, be considered to be knowledge. They bear the same relation to knowledge that pure geometry does to applied, or that pure mechanics does to applied. We may describe "space" as isolated from the conditions of conception. We may describe the categories as isolated from the conditions of sensibility. Such descriptions are the "pure geometry" of knowledge. The arguments of the *Aesthetic* assume significance as such descriptions if they are interpreted only from the point of view of the *Analytic*. This is the unity which might be pointed out in the diversity of Kant's doctrines in the *Aesthetic* and *Analytic*. The value of such an interpretation is obvious. Its disadvantage is that by simplification it omits as much of Kant's teaching as it includes. As Professor Kemp Smith says: "The *Critique* contains too great a variety of tendencies, too rich a complexity of issues, to allow of such simplification."[29]

Any unified account of Kant's theories of space obscures four

[29] Kemp Smith, *A Commentary,* p. 102.

different positions. First, space has a necessary, intuitive nature; it is not generated by a synthesis but is given or presented temporally prior to experience. Secondly, space has a necessary, intuitive nature; it is not yielded by a synthesis but is given or presented upon the occasion of experience.[30] In these first two positions, space is given as an infinite whole. Thirdly, space is yielded by a synthesis of the parts beginning *with* the materials of sense and not merely *on the occasion* of our apprehension of those materials. The resulting space would not be given or presented, since no whole would be reached. Hence the parts would determine the whole, and space would be nonintuitive. Space would have a necessary nature, although there would be denotatively many spaces.[31] Fourthly, if the synthesis beginning *with* the materials of sense does not even yield a necessary nature, spaces would be not only nonintuitive and denotatively many, but possibly of different kinds. Space would be merely the arrangement of objects as set together.[32]

Is there any further evidence in the *Analytic* that Kant was trying to work out a unified doctrine of space? In one place, he held:

Aber Raum und Zeit sind nicht bloss als *Formen* der Sinnlichen Anschauung, sondern als *Anschauungen* selbst (die ein Mannigfaltiges enthalten) also mit der Bestimmung der *Einheit* dieses Mannigfaltigen in ihnen a priori vorgestellt (siehe trans. Ästhet.) .[33]

Here he was certainly not claiming that space is merely the form in which objects are set together, and his stand is to some extent harmonious with the teachings of the *Aesthetic*. Space, as he had held in the *Aesthetic,* is both an intuition and a form of empirical intuition. Space, as an intuition, contains a manifold whose unity can be represented *a priori*. Such a manifold is different from the manifold of sense. Space is a conscious representation although it is not given prior to sense experience. In amplification of this view, Kant proceeded in a footnote to hold:

[30] This view is similar to S. Alexander's. Cf. below, Chapter IX, § 1.
[31] This view is similar to A. N. Whitehead's. Cf. below, Chapter IX, § 2.
[32] This view is similar to C. D. Broad's. Cf. below, Chapter IX, § 3.
[33] Kant, *Kritik der reinen Vernunft,* B 160.

Der Raum, als *Gegenstand* vorgestellt, (wie man es wirklich in der Geometrie bedarf,) enthält mehr, als blosse Form der Anschauung, nämlich *Zusammenfassung* des Mannigfaltigen, nach der Form der Sinnlichkeit gegebenen, in eine *anschauliche* Vorstellung, so dass die *Form der Anschauung* bloss Mannigfaltiges, die *formale Anschauung* aber Einheit der Vorstellung gibt.[34]

Space is represented as an object, and geometry is an example of this procedure. Such a procedure is more than a setting together of objects (*Zusammensetzung*), being rather a comprehension (*Zusammenfassung*) of the manifold as one.

Diese Einheit hatte ich in der Ästhetik bloss zur Sinnlichkeit gezählt, um nur zu bemerken, dass sie vor allem Begriffe vorhergehe, ob sie zwar eine Synthesis, die nicht den Sinnen angehört, durch welche aber alle Begriffe von Raum und Zeit zuerst möglich werden, voraussetzt. Denn da durch sie (indem der Verstand die Sinnlichkeit bestimmt) der Raum oder die Zeit als Anschauungen zuerst *gegeben* werden, so gehört die Einheit dieser Anschauung a priori zum Raume und der Zeit, und nicht zum Begriffe des Verstandes.[35]

It would be idle to deny that Kant was attempting here[36] to work out a co-ordinated view of space in the *Critique* as a whole. Either he was aware of the gap to be bridged and, as Kemp Smith[37] suggests, was grafting one view upon the other, or he was unaware of the extent of the discrepancies involved. In either case, he was attempting to combine his four metaphysical arguments of the *Aesthetic* with the contention that there is a synthetic activity of the intellect which yields space. How successful was his attempt? If my analysis of the views of space in the *Dissertation* and in the *Aesthetic* is correct, his main position in the one, and his sole position in the other, is based upon the contention that space is given and not generated and upon the contention that it is given temporally prior to experience. In this footnote to B 160, however, he said explicitly that the doctrines of the *Aesthetic* are to be taken as implying a synthesis which does not involve the sensuous manifold. Whatever is the nature of the materials with which such a synthesis could begin, space is both generated by a synthetic ac-

---

[34] *Ibid.*, B 160 *n*.   [35] *Ibid.*

[36] As well as at B 136; A 169–70 = B 211; and *Über die Fortschritte der Metaphysik*, 1790, *Phil. Bib.* Bd. 46 c, p. 102.

[37] Kemp Smith, *A Commentary*, p. 96.

tivity of the understanding and yielded as an object, once it has been generated. He meant that in the order of our apprehension the parts of space are given first in the synthesis, whereas upon the completion of the unity of space the whole is found to determine the parts. Space is logically prior to sense experience, generated by an activity of the mind, and contemplated as an object once it has been generated. Once the whole is yielded the parts are in it as limitations, but in the process of apprehension its parts are given as determining the whole. The arguments of the *Aesthetic* would hold for space after it is generated; those of the *Analytic* refer to its nature as we construct it.

I have already dealt with some of the difficulties involved in such an attempted union of Kant's divergent theories. Even if his views in the *Aesthetic* are stripped of every indication of the theory of temporal priority, the further difficulties involved in combining the necessary and the intuitive nature of space with the doctrine of synthesis would seem to be insurmountable.[38] In addition, there would remain the further, more general difficulty in regard to the nature of the materials with which a synthesis yielding space could begin. What is the nature of the nonsensuous manifold with which such a generative activity would start? As I have pointed out,[39] Kant could mean an intellectual synthesis beginning with the materials of intellectual intuition and yielding the pure intuition of space, which is entirely sensitive. With all of the difficulties of this dualism, certain advantages follow from it. Once the dualism is assumed, space is determined by two sets of conditions, each of which is complete in itself. Space conforms to the conditions of the intellect in so far as it is yielded by an intellectual activity. The completeness of these intellectual conditions is in no way disturbed by the conditions of sense. Space conforms also to the conditions of sense. It is uniquely related to these conditions, as described in § 15 of the *Dissertation* and the four arguments of the *Aesthetic*. The completeness of these conditions is in no way disturbed by the conditions of intellect. The linchpin of the argument in § 15 of the *Dissertation* and in the *Aesthetic* is this dualism between sense and intelligence. Once it is granted,

[38] Cf. above, pp. 222–24. [39] Cf. above, pp. 210–12.

the arguments follow validly. Whatever are the difficulties with the dualism itself, its chief advantage is the support which it lends to these fundamental arguments. Most of the obscurities in Kant's later teaching result from his attempt to retain the views of the *Aesthetic* and of the *Dissertation* and to discard the dualism upon which they are grounded. Many of his difficulties would have been avoided had he realized that his teaching in the *Dissertation* and in the *Aesthetic* is based upon the dualism, and must stand or fall with it. Had he faced this fact and retained the dualism (admitting its incompatibility with his more mature views) the result would have been much less unsatisfactory than his teaching in the *Analytic* at B 160 and B 211.

I do not mean that the doctrine of an intellectual synthesis, if closely analyzed, turns out to be any more coherent than any other doctrine of a synthesis which does not begin with the sensuous manifold. What is the nature of such an activity? What is the nature of the nonsensitive (that is, intellectual) elements with which it could begin? Unless intelligible, nonsensuous things in themselves are given to the mind in intellectual intuition, there would be no such elements. In the *Dissertation* the theory of the intellectual synthesis rests upon the assumptions that there is knowledge in metaphysics which is in no way concerned with the world of space and time and that the conceptions involved in such knowledge presuppose a synthesis which in no way involves the senses, or even the forms of sense experience. These assumptions were possible for Kant as long as he believed in a set of materials given in intellectual intuition. Once he abandoned this belief, the materials of sense were the only materials with which a synthesis could begin.

After his rejection of the dualism of 1770, Kant formulated the doctrine of a second type of synthesis in the vain hope of retaining the views of the *Aesthetic* as a body of teaching, in spite of the doctrine that conceptions and intuitions necessarily condition each other. Instead of facing the fact that the rejection of the dualism of 1770 involves the rejection of the arguments of the *Aesthetic*, he formulated in the *Analytic* at B 160 *n* and B 211 a doctrine of synthesis which he believed to be compatible with the teachings of the *Aesthetic*. He believed that in spite of the union of conception and intuition, he could work out a doctrine of synthesis which would leave the arguments of the *Aesthetic* intact.

The result is a tautologous doctrine, compatible neither with the theory in the *Analytic* of the union of conception and intuition nor with the arguments of the *Aesthetic*. At B 160 *n*, he said that a synthesis yields a sensitive whole of space. This synthesis cannot be intellectual, for there can be no isolation of conception from intuition. It must not only yield the sensitive whole of space; it must begin with something sensitive. Yet it does not—Kant claimed—begin with the sensuous manifold. The obvious question (which he apparently never faced) is: If such a synthesis is not intellectual and does not begin with the sensuous manifold, with what does it begin?[40] There may be some justification for Kant's omission of this question in 1770, when his isolation of sense and intellect left open—as he admitted—many questions concerning the nature of the latter. But in 1787 it was quite different. His union of conception and intuition involves necessarily the problem of the nature of the synthetic activity of the mind which yields space. His insistence that space is yielded by a synthesis is equaled only by his persistent omission of the question concerning the nature of the elements with which such an activity could begin. Had he faced this question, he would have realized that a synthesis must begin either with the sensuous manifold, in which case it is preceded and determined by that manifold, or it must begin with the very thing it is supposed to yield, namely, space. In the latter case, the doctrine of synthesis not only is incompatible with the teachings of the *Aesthetic,* but also is tautologous. If a pure manifold, space, is given with which a synthesis may begin, then space is not derived from the synthesis, but precedes and determines it. Either there is no pure manifold given with which a synthesis can begin, or space is prior to all synthesis. A pure manifold is "space" as much before a synthetic activity as afterwards.[41] A particular space is "space" as much as is another greater or smaller, particular

[40] Cf. Kemp Smith, *A Commentary*, p. 97: "Nor does [Kant] show what the simple elements are from which the synthesis of apprehension and reproduction in pure intuition might start."

[41] Cf. above, Chapter VI, § 2.

space. Granting a pure manifold, then space is prior to sense experience, the parts of space are limits, and all particular representations of space are *in* it and not *under* it. To assume a manifold (other than the sensuous manifold) from which a synthetic activity can begin is to restate the arguments of § 15 of the *Dissertation* and of the *Aesthetic,* which preclude any synthetic activity. To assume that a synthetic activity yields space is to deny that the manifold from which it began is pure. A synthetic activity must begin either with the sensuous manifold or with the very "space" which it is supposed to yield.

§ 5

KANT FAILED to unify his doctrines of space in the *Critique.* Either space is temporally prior to the manifold of sense—in which case, it is not determined by any kind of synthesis;[42] or space is determined by a synthesis which begins with the prior existing manifold of sense.[43] Either space has a necessary nature as given, or the possibility remains that it has a contingent nature as derived. Either the whole of space determines the parts—in which case, there is no synthesis beginning with the parts; or the parts precede the whole, and the whole is determined by a synthesis of them.[44] If the whole has been reached by a synthesis, it may have a necessary nature, but there is no assurance that it is an intuition. The parts may be constitutive (*Bestandteile*) and may precede it logically as well as temporally. If the whole has not been reached, the synthesis may be carried further, and what was previously considered to be the whole might be found to be merely an aggregate, determined by the extent of the previous synthesis of the parts. If the nature of space presupposes an activity of the understanding, there is no assurance that the parts of space are not *under* rather than *in* the whole.[45] Kant was trying to hunt with the hounds and

---

[42] The view of the *Aesthetic.*   [43] The view of the *Analytic.*
[44] The view of the *Analytic.*
[45] Hartmann, *Kritische Grundlegung des transcendentalen Realismus,* p. 154, quoted by Vaihinger, *Kommentar,* II, 228: "Diese erklärungen [at B 160 *n*] genügen, um Kants Schlussfolgerung in ihr Gegentheil zu verkehren. Wenn der einige Raum als gegebenes Ganzes erst Product einer vom Verstande ausgeführten Synthese des räumlichen Mannigfaltigen ist, so ist er später als diese, aber nicht früher; es

run with the hare. He was trying to show that space is prior (temporally or logically) to the sensuous manifold, and yet that it presupposes a synthesis. He was trying to show that the parts of space are dependent upon the whole, and yet to say that the whole of space is determined by a synthesis of the parts. It cannot be done. His attempt to combine these views failed. His only alternative was the view of the *Dissertation* that the conditions of synthesis can be entirely intellectual and the conditions of the resulting whole can be entirely sensitive. In such a view, sense and intellect are dogmatically assumed to be separated and complete in themselves. But, according to Kant's view in the *Analytic,* they are bound together inseparably, and the assumption is false.

These conflicting views of space in the *Critique* make clearer Kant's two views of space in the *Dissertation.* In 1770, he could answer Euler's question in two ways. Space is not abstracted from sensation; from the conditions of the sensible world, it is not abstracted at all. There is, however, an intellectual synthesis which yields it. It is determined by this synthesis. Kant reconciled these two answers by means of his dualism of 1770. To know the sensible world, the intuitions of space and time are required. To know the intelligible, real world, intellectual intuitions are required. In both cases, conceptual analysis clarifies but does not amplify such knowledge. Knowledge of the two worlds does not overlap. To know appearances, the mind must cut itself off from intellectual intuitions; to know realities, the mind must cut itself off from temporal and spatial conditions. This, Kant held in 1770, it is capable of doing. The conditions of sense and the conditions of intellect are each complete in themselves. Knowledge in both cases is synthetic, involving more than a conceptual analysis, but the two kinds of knowledge are entirely different. The synthesis yielding space and time, while not beginning with the senses, is

müssen dann die durch die sinnliche Anschauungsform allein aus der Empfindung formirten endlichen Anschauungen (das räumliche Mannigfaltige) das frühere sein, aus welchem erst der einige Raum sich bilden kann, und nimmermehr können sie ihrer Entstehung nach blosse Einschränkungen dessen sein, was erst vermittelst ihrer zu Stande kommen kann, indem der Verstand sich dieses ihm gegebenen Stoffes combinatorisch bemächtigt. Kant hat leider nicht bemerkt, dass er in dieser Anmerkung zur 2. Aufl. der Analytik selbst seine frühere verkehrte Auffassung überwunden und berichtigt hat."

nevertheless different from the synthesis which yields intellectual intuitions. In the same way that the former synthesis precedes the conditions of sense, so the latter precedes the conditions of reality. Space can thus be yielded by a synthesis, and yet not abstracted from sense.

In the *Analytic* Kant's theory is quite different. Human minds are not capable of intellectual intuitions. Therefore, the only kind of synthesis yielding knowledge is that yielding space and time. The conditions of such knowledge are twofold, the conditions of conception and the conditions of intuition. Conceptions and intuitions, the two functions or determinants of our knowledge, do not occur independently. There are not, as Kant held in 1770, two moments of knowledge, the intuition and then the clarification and conceptual ordering. No such ideal isolation of the two processes actually occurs in knowledge. Sense and intellect mutually condition each other; one is indispensable to the other. Hence it is impossible for a synthesis to yield space, unless it at the same time conforms to the conditions of sense. Any synthesis other than one involving the materials of sense is an abstraction, determining perhaps knowledge in form, but never knowledge. Therefore, if space is the product of a synthesis, it is abstracted from, or yielded by, the manifold of sense. If it is not abstracted from the world of sense, it cannot be abstracted at all but must be presented or given, as Kant had held in the *Aesthetic*. Kant could retain the theory that a synthesis not beginning with the materials of sense yields space only on the assumption of the thoroughgoing dualism between sense and intellect which he had rejected after 1770.

In every passage of § 15 of the *Dissertation* save two, Kant treated the pure intuition of space as presented or contemplated and not constructed. In two places,[46] he treated it as yielded by an activity of the mind. In this treatment, he discovered the weakness in his dualism. At the end of the corollary, he suggested that the conceptions of space and time, which are not abstracted from sense and which are not gained by reflection (like the usual general conceptions), are abstracted from an activity of the mind on the occasion of sensation. He assumed that an intellectual activity can

---

[46] Kant, *Inaugural Dissertation*, § 15, C (in part), §§ 14–15, corollary (end).

yield a sensitive whole. After 1770, he realized that this is impossible. He realized, however, that the fault lay not in the assumption of an activity of the mind but in the deeper assumption of a thoroughgoing dualism. The assumption of an activity of the mind must—he realized—be retained, but the dualism rejected. He could not isolate sense and intellect. There is an activity of the understanding which begins with the manifold of sense and which determines space. The understanding represents space as a pure manifold in contrast to the sensuous manifold and as a pure form of the sensuous manifold. From his point of view in the *Analytic*, Kant had been correct in 1770 in holding that there is an activity of the mind. He had been wrong only in regard to its nature. The rest of § 15 of the *Dissertation* is based upon the assumption that there is no activity of the mind. The *Dissertation,* as a whole, is based upon the assumption that conception and intuition can be isolated. The doctrine that space is prior to sensation is also based upon this assumption. The doctrine that the whole of space determines the parts is also based upon it. The same is true of the doctrine that an infinite number of representations are *in* space instead of *under* it. Once Kant abandoned this assumption and joined conceptions and intuitions, the representations of space and time are subjected to the conditions of conception as well as to the conditions of sense. He could preserve the doctrines of space in the *Aesthetic* only by reverting to the point of view of the *Dissertation* and separating sense from intellect. He would never have done this. He retained the views of the *Aesthetic,* either because he did not realize how completely he had contradicted them; or because, realizing it, he knew that the alteration required was too far-reaching to be undertaken.

CHAPTER IX

KANT AND THE PRESENT

§ 1

WE HAVE FOUND[1] that in 1770 Kant formulated two criticisms of the relational view of space of the Leibnizians. In the first place, such a view involves, he held, a circular definition; in the second, it tears geometry down from the heights of certainty, reducing it to an empirical science. With the development of the non-Euclidian geometries and the theories of relativity in physics, the problem of the conflict between the absolute and the relational views of space has taken on a new significance. In such divergent views of space as those of Alexander, Whitehead, and Broad, the usual account of the conflict between these two theories (since the time of Newton) is given. In all three of these views, the absolute theory of space as ontologically independent of, and subsisting apart from, time is quickly disposed of, and the Newtonian account of one, unique, empty space rejected.

Apart from this common point of departure, the views of the three men vary widely, and we shall now turn to each of them. In doing so, we must bear in mind several distinctions. First, "absolute" space may mean the theory that space is necessarily what it is and not otherwise. This theory merely means that there is a unique, singular space, connotatively and denotatively one. It does not mean that such space necessarily has "this" or "that" connotation, but that it has one and only one connotation, as well as being singular. Secondly, superimposed upon this doctrine of the general "absoluteness" of space, there has been made historically the additional assumption that this unique nature is Euclidian and Newtonian. In being Euclidian, it would have necessarily a specific nature (chiefly three-dimensionality), but it would not necessarily be independently real; in being Newtonian, it would be Euclidian

[1] Cf. above, pp. 149–150.

and real, independently of time and matter. This difference becomes highly important in connection with the views of Alexander, Whitehead, and Broad. Thirdly, space may be "absolute" in still a third sense. According to this theory space is not, in the last analysis, in itself necessarily what it is and not otherwise. It lacks the final, independent ontological status accorded to it by the first theory. Furthermore, it is not Euclidian since it cannot be considered to subsist in its own right, and *a fortiori* it is not Newtonian since it is not real as a receptacle of nature, independent of time and matter. According to this third theory of the "absolute" nature of space, space by itself is not necessarily what it is and not otherwise; but in conjunction with time, or rather as an aspect of space-time, it is what it is and not otherwise. The space of space-time is connotatively and denotatively one. It is independent of matter only in the sense of being the stuff out of which matter is formed. To this theory (Alexander's) we will shortly return. Fourthly, there is a very different general doctrine of space which cannot properly be called a theory of "absolute" space, but which is also not a theory that space is relational in the usual sense of the term. This theory of the relative, "nonrelational" nature of space means that space is denotatively relative, or many, but connotatively it is singular and homaloidal. There are many spaces, each relative to something else, usually time, but these relative spaces have a common nature, perhaps Euclidian, perhaps hyperbolic, perhaps elliptical, but in any case not more than one of these. Whitehead holds this view. Fifthly, there is a second form of this relative theory of space, which holds that space is denotatively many and, in addition, connotatively various or nonhomaloidal. On this theory, there are many spaces, each of them relative to something else, usually time, and there are various kinds of space all ontologically on a par, such as Euclidian, hyperbolic, and elliptical. This is the view of Broad. Lastly, there is the older relational theory of space of Leibniz.

Of these six alternatives, we shall now consider the three which are adopted by Alexander, Whitehead, and Broad, respectively. It will be our contention that Kant's theories of space are important in relation to the ideas of each of these men: his views in

the *Aesthetic* are more closely akin to those of Alexander; his views
in the *Analytic* are more like those of Broad.

S. Alexander takes his stand in opposition to the "absolute"
theories in the first two senses indicated above. Space, by itself, is
not unique and singular, connotatively and denotatively one.
Euclidian or any other type of space is a legitimate abstraction
from space-time, but it is only an abstraction. Furthermore, Alexander opposes both variants of the second type of "absoluteness."
Space is not uniquely Euclidian, even as subsisting merely, nor is
it Euclidian and Newtonian. It is not an infinite receptacle or
container of things. It is not independent of time, and no part of
it is empty. He defends, however, the "absolute" nature of space
in the third sense against all theories of the relativity of space,
including the relational type, and his defense is very important in
relation to Kant. Space is intimately tied up with time. Space-
time is absolute; it is what it is and not otherwise; it is connotatively and denotatively one. It is homaloidal and its spatial aspect
is three-dimensional and Euclidian. It is not a container of nature,
but it is the very stuff out of which nature is made. There is a
distinction between the space[2] of empirical metaphysics and the
space or spaces (abstracted therefrom) of physics and mathematics.
While quite legitimate in their place, mathematical treatments of
space are, Alexander holds, limited in their scope and significance.
In its simplest forms, mathematics is dealing with the same space
which is given in experience and analyzed in metaphysics (philosophy of space). The more generalized forms of mathematics
take us away from this simpler space and seem to reduce all space
to relations. But the notion of relation is, Alexander holds, highly
complex and itself involves simpler empirical elements. The relations to which space is apparently "reduced" are in fact composed
of the simpler elements of the originally given, empirical space.
To treat space as relational is a valid procedure, but to do so
exclusively is to put the cart before the horse: for the very nature

[2] More fundamentally in this entire discussion, it would be space-time, rather
than space, with which we are dealing. It is necessary to remember this fact in
order to distinguish Alexander's position from the other two types of "absolute"
space, but since he admits that space may be treated apart from time, I shall refer,
from now on, simply to space. Alexander, *Space, Time and Deity*, I, 170–80.

of the things related (in some cases spatially) is space-time, of which all things are ultimately constituents. Such space-time is apprehended immediately in experience. The three-dimensionality of its spatial aspect is discoverable in and through time; the nature of its temporal aspect, in and through space.[3] Its nature is one of the "necessary" elements presented in experience, to be disentangled from the contingent ones by empirical metaphysics.

In connection with Kant's views of space, Alexander says:

An eminent philosopher, Kant, declares that things in space can be thought away but Space cannot, and at the same time regards this Space as a "form" of intuition. . . . If [he] had maintained pure Space to be conceivable by some kind of apprehension and had not asserted it to be a subjective form . . . [he] would have been in fact right.[4]

In relation to this remark, the outcome of our study of Kant may be briefly recapitulated. Alexander is correct in saying that Kant made all three of these claims: (a) space, unlike things, cannot be thought away; (b) space is a form of intuition; and (c) space is subjective. We have found, however, that in addition to his doctrine that space is a form of intuition, Kant formulated as early as 1769, and held in the *Critique,* the doctrine that space is itself a pure intuition, contemplated in all of its immediacy, prior to experience, as well as in geometry. The fact that space is necessarily represented was not used by Kant in the *Aesthetic* as evidence that space is a form, but rather as an intrinsic feature of the view that it is given to the mind as a pure content. Consequently, besides his theory of a form of intuition, Kant taught very explicitly that space is "conceivable by some kind of apprehension," in fact by a kind differing in only one respect from the kind espoused by Alexander. For both men, space is presented immediately to the contemplative gaze of the mind; according to Kant, however, it is given outside experience, narrowly defined; while according to Alexander, inside experience, widely construed. As regards the very different theory of the "subjectivity" of space, I have tried to show that such a doctrine was extrinsic to Kant's thinking in 1770, being based upon a dualism between sense and intellect and between their forms, space and an "intellectual intuition" (which Kant never found). I do not claim that Kant ever reached such realism as that of Alexander, the two chief hindrances being his narrow view of experience and his retention of the doctrine of appearances; but, stripped of these two views, the Kantian theory of space in the *Dissertation* and the *Aesthetic* approaches, in my opinion, very close to a view that Alexander would say is "in fact . . . right." The doctrine of the *Analytic* that space is bound up with the materials of sense and is constructed rather than given is, of course, quite different.

Kant's hint in 1770 concerning the circular reasoning of the Leibnizians in considering space as relational, implies precisely such a position as Alexander's. Of course, Kant had in mind no such theory of space-time (or even space and time) as the ultimate constituent of things. But Alexander means, apart from his wider theory, precisely what Kant did, namely, that space is prior to, and at the basis of, the relations of things in it. Alexander goes on to add what Kant of course did not consider, namely, that in spite of its essentially nonrelational nature, space may be considered as relational in mathematics. Space, in Kant's view, although the form of the world of sense and prior to the objects in it, is not, as Alexander holds, the source and determinant of that world. Space, in Kant's view, being prior to the objects of sense and the relations among them, can in no way be the relations of objects in it. Kant considered space to be at the basis of matter merely in the sense that it is one of the forms, admittedly fundamental, in which matter exists, whereas Alexander believes it to be the very material of which nature consists. Considering Euclidian geometry as the fundamental form of mathematics, Kant held that that science involves a nonrelational theory of space and rejected relational space not only on philosophic grounds, but also because of the nature of mathematics. Alexander, on the other hand, admitting that mathematics involves relational space, sees nothing in this fact to prevent it from having a more basic nonrelational nature.

We can now appreciate the significance of the question of the relation of space to the sciences of geometry and mechanics in Kant's views of space in 1770 and in the *Aesthetic*. Important commentators[5] who differ in regard to details agree that Kant's chief concern in both of the expositions of space in the *Aesthetic* was with the space of mathematics, pure, applied, or both. If this view is correct, nothing in the Kantian philosophy of space can be taken to imply the possibility of a consideration of nature more basic than that of physics and mathematics. Even Kant's emphasis upon the basic relation of space to the contents of experience must be considered as concerning merely the highly sophisticated "experience" of the physicist. According to this view, the problem of synthetic, *a priori* truth was Kant's chief problem in his treatments of space. On the other hand, if our contentions have been correct, Kant's concern in 1770 and in the *Aesthetic* was a much wider one. Space is given as a pure intuition not merely in pure geometry, but in other cases as well. Space is the form of all empirical intuition and not merely of the highly specialized objects in applied science. Like Alexander, Kant implied an apprehension of space more basic than that of pure and applied science. The cases in which space is given both as an object and as a form outrun those in which it is given in mathematics and in mechanics. There is a more basic approach to nature than that of the physicist. This likeness between the views of Kant and Alexander dwarfs their differences. Kant held that space is nonempirical, but his conception of experience was limited. Kant held that space is subjective, but this contention was extrinsic to his views. Kant held that space is a form, but he also held that it is a content. For both men, space has a necessary, given nature. Like Alexander, Kant was examining and describing the necessary features of what is given. The fact that he did not consider those features to be in experience, as well as the fact that he believed them to be bound up with appearances rather than realities, should not obscure from us the fact that he was assigning to space a leading role in a metaphysics of nature.

Kant's second criticism of the relational view of space depends for its validity upon his view that space is a pure intuition. The gravest error of the Leibnizians consists, he held, in the fact that they tear down geometry from its heights of certainty and reduce

<hr>

[5] Cohen, Fischer, Vaihinger, Adickes; cf. above, pp. 184–85.

its truths to an empirical status.[6] As we have found, Newton's unquestioning acceptance of Euclidian geometry as involving necessary truth about space is incompatible with his inductive method. A strict and thoroughgoing application of that method offers as little justification for the assumption that space has a necessary nature as it offers for the assumption that the laws governing motions in space have such a nature. Yet Newton unhesitatingly assumed such a necessary nature for space. His doctrine of "absolute" space means in its widest significance, that space is necessarily what it is and not otherwise, and *ipso facto* that it is Euclidian. Kant's doctrine of space as a pure intuition was, on the contrary, not an assumption, but an exposition of the given nature of space. In spite of the fact that Kant, unlike Newton, did not merely assume that space is necessarily what it is and not otherwise, but also set out to give an exposition of this view, he failed to distinguish between this wider doctrine and the more specific theory that its necessary nature is Euclidian. In other words, it would be quite possible to maintain with Kant that space has *a* necessary nature and then to raise, as Kant did not after 1747, the narrower question of whether that nature is Euclidian? In regard to this narrower question Kant was, in 1770 and later, as uncritical as Newton. From 1747 onwards, he was convinced that the necessary nature of space, if it could be established, would be Euclidian. After 1747 he did not consider the possibility of a homaloidal, non-Euclidian space.

Because of this fact, Kant appealed unquestioningly in 1770 to the doctrine of *a priori* truth in geometry to support his theory that space is a pure intuition, and to refute any relational theory of space. In the face of the various post-Kantian non-Euclidian geometries, such an appeal to the nature of geometrical truth, far from constituting a refutation of the relational theories of space, would seem to be an argument in their favor. Kant's conclusion that space is nonrelational can be valid only if some such deduction of the three-dimensionality of space as Alexander's is correct and even then not in the sense that space cannot in a derivative sense also be relational. Kant's claim that space has a given nature

[6] Kant, *Inaugural Dissertation*, § 15, D.

can be confirmed only if there is a kind of empirical metaphysics like Alexander's, yielding a more basic insight into the nature of space than all subsequent mathematical treatments. In such a case, there would be a first philosophy more basic than mathematics and physics, with space as one of its fundamental conceptions. On the other hand, Kant's conclusion that space is nonrelational collapses if no such deduction of its three-dimensionality is possible. Kant's contention that space is given is unwarranted if there is no such empirical metaphysics as that of Alexander. In such a case, the nature of space is determinable solely by the physicists and the mathematicians. Space would be relational or nonrelational, Euclidian, hyperbolic, or elliptical, solely upon grounds that the physicist could give. Physics would be first philosophy.

It is significant that both Alexander and Whitehead arrive, although in very different fashions, at the conclusion that physical space is three-dimensional and Euclidian. While both men deny that space is a container, and link space and time inextricably, both of them (unlike Broad) hold that the space (or, in Whitehead's case, the spaces) of space-time is three-dimensional.[7] According to Alexander, the one space (of space-time) is ontologically prior to, and constitutive of, the world of matter. From the one-dimensionality of time, the three-dimensionality of space is derived, and vice versa. In the light of this contention—paralleled, as we shall find, by Whitehead's treatment of the three-dimensionality of spaces within various time series—it is difficult to say that the final verdict has yet been given against the three-dimensionality of space, much less against its homaloidality in some sense.

§ 2

IN TURNING TO the views of Whitehead, we must recall the three different theories of "absolute" space which we mentioned above. According to the first, space has *a* necessary nature. According to the second, it is a Newtonian container. According to the third, it

[7] Whitehead admits, however, that it might be uniformly elliptical or uniformly hyperbolic if simpler explanations of nature resulted. *The Principle of Relativity*, p. v; cf. *Process and Reality*, p. 442.

is an aspect of space-time. Alexander accepted the third theory, adding that space is three-dimensional; that it may be treated in mathematics as relative and relational, although basically it is neither; and finally, that it is the very stuff of nature. On the other hand, there is a fourth theory, which holds that space is relative rather than absolute and yet that it is not a relation. According to this theory, space is denotatively relative. There are many spaces, each relative, not merely to time, but to a particular time series. In this view, however, space is still considered as connotatively one, or homaloidal, whether its one nature should turn out to be Euclidian, hyperbolic, or elliptical. This is the view of Whitehead, who makes it more specific by contending that space is Euclidian. It is with reference to the homaloidality of space that he parts company with Einstein and Broad.

Like Alexander and Broad, Whitehead begins his account of space by rejecting the Newtonian theory of an absolute space, because it separates space and time and because it involves the notion of a container. Unlike Alexander, his general view commits him later to the theory of empty space, but such emptiness refers merely to events whose ingredient objects escape our recognition.[8] He holds that both the absolute and the relative theories of space grow out of the mistaken subservience of scientific thinking to the notion of "substance" and "attribute." Both theories assume a sort of substratum in nature. The one abstracts space from substance and then turns around and puts substance, in some sense, back *into* space as a container. The other, the less untenable of the two, tries "to slip substance into space on the plea that space expresses relations between substances" whereas actually, even in that view, it would be only a relation between attributes.[9] I do not propose to undertake either an exposition or a criticism of Whitehead's attack upon substance. Kemp Smith, in defending "metaphysical postulation," holds[10] that such wider categories as whole, part, and necessitation require to be further specified before they become substance and that such specification "is only such as they themselves

---

[8] Whitehead, *The Concept of Nature*, p. 145; cf. below, p. 249; cf. Clarke's account of substances in empty space, Clarke, Paper IV, § 9.

[9] Whitehead, *The Concept of Nature*, p. 21.

[10] Kemp Smith, *Prolegomena to an Idealist Theory of Knowledge*, pp. 176–77.

prescribe, in their relation to other aspects of sense-experience." The category of substance yields more than formal insight into nature only to the extent that "empirical data are available for this purpose." Kemp Smith seems to mean that such data are forthcoming. Whatever is the answer to the question of the relative ontological status of "events" and "things," Whitehead's exposition of space in terms of the former has many significant features.

Space, he holds, is an abstraction from events. An event-particle is an abstractive element and a point in timeless space is a class of event-particles. There is a separate timeless space corresponding to each separate temporal series. These views are entirely in the direction of relativism. But unlike Broad, he makes a very interesting shift, which, if I am not mistaken, has significant implications with reference to some of Kant's views. Instead of considering kinematics—and the special theory of relativity—as an abstraction of the same order as the views of traditional mechanics, he calls a halt, contending:

Unless motion is something as a fact in nature, kinetic energy and momentum and all that depends on these physical concepts evaporate from our list of physical realities. Even in this revolutionary age my conservatism resolutely opposes the identification of momentum and moonshine.

Accordingly I assume it as an axiom, that motion is a physical fact. It is something that we perceive as in nature. Motion presupposes rest. . . . Now you cannot have a theory of rest without in some sense admitting a theory of absolute position.[11]

Of course, he does not proceed to define absolute position with reference to an absolute space and time, but he holds that the doctrine of relative space is mistakenly considered to run counter to any conception of absolute position whatsoever. There may be "alternative definitions of absolute position." In his view there is such absolute position within a temporal series. There are, of course, alternative time systems, but within each there is absolute position, and the space involved, while relative to the time system, is not relational in the usual sense of the term.

Whitehead works out a theory of timeless space for each time

[11] Whitehead, *The Concept of Nature*, p. 105.

system and a uniformity of each of those timeless spaces. From these considerations, he holds that knowledge of a whole time system is possible, including even the unobserved characters of remote events. In this way he accounts for many features of nature. His view, he claims:

(a) . . . explains the differentiation of the one quality of extension into time and space. (b) It gives a meaning to the observed facts of geometrical and temporal position, of geometrical and temporal order, and of geometrical straightness and planeness. (c) It selects one definite system of congruence embracing both space and time, and thus explains the concordance as to measurement which is in practice attained. (d) It explains (consistently with the theory of relativity) the observed phenomena of rotation, *e.g.* Foucault's pendulum, the equatorial bulge of the earth, the fixed senses of rotation of cyclones and anticyclones, and the gyro-compass. . . . (e) Its explanations of motion are more fundamental than those expressed in (d) for it explains what is meant by motion itself.[12]

While this view is not a defense of absolute space, time, or motion, it is certainly a long way from the doctrine of Broad in which, as we shall see, only the formulae of the general theory of relativity are concerned with physical space. Space, according to Whitehead, is admittedly an abstraction from events; it is inextricably bound up with time; but within one time system it would seem to have a necessary character. The space in which motion and rest are found may be as legitimately considered to be a feature of reality (within a time series) as the spaces of kinetics in the general theory of relativity.

Space is not a relation between "substances," but it would also seem to be more than a relation between events. It (or rather space-time) is an abstraction from events, but within a time series it is not relational at all. It is the path of an event-particle, but not a relation of any one thing to another. Hence space is relative, in regard both to time and to a particular event, but not, in the strict sense of the word, relational. Furthermore, a timeless space (in a time series) is continuous. This important fact means that within the time series, physical calculations may proceed in a way quite similar to the traditional mechanics. Whitehead goes to great pains

[12] *Ibid.*, pp. 194–95.

to show how this view allows accurate measurement. It would be difficult, he holds, to see how the facts of measurement could be accounted for if the objects of nature are "substances." Poincaré's[13] contention that the choice among various geometries depends upon convention would, he says, in such a case be a strong one, not because of difficulties in reaching exactitude, but because such a choice would depend solely upon "the volitions of the mind at the other end of the sense-awareness."[14] In such a case, there would be no way of measuring accurately. On the other hand, he goes on to say, Russell[14] is right in claiming that measurement actually occurs. Measurement is possible, Whitehead holds, because objects are only abstractions which may be situated in many events and which may repeat themselves. In special cases "identity of quality between congruent segments" is directly perceived, but, as a rule, such identity involves sense awareness only of selected cases and a logical inference from them. The facts of congruence and measurement are based upon the reality of motion and the continuity of space-time with motion, and such space is three-dimensional. The congruence of objects—and the possibility of measurement—is based upon the nature of timeless spaces in a time series and upon the nature of motion.

Unlike Alexander, Whitehead does not extract the three-dimensionality of space from time. He merely maintains that it is a "fundamental fact of nature."[15] "If space has only three dimensions we should expect all mankind to be aware of the fact, as they are aware of it."[16] He claims that he is able to explain the theory of relativity without recourse to a "curvature in the space-time manifold."[17] He is not contending for an "absolute" theory of space in any of the three meanings of the term. Space is relative, in every case, to a time series; denotatively we should speak of space only as within one of these series. Within each series, however, space is uniform, continuous, and three-dimensional. There are many spaces, but each of them is homaloidal and Euclidian. There is no one Newtonian space; neither is there one space-time as the stuff of all nature. In these regards, Whitehead is unreserv-

---

[13] *Ibid.*, pp. 121–24.   [14] *Ibid.*, p. 122.
[15] *Ibid.*, p. 123.   [16] *Ibid.*, p. 124.   [17] *Ibid.*, pp. 181–82.

edly on the side of the relativists. Space is as little prior to events ontologically as it is prior to fictitious substances. It is an abstraction from events, and a highly relative one. On the other hand, however, he differs sharply from Broad, who denies the reality of motion apart from force and rejects the homaloidality of space.

The findings of our study in regard to the various views of Leibniz are significant in relation to Whitehead's view of space. There were, as we have found,[18] four different meanings of "ideality" in Leibniz's various doctrines: (1) Space is metaphysically ideal, concerning phenomena rather than monads. (2) Even with reference to phenomena, space is an abstraction. (3) Unlike place, space is fictitious, involving the assumption of absolute rest. (4) Unlike relations of situation, space is subjective, involving an identity of relations feigned by the mind. The metaphysical unreality of phenomena involves a distinct parallel in the views of Leibniz to the status of recurrent objects in Whitehead's view. According to Leibniz, only monads as centers of spiritual force, are real; phenomena, involving derivative forces and mechanical motion, while certainly not empirically unreal, are "metaphysically" ideal. They are a part of nature in its secondary aspect. Similarly, according to Whitehead, the factors of nature without passage, the objects and relations between objects, are in events but are not themselves events. Events as the sole reality, nevertheless, in some way manifest themselves in those factors. In a sense, such objects and the spatial-temporal measurements of them are metaphysically ideal.

Again, in Leibniz's views, space and time are not even real as concrete features of phenomena. There are not two extensions, one abstract (space) and the other concrete; yet space is, in a certain sense, the abstract measurement of the concrete extensions. Similarly, according to Whitehead, the method of extensive abstraction yields certain ideal limits, certain "rects and levels as merely loci of event-particles."[19] Such abstraction yields time systems, with eternal, unchanging spaces. Such spaces are not even real in the sense that the objects (not events) in them are real. To Whitehead, spaces are abstract just as they were to Leibniz.

[18] Cf. above, pp. 50–52.   [19] Whitehead, *The Concept of Nature*, p. 94.

Again, the assumption of absolute rest is, in the opinion of
Leibniz, illicit. Places, not being based upon such an assumption,
are nonfictitious, but space, involving it, is fictitious. Similarly,
Whitehead's conception of absolute position means position
merely with reference to one time series. Of course, Leibniz did
not state his view in precisely such terms, but his theory of the relativity of motions, spaces, and times is the same as Whitehead's.

Finally, Leibniz contended that relations of situation are "real,"
or concrete, aspects of phenomena. One body has a relation of
situation to a group of others, and a second takes over that relation. Such "taking over" is, however, only approximate, and the
two relations of situation are different, even assuming the other
bodies to have remained unmoved. Space, on the other hand, is
the "feigned identity" between these two relations of situation.
Hence space is, in a certain sense, subjective. Leibniz stated this
theory of space only in the Controversy with Clarke, and such
subjectivism is out of harmony with the rest of his views. On
the other hand, Whitehead nowhere took any parallel subjective
stand. Avoiding any theory of a "feigning by the mind," he
worked out a doctrine of relations of situation which is quite
similar to Leibniz's more objective account. In general, Whitehead held: [20]

The ingression of an object into an event is the way the character
of the event shapes itself in virtue of the being of the object. . . . I call
the relation between the two "the ingression of the object into the
event."

One special form of ingression is position in space.[21]

I will call this special form of ingression the "relation of situation";
also by a double use of the word "situation," I will call the event in
which an object is situated "the situation of the object."

In other words, one special type of the ingression of an object into
an event is the relation of situation. Like Leibniz, Whitehead was
attempting to explain the nature of the relations of objects to each
other in a universe in which they are not intrinsically real and in
which their relations of situation are even more abstract. Unlike
Leibniz, he was not attempting to account for uniformities in the re-

[20] Whitehead, *The Concept of Nature,* p. 144.   [21] *Ibid.,* p. 147.

lations of objects considered as real (even in a secondary sense) in a mechanical realm. The ingression of objects into events must not be confused with sets of mechanical conditions imposed upon the objects from without. From Whitehead's point of view, Leibniz (like Poincaré) was forced to resort to a "feigning of the mind" in order to account for an "identity" of relations precisely because he assumed that objects possess a kind of reality within a mechanical framework. When such an assumption has been made, some kind of appeal to the "feigning mind" or the "volitions of the mind at the other end of the sense-awareness" becomes necessary to account for the possibility of measurement. Such subjectivism can be avoided only by a different conception of the nature of objects in such a way that the observed relations of situation (positions in space) may be explained. Since relations of situation are, in Leibniz's opinion, merely in agreement and never identical, he was forced to appeal to precisely the sort of arbitrary element that Whitehead claims must be appealed to if the objects themselves are considered to be real. From this fact, Whitehead did not go on to hold that space itself must be considered to be subjective, but otherwise his position is quite similar to Leibniz's.

§ 3

LIKE ALEXANDER AND WHITEHEAD, Broad begins[22] his considerations of the problems of space and time with a sketch of the traditional conflict between the absolute and relational theories of space since the time of Newton and shows why the view of an ontologically independent space, a sort of container, must be rejected. Aside from this starting point in common with the other two men, Broad's approach to a philosophy of space is very different from theirs. In addition to a treatment of the nature of sensa designed to throw light upon the ontological status of the spaces (or space-times) of present-day mathematical physics, his position involves a fourfold development of his views of space. This development proceeds by limitation—or, rather, by elimination. (1) In a sketch of the traditional absolute space of New-

[22] Broad, *Scientific Thought.*

tonian physics, he admits that there can be no *a priori* grounds for rejecting it, but he claims (2) that everything explained by it can be equally well explained by the traditional relational view and that the latter view has certain additional advantages. Both of these points of view have been, he holds, superseded (3) by the requirements of the special theory of relativity in reference to kinematics. In that field, which is highly restricted and an abstraction from physical nature, there are various space-times within bounds prescribed by the speed of light. Each of these spaces is homaloidal and Euclidian. However, even such a view is inadequate in (4) the wider account of nature implied in the general theory of relativity, and must be abandoned in favor of a theory of nonhomaloidal spaces.

It is not necessary to trace in detail Broad's critical elaboration of the views of space of the traditional mechanics (1) as absolute, or (2) as relational; or his discussion of (3) the homaloidal, Euclidian spaces of the special theory of relativity and (4) the nonhomaloidal spaces of the general theory. For our purposes, it is sufficient to note that he rejects the second and the third no less than the first, and for the same type of reasons.

The passage from one to another view of the structure of physical Space-Time, so long as this structure is assumed still to be homaloidal, is of no particular philosophical importance. But the jump from a homaloidal to a non-homaloidal structure ought not to be taken lightly. It does involve, so far as I can see, the definite abandonment of a certain concept of Nature, which has so far been universally held. This is, roughly speaking, the concept of Space and Time as inert indifferent "containers," distinguishable from the material which happens to occupy them. This view appears in a very crude form in the Absolute theories of Space and Time. But it survives, and can be restated, in the Relational theories and in the Special Theory of Relativity.[23]

The older theories of the absolute and the relational nature of space, as well as the much more relativistic theory of various space-times each with a Newtonian or Euclidian three-dimensional frame, are lumped together by Broad as involving, all of them, an outmoded view of nature as a "container." He does not mean that

[23] *Ibid.*, pp. 485–86.

the inadequacy of each of them is of the same degree. The older relational view is less inadequate than the "absolute" one, and the conception of many Euclidian spaces, each conjoined with, though distinct from, time, is less inadequate than the older relational view. Yet they all involve, in one form or another, the view that space, however denotatively varying, is connotatively unique, that is, homaloidal. Thus they all presuppose the same type of neutral model or "container."

In other words, Broad rejects all of the theories of "absolute" space that we have listed above, the traditional relational theory of Leibniz, and any modern theory of various spaces of one single kind. He denies that space is what it is and not otherwise in the quite general sense of having some general, necessary nature, independent of, and yet undetermined by, anything else. Space is not, as was historically assumed, Euclidian (and merely subsisting) or Euclidian and Newtonian (and existing as a container). More important, however, is Broad's claim in opposition to Alexander that space, even in relation to time, is not denotatively one and, in opposition to him and to Whitehead, that it is not connotatively one and homaloidal. In fact, Broad would consider the views of both of these men as not intrinsically different from the Newtonian view that space is independent of time, or at least a container of things. Alexander, in the opinion of Broad, would be mistaken, first in referring to one space-time, and secondly in assuming that such space is Euclidian. Whitehead's view, while not avowedly·involving the first fallacy, since it distinguishes between the various spaces in various time series, reduces in the end to the same result, since it expressly involves the second error, by making all of these spaces Euclidian; and it would continue to involve this error, if it made them all elliptical or hyperbolical, as Whitehead says he would be, under certain conditions, willing to do.[24] If each of the allegedly different space frames is Euclidian, the resulting conception is, in Broad's opinion, not essentially different from the one absolute space-time of Alexander or from the one absolute space of Newton. Broad's own view, involving various types of space as well as various existing examples of each, introduces space

[24] Whitehead, *The Principle of Relativity*, p. v; cf. *Process and Reality*, p. 442.

into nature as an active feature, manifesting itself as one sort in reference to one set of phenomena, and another in reference to another. Only such a view of space is adequate, he says, in the general theory of relativity, and only a corresponding conception of nature is philosophically sound.

If Broad is correct in claiming that spaces are nonhomaloidal, Kant was mistaken in reference to both the singular, denotative oneness of space, and its connotative "absoluteness," its homaloidality. If, on the other hand, Whitehead is right in claiming that spaces are homaloidal although denotatively many, such a theory is not out of harmony with an important portion of Kant's position in the *Aesthetic*. In such a view, space would have a necessary nature, although that nature would not be found in one singular space, but in the various spaces of different time series. Space would be necessary but nonintuitive. Within each time series, the likeness would be even greater; for if space is not only homaloidal, but Euclidian, then each space would have many of the characteristics that Kant believed to be found in the one space. According to Broad, such a conception of nature is not intrinsically different from Newton's. Assuming a uniformity of nature, the entire event of which a time series is a feature, could be treated, admittedly abstractly, as involving a sort of absolute Euclidian nature. Would not the likeness between such an event as a part of nature and the "absolute" nature of Newton overshadow the background of differences, such as processes rather than objects, the tie of space to time, and the relativity of the series?

Broad's sketch of the spaces of the special theory of relativity illustrates a sense in which he believes there may be denotatively many spaces each with a Euclidian nature, in a study which, in his opinion, involves an abstraction from nature. Two points may be simultaneous, he holds, with reference to one Euclidian space frame, and with reference to another they may be successive. An infinite number of such frames in reference to which those two points would be more and more successive is mathematically possible. From the point of view of kinematics, the fact of the speed of light limits, however, the possible amount that the two points may be temporally successive while remaining simultaneous with reference to any one frame. Hence the number of possible Euclidian frames is limited even in regard to such an abstract nature as the special theory describes. Beyond this limit, the Euclidian space frames are mere mathematical possibilities. In this way, Broad holds, space, according to the special theory, is Euclidian but denotatively various in the various frames.

We must remember that Broad himself rejects this whole conception as incompatible with the findings of the general theory of relativity which requires nonhomaloidal spaces, one type in one "field" and another type in another. According to Whitehead, no such abandonment of a homaloidal space is necessary, although he does not commit himself finally to the theory of Euclidian homaloidality. It is not merely Whitehead's wider philosophic position which constrains him to such a view, but also his own way of accounting for the data upon which the general theory of relativity is based. He claims that his view will account for other special phenomena, extremely difficult to treat if the notions of motion, absolute position in a time series, etc. are given up.

Does the theory of the homaloidality of space reduce to the notion of a container as Broad holds? It would be insufficient for Whitehead to appeal to the reality of process and events rather than of objects in order to avoid this charge. Admittedly, such a container would not be a container of objects in the Newtonian sense. Nor does the crux of the issue lie in the problem of the separateness or the relatedness of space and time. The question is rather: would not the denotatively various spaces of the various time series all fall within one infinite event, with one time series and one space? In other words, does not the position of Whitehead reduce, at least in regard to space-time, not to the Newtonian view, but to a conception very similar to Alexander's? Is not space a kind of form, subtly modified in regard to its contents and its relation to them but nonetheless still intrinsically a type of container? If this is the case, then in spite of the wide discrepancy between the general points of view of Kant and Whitehead, in spite of a complete unlikeness of their metaphysical positions, nevertheless, in opposition to the view of Broad, their conceptions of space and nature are basically alike. The same type of space-time would be involved in the abstractive process of Whitehead as is contemplated in the "experience" of Alexander, or given to the mind prior to the "experience" of Kant. According to Whitehead, the relation of space to nature would be extrinsic; according to Alexander, intrinsic. According to Kant's view, purged of the doctrine of appearances, its relation to nature would be intrinsic; without such a purge, extrinsic. The views of space of the three men would be essentially alike. Broad's view of connotatively various spaces would be in opposition to them all.

Evaluation of the three theories which we have briefly traced is beyond the scope of this study. It is clear that Alexander's contentions must stand or fall with the validity of his theory that a kind of empirical metaphysics is possible. On the contrary, both Whitehead and Broad claim as the special basis for their views the requirements of the general theory of relativity. Thus the relative strength of the contentions of these two men can be decided only by the physicist.

If Whitehead's view cannot be reduced to the theory of one space-time, then the issue between Alexander, on one side, and Whitehead and Broad, on the other, would seem to be: is there one space-time which is empirically observable, or are there various relative space-times—perhaps even various types of space-times? Is space immediately apprehensible in its own person, as an intrinsic feature of nature, or must such apprehension await corroboration and correction by the physicist?

If it is admitted that there is no one space-time, and if it is admitted that the nature of various space-times depends exclusively upon the requirements of the general theory of relativity, the issue between Broad and Whitehead would seem to be: do the data of relativity physics compel the acceptance of a theory of nonhomaloidal spaces (as aspects of space-times) or may those data be equally well, if not better, interpreted by a theory of denotatively various, yet homaloidal spaces? Broad believes that the only conception of nature adequate to account for the findings of relativity physics involves many nonhomaloidal spaces, each placing its own stamp on particular natural phenomena in a special "field." Whitehead holds that the theory of numerous homaloidal spaces not only adequately explains the data involved in the general theory of relativity, but also accounts for other phenomena which have been left by Einstein mysterious and unexplained.

The issue between Alexander and the other men is purely a problem for philosophy: only if Alexander is wrong does the second issue arise. If it does arise, it is a problem for physics. If Alexander is wrong, the philosophy of space must not merely accept the findings of the mathematical physicists as final in their own field, but must itself adopt their point of view as the only philosophically adequate one. Is it possible that even in such case, the views of Kant are significant? It is to this possibility that we must now turn.

§ 4

CASSIRER HAS ANALYZED the question of the possibility of a reconciliation of Kant's views and the general theory of relativity. He makes out a strong case for the view that Kant's critical position is quite compatible with that theory. He claims further that while the theory of relativity seems to involve in some ways a departure from the Kantian point of view, it, in fact, merely represents an advance beyond it along lines definitely in harmony with it. It is our task now, in concluding this study, to appraise these contentions of Cassirer. Kant, he held, worked out

. . . his own interpretation of the critical concept of the object, in which the relativity of knowledge was affirmed in a far more inclusive meaning than in ancient or modern skepticism, but in which also this relativity was given a new positive interpretation. The theory of relativity of modern physics can be brought without difficulty under this interpretation. . . .[25]

It is a mistake, Cassirer holds, to consider the theory of relativity as meaning a sort of indefinite indeterminateness in our knowledge of nature. That theory teaches instead that appearances as viewed within any particular system must not be confused with

[25] Cassirer, *Substance and Function, and Einstein's Theory of Relativity,* p. 392.

"an inclusive and final law of experience."[26] In the general theory of relativity "we can rise above the fragmentariness of the individual views to a total view of natural processes." In doing so, we must abandon any pictorial view of an "object," and substitute for such a view "a physical theory, in the form of equations and systems of equations. . . ." It is precisely such a conception of nature that Kant's critical position yields. An object is a sort of synthetic unity posited by a rule of the understanding. Space, time, and the categories are functions of knowledge. Kant's "transcendental philosophy" yields in a general form the same results the theory of relativity arrives at empirically. The conditions set up by Kant concerning the possibility of experience provide precisely the theoretical scaffolding for the empirical results of present-day physics.

I do not wish to quarrel with Cassirer's interpretation of the Kantian critical position. As I have said above,[27] Cassirer brings into clear focus the tenets of Kant's views of space in the *Analytic*. On the other hand, it seems to me a mistake to ascribe to Kant a unified teaching (at least in regard to space) in the *Critique*. Indeed, Cassirer recognizes the manifold problems that Kant encountered and manifold points of view that he held. In spite of this recognition, Cassirer emphasizes the view of the *Analytic* as regards the nature of knowledge and interprets the *Aesthetic* as if Kant had written it from that point of view. He follows the same tactics in his comparison of the Kantian position with the findings of modern physics. He grants, to begin with,[28] that "pure space" has no meaning in modern physics apart from some "invariant with regard to all transformations of the doctrine of the empirical measurement of space and time." The conclusion which he draws from this fact is not that the Kantian doctrine of a pure intuition is, hence, entirely out of harmony with modern teachings, but that Kant, after having passed through more dogmatic and uncritical theories of space, arrived at a critical conception of "pure intuition" compatible with modern relativity.

[26] *Ibid.*, p. 393. Cf. Geiger, *Die philosophische Bedeutung der Relativitätstheorie*, pp. 45–46.
[27] Cf. above, pp. 225–26.
[28] Cassirer, *Substance and Function, and Einstein's Theory of Relativity*, p. 409.

What the physicist calls "space" and "time" is for him a concrete measurable manifold, which he gains as the *result* of coördination, according to law, of the particular points; for the philosopher, on the contrary, space and time signify nothing else than the forms and *modi,* and thus the presuppositions, of this coördination itself. They do not result for him from the coördination, but they *are* precisely this co-ordination and its fundamental directions. It is coördination from the standpoint of coexistence and adjacency or from the standpoint of succession, which he understands by space and time as "forms of in-tuition." In this sense, both are expressly defined in the Kantian In-augural Dissertation.[29]

Cassirer proceeds to quote in this connection the relevant portions of the opening lines of § 14, 5 and § 15, D of the *Dissertation,* in which Kant holds that space and time are not objective and real, but subjective and ideal, a sort of subjective condition or schema for co-ordinating the sensa (or outer sensa) according to a fixed law of the mind. Now, it has been our contention that Kant reached this doctrine of the "subjectivity" of space only in the third phase of his thinking of 1769, that he superimposed it upon his already formulated doctrines of space because of his hope that he would find other "pure intuitions," intellectual rather than sensitive. On the other hand, the major doctrines of the *Disserta-tion* are the doctrines of the pure intuition and the pure form of empirical intuition. Kant formulated these doctrines, in the first instance, not only independently of such a dualism between the sensible and intelligible worlds, but even independently of the re-enforcing evidence from the nature of mathematical truth. Those passages of the *Dissertation* which refer to the "subjec-tivity" of space, as well as those passages based upon mathematical examples, were superimposed, without essential alteration of meaning, upon a doctrine formerly and independently arrived at. It is true that space as a "form" is not, as such, a pure "content." But in § 12 of the *Dissertation* Kant held that space and time as the objects of mathematics are "not merely formal principles of all intuition, but themselves original intuitions." Again in § 15, C, he mentioned the "intuition which [geometry] is occupied in contemplating." Contemplated space is, as such, a content rather

[29] *Ibid.,* p. 417.

than a form. In his second space argument in the *Aesthetic,* he held explicitly that objects in space may be thought away but space may not be thought away.

If Kant meant merely a sort of formal principle when he referred to the pure intuitions in the *Dissertation* and in the *Aesthetic,* we have stumbled upon another of those cases in which Kant was nodding as he wrote, so noticeably nodding that Cassirer could say of him: "The most general meaning of [pure intuition] *which indeed was not always grasped by Kant with equal sharpness, since more special meanings and applications were substituted involuntarily in his case,* is merely that of the serial form of coexistence and of succession." [30] Concerning which statement the inevitable question arises, *whose* meaning? The critical Kant's meaning, not yet worked out and not to be formulated for some eleven or seventeen years? A Neo-Kantian's meaning? It seems to me idle speculation to claim that Kant's doctrine of pure intuition meant from 1769 to 1787 what it must now mean if it is to receive confirmation from present-day physical teachings. It seems to me to be an unwarranted distortion of fact to claim, that except for "involuntary substitution," it meant from 1769 to 1787 something compatible with his critical teachings in the *Analytic.* I have great sympathy for the type of commentator who, baffled by the contradictions in Kant's views, tries to account for them in terms of presuppositions from which Kant was trying to break away and in terms of unformulated critical teachings which he later worked out. But it seems to me to be stretching this type of analysis rather far to claim that Kant "substituted meanings involuntarily." Our account does not resolve all of the difficulties even in his philosophy of space, but at least it proceeds on the assumption that he meant what he said when he said it.

In the *Dissertation* Kant held that there is a pure intuition, space, given immediately to the mind and not generated; in addition, space is a pure form of intuition. These two fundamental tenets were formulated first with, and then without, the re-enforc-

---

[30] *Ibid.,* p. 418. Italics mine; cf. *Zur Einstein'schen Relativitätstheorie,* p. 85: ". . . weil sich ihm unwillkürlich speziellere Bedeutungen und Anwendungen unterschieben. . . ."

ing evidence involved in the nature of the truths of geometry and mechanics. Superimposed upon this view and based upon a hope that was doomed to failure was the doctrine of the "subjectivity" and "ideality" of space. The sole ambiguity arises in reference to the question of the manner in which the representation of space is arrived at. According to Kant's main view in the *Dissertation* and according to his sole view in the *Aesthetic,* space is presented to the contemplative gaze of the mind and not generated. Space is not merely a formal principle, nor is it merely a function of knowledge in mathematics. This view is incompatible with the findings of the modern theory of relativity and is also out of harmony with Kant's own critical position. According to his second view in 1770, space is generated by the mind on the occasion of experience.[31] Out of this view grew the teachings of the *Analytic.*

It is doubtless to the credit of Cassirer and others to have pointed out that this second view of Kant's, as well as the general theory of knowledge in the *Analytic,* is compatible with the general theory of relativity. I fail, however, to discover any justification for the claim that such unique, critical insight represents a position from which Kant departed only involuntarily; for the interpretation of the views of the *Aesthetic* solely from that point of view; or for the distortion of the doctrine of a pure intuition in the *Dissertation* and in the *Aesthetic* into a meaning that they do not have. The space which Kant was describing in 1770 and in the *Aesthetic* as a pure intuition is, in my opinion, as different from mathematical space, a function of knowledge imposed by the understanding upon nature solely in that highly sophisticated type of "experience," physics, as the ordinary man's apprehension of empirical objects in space is from a mathematical description of those objects. Neither pure nor applied mathematics—separated, or mixed, or melted into one—was Kant's primary concern in 1769 when he first formulated the theory of a pure intuition. Fischer, Cohen, Adickes, Vaihinger, and Cassirer[32] are, in my opinion, mistaken in their descriptions of the "Wendung von 1769." Only

[31] Found in the example of incongruent counterparts in Kant, *Inaugural Dissertation,* § 15, C, psychologically interpreted, and at the end of the corollary to §§ 14–15, possibly as an afterthought.

[32] Cf. above, pp. 131–35, 184–86, 240–41.

after the doctrine of space as a pure intuition and a pure form of the empirical world had been formulated did Kant realize that the nature of truth in geometry and mechanics forms important *re-enforcing* evidence for that theory. Experience was for Kant not merely Newtonian physics, at least not in the *Dissertation* and the *Aesthetic.*

In the critical position in the *Analytic,* it is otherwise. Space is referred to as a conception. It is a function of knowledge like the categories. As to this position, Cassirer's view of the relation of relativity physics to Kant is illuminating. Space and time in relativity physics have become connected. Is not this anti-Kantian, he asks? As anti-Kantian as it is, in my opinion, with reference to the *Dissertation* and the *Aesthetic,* it is decidedly Kantian, *if we restrict ourselves to his view in the Analytic.* It is true that Kant did not link space and time in the same fashion that modern physicists do, but his result is the same as theirs. Space is indissolubly linked with matter; time is similarly indissolubly linked with matter; hence, as functions of our knowledge, both being related to the sensuous manifold, they become linked with each other. There is only the "synthetic unity of phenomena according to temporal relations" and according to spatial ones. Space becomes in the *Metaphysical First Principles of Natural Science* an Idea involving a logical universality which precludes absolute motion. Space is merely at the basis of the movements of empirical bodies relative to each other.[33] Both in Kant's view and in modern physics, space (along with time and the categories) is a function of knowledge, a tool of the understanding enabling it to achieve an objective determination of phenomena.

In rejecting Cassirer's suggestion that Kant's views are compatible with modern physics, Scholz[34] points out that the nature of the relation between space, time, and matter is in Kant's views *a priori,* while in modern relativity theory it is determined first by empirical observations of particular "configurations and field-generating masses." With reference to the *Analytic,* Scholz's criticism is wide of the mark. Cassirer would be the first to admit

[33] Kant, *Metaphysische Anfangsgründe der Naturwissenschaft,* ed. by Hartenstein, VIII, 486, 561.

[34] *Kant-Studien,* 1924, Bd. XXIX, Heft, 1-2, p. 67.

the different manner in which space, time, and matter are united by Kant and by Einstein; but that difference merely means that the philosopher considers space and time as functions and "modi" of knowledge in general, while the physicist is interested in them solely in their empirical contexts. Not only are the results of the two methods reconcilable; they must conform, if the philosophy of space is to remain critical. Furthermore, as we have found, Kant held, in the *Analytic,* that the nature of space and time receive their confirmation as functions of knowledge in and through experience. The *a priori* determination of their nature is not, as he had earlier held, cut off completely from the sensuous manifold but involves a synthesis beginning with that manifold. This theory of knowledge is quite easily reconcilable with the findings of modern relativity physics, as Cassirer holds.

Cassirer says, further, quoting Laue:

The boldness and the high philosophical significance of Einstein's doctrine consists in [the fact] that it clears away the traditional prejudice of one time valid for all systems. Great as the change is, which it forces upon our whole [manner of] thought, there is found in it not the slightest epistemological difficulty. For in Kant's manner of expression time is, like space, a pure form of our intuition; a schema in which we must arrange events, so that in opposition to subjective and highly contingent perceptions they may gain objective meaning. This arranging can only take place on the basis of empirical knowledge of natural laws.[35]

An acceptance of this account of the significance of Kant's critical philosophy in reference to Einstein is not, in my opinion, incompatible with a rejection of Cassirer's account of Kant's theory of a pure intuition in the *Dissertation* and the *Aesthetic.* Furthermore, such an account of the relation of Kant to modern physics stands independent of the question of the homaloidality of space as differently treated by Broad and Whitehead. It is true that if Whitehead is right and space is homaloidal and Euclidian, there would be an element of truth in the earlier intuitive theory of Kant, which would be completely lacking, if the spaces of the various space-times are nonhomaloidal.

On the other hand, precisely to the extent that the modern

[35] Cassirer, *Substance and Function, and Einstein's Theory of Relativity,* pp. 414–15.

physical theories of space of Einstein and Broad turn out to hold the field, and with them the Kantian epistemology of Cassirer, precisely to that extent must we discard such a view as that of Alexander, and with it the (in my opinion) equally Kantian contention that space is given immediately to the contemplative gaze of the mind. As far as Kant is concerned, it is "heads I win, tails you lose," which is one of the advantages of being inconsistent. I have already pointed out the sense in which the Kantian doctrines of the *Aesthetic* might be modified in the light of a wider conception of experience to make space empirical and yet necessary: "*a priori*" in Alexander's sense of the term. In such a view there would be a face-to-face intuitive apprehension of space (in its essential relation to time) independently of the objects of sense, although possibly only in and through our experience of them. Space-time would be, as Alexander holds, the stuff out of which nature is shaped. In this view, the teachings of the mathematical physicists would be quite a valid abstractive procedure, but it would begin with, and in the end would return to, the space of this more primitive, metaphysical experience. On the other hand, if the views of mathematical physics give us the sole clue to the nature of space, the Kantian philosophy of space in the *Aesthetic* must be entirely abandoned as outmoded. In this case, however, his critical theory of knowledge in the *Analytic*, involving the indissoluble link between space, time (as schema or functions of knowledge), and phenomena, remains, forming an epistemological basis for relativity physics in a way that he himself never envisioned. Spaces and times are the "forms and modi" of knowledge. In this view, "in this very advance [made by physics today] the doctrine that it is the 'rule of the understanding,' that forms the pattern of all our temporal and spatial determinations, is verified anew."[36] It is true that, in this view, the physicists have yet to decide whether the many spaces (of the space-times) are homaloidal or not, but, pending their answer to this question, the task of the philosophy of space is finished, and with it our study.

[36] *Ibid.*, p. 415.

BIBLIOGRAPHY

Adamson, Robert, On the Philosophy of Kant. Edinburgh, 1879.

Adickes, Erich, Kant-Studien. Kiel and Leipzig, 1895. (Not so important with reference to the problems of space.)

Alexander, Samuel, Space, Time and Deity. 2 vols., London, 1934. (A study of space that is in harmony with some of Kant's views.)

Aristotle, Metaphysica, in The Works of Aristotle, Vol. VIII, translated by W. D. Ross. Oxford, 1928. (Significant for our study because it raises the possibility of some first philosophy other than physics.)

Béguelin, Nicolas, Conciliation des idées de Newton et de Leibniz sur l'espace et le vuide. Berlin, 1769. (Written in an important year in Kant's thinking.)

Broad, Charlie Dunbar, Scientific Thought. New York, 1927. (A study of space in harmony with Kant's critical views.)

Burtt, Edwin Arthur, The Metaphysical Foundations of Modern Physical Science. New York, 1932. (A valuable study of some of the problems in Newton's theory of space.)

Caird, Edward, The Critical Philosophy of Immanuel Kant. 2 vols., Glasgow, 1877–89. (An older commentary written from the Hegelian point of view.)

Cassirer, Ernst, Das Erkenntnisproblem in der Philosophie und Wissenschaft der neueren Zeit. 3 vols., 3d ed., Berlin, 1922–23. (Vol. II traces many of the crosscurrents in the philosophy of space between Newton and Kant.)

——— Substance and Function, and Einstein's Theory of Relativity, translated by William Curtis Swabey and Marie Collins Swabey. Chicago, 1923. (A valuable study of the relation of Kant to Einstein.)

——— Zur Einstein'schen Relativitätstheorie. Berlin, 1920.

Clarke, Samuel, A Collection of Papers Which Passed between the Late Learned Mr. Leibniz and Dr. Clarke. London, 1717. Cited in this book as Paper I, Paper II, etc. (This includes an appendix of short translations by Clarke from pertinent works by Leibniz. The papers form a significant chapter in the history of the philosophy of space.)

Cohen, Hermann, Kants Theorie der Erfahrung. Berlin, 1873.

——— Kommentar zu Immanuel Kants Kritik der reinen Vernunft. 3d ed., Leipzig, 1920. (An older, more simplified version of Kant's views.)

Cunningham, G. Watts, "Meaning, Reference, and Significance," in *The Philosophical Review*, Vol. XLVII (1938), No. 2.

Dietrich, Konrad, Kant und Newton. Tübingen, 1876. (Eclectic.)

Elsbach, Alfred ·Coppel, Kant und Einstein. Berlin and Leipzig, 1924. (Eclectic.)

Erdmann, Benno, Reflexionen Kants zur kritischen Philosophie. Leipzig. Bd. I, 1882; Bd. II, 1884. (The Reflexionen are arranged according to Kant's various periods of thought.)

———— Die Stellung des Dinges an sich in Kants Aesthetik und Analytik. Berlin, 1873.

———— Kants Kriticismus in der ersten und in der zweiten Auflage der Kritik der reinen Vernunft. Leipzig, 1878. (Important contributions to Kantian literature.)

Euler, Leonhard, Réflexions sur l'espace et le temps. Berlin, 1748. (The major source of Kant's theory of pure intuition.)

———— Lettres à une princesse d'Allemagne sur divers sujets de physique & de philosophie. St. Petersburg, 1768–72.

Fischer, Kuno, A Commentary on Kant's Critick of Pure Reason, translated by John Pentland Mahaffy. London, 1866. (Older, one-sided.)

Fite, Warner, Moral Philosophy. New York, 1925.

Gattermann, H., Über das Verhältnis von Kants Dissertation vom Jahre 1770 zu der Kritik der reinen Vernunft. Halle, 1899. (Eclectic.)

Geiger, Moritz, Die philosophische Bedeutung der Relativitätstheorie. Halle, 1921. (Popular, but keen.)

Hartmann, Eduard von, Kritische Grundlegung des transcendentalen Realismus. Berlin, 1875. (Marked a new turn in Kantian literature.)

Hume, David, An Enquiry Concerning Human Understanding. Chicago, 1921.

Kant, Immanuel, Briefwechsel. Der philosophischen Bibliothek Bd. 52a and 52b, Leipzig, 1924. (Contain an important reference to the year 1769.)

———— Cosmogony, Including his Natural History and Theory of the Heavens, edited and translated by W. Hastie. Glasgow, 1900.

———— Critique of Pure Reason, translated by Max Müller. New York, 1925.

———— De mundi sensibilis atque intelligibilis forma et principiis, in Werke, Vol. III, edited by Gustav Hartenstein. Leipzig, 1838. (Referred to in this study as the Inaugural Dissertation.)

———— Eine neue Beleuchtung der ersten Prinzipien der metaphysischen Erkenntnis. Der philosophischen Bibliothek Bd. 46a, Leipzig, 1921.

———— Inaugural Dissertation and Early Writings on Space, translated by John Handyside. Chicago, 1929. (This includes selected passages from Thoughts on the True Estimation of Living Forces and the whole of On the First Ground of the Distinction of Regions in Space.)

———— Kritik der reinen Vernunft. Der philosophischen Bibliothek Bd. 37a, Leipzig, 1926.

———— Lose Blätter aus Kants Nachlass, edited by Rudolf Reicke. Königsberg, 1887.

———— Metaphysische Anfangsgründe der Naturwissenschaft, in Werke, Vol. VIII, edited by Gustav Hartenstein, Leipzig, 1838.

———— Opus postumum. 2 vols., Berlin and Leipzig, 1938.

———— Prolegomena zu einer jeden künftigen Metaphysik, die als Wissenschaft wird auftreten können. Der philosophischen Bibliothek Bd. 40, Leipzig, 1926. (Stresses the relation of space to mathematics.)

———— Reflexionen Kants zur kritischen Philosophie, Leipzig. Bd. I, 1882; Bd. II, 1884. (Arranged according to the periods of Kant's thought.)

———— Träume eines Geistersehers, erläutert durch Träume der Metaphysik. Der philosophischen Bibliothek Bd. 46b, Leipzig, 1921.

———— Über die Form und die Prinzipien der Sinnen- und der Verstandeswelt. Der philosophischen Bibliothek Bd. 46b, Leipzig, 1921.

———— Über die Fortschritte der Metaphysik seit Leibnizens und Wolfs Zeiten in Deutschland. Der philosophischen Bibliothek Bd. 46c, Leipzig, 1921.

———— Über eine Entdeckung nach der alle neue Kritik der reinen Vernunft durch eine ältere entbehrlich gemacht werden soll, in Werke, Vol. III, edited by Gustav Hartenstein. Leipzig, 1838.

———— Untersuchung über die Deutlichkeit der Grundsätze der natürlichen Theologie und der Moral. Der philosophischen Bibliothek Bd. 46a, Leipzig, 1921.

———— Von dem ersten Grunde des Unterschiedes der Gegenden im Raume. Der philosophischen Bibliothek Bd. 46b, Leipzig, 1921.

Kemp Smith, Norman, A Commentary to 'Kant's Critique of Pure Reason.' London, 1918. (The standard commentary in English. Follows Vaihinger on many issues.)

———— Prolegomena to an Idealist Theory of Knowledge. London, 1924. (An important contribution to modern epistemology containing important Kantian features.)

Latta, Robert, Leibniz: The Monadology and Other Philosophical Writings. Oxford, 1898. (A valuable general commentary on Leibniz.)

Leibniz, Gottfried Wilhelm, Freiherr von, A Collection of Papers

Leibniz (*Continued*)

Which Passed between the Late Learned Mr. Leibniz and Dr. Clarke, edited by Clarke. London, 1717. Cited in this book as Paper I, Paper II, etc. *See* Clarke, Samuel.

———— Discourse on Metaphysics, translated by George R. Montgomery. Chicago, 1931.

———— Essays on Dynamics, in New Essays concerning Human Understanding, translated by Alfred Gideon Langley. New York, 1896. (Important in contrast to Kant's views in 1747.)

———— Examen des principes du R. P. Malebranche, in Leibnitii Opera philosophica omnia, edited by Johannes Eduard Erdmann. Berlin, 1840. (A much neglected exposition of a little known variant of Leibniz's views of space.)

———— Lettre à Mr. Bayle, in Leibnitii Opera philosophica omnia, edited by Johannes Eduard Erdmann. Berlin, 1840.

———— The Monadology and Other Philosophical Writings, translated by Robert Latta. Oxford, 1898. (Also a valuable general commentary on Leibniz.)

———— New Essays Concerning Human Understanding, translated by Alfred Gideon Langley. New York, 1896. (Contains two different accounts of space.)

———— Nouveaux essais sur l'entendement humain, in Leibnitii Opera philosophica omnia, edited by Johannes Eduard Erdmann. Berlin, 1840.

———— On Nature in Itself, in The Philosophical Works of Leibniz, translated by George Martin Duncan. New Haven, 1908.

———— On the Active Force of Body, on the Soul, and on the Souls of Brutes, in The Philosophical Works of Leibniz, translated by George Martin Duncan. New Haven, 1908.

———— On the Reform of Metaphysics and on the Notion of Substance, in The Philosophical Works of Leibniz, translated by George Martin Duncan. New Haven, 1908.

———— Réplique aux reflexions contenues dans la second édition du Dictionnaire de Mr. Bayle, in Leibnitii Opera philosophica omnia, edited by Johannes Eduard Erdmann. Berlin, 1840.

———— The Philosophical Writings of Leibniz, selected and translated by Mary Morris. New York, 1934. (Contains a portion of Leibniz's correspondence with Clarke.)

Maupertuis, Pierre Louis Moreau, Examen philosophique de la preuve de l'existence de Dieu. Berlin, 1756. (Shows the influence of Hume; may have influenced Kant.)

Moore, George Edward, Philosophical Studies. New York, 1922. (Disentangles an epistemological difficulty; valuable in reference to Kant's treatments of the infinitude of space.)

Newton, Sir Isaac, The Mathematical Principles of Natural Philosophy, translated by Andrew Motte. New York, 1846.

——— Optics. London, 1730.

Paton, Herbert James, Kant's Metaphysic of Experience. 2 vols., London, 1936. (Stimulating. Possibly important in reference to Kant's general views. Gives a very different account of Kant's views of space from our own.)

——— "Critical Notice of La Déduction transcendentale dans l'oeuvre de Kant, par H. J. de Vleeschauwer in Mind, Vol. XLVII (April, 1938), No. 186.

Pratt, James Bissett, Personal Realism. New York, 1937. (American Critical Realist. Important in reference to Leibniz's theory of perception.)

Riehl, Alois, Der philosophische Kritizismus. Bd. I. Leipzig, 1908. (A main Kantian commentary.)

Scholz, Heinrich, "Das Vermächtnis der Kantischen Lehre vom Raum und von der Zeit," in Kant-Studien, Bd. XXIX, Heft 1–2, Berlin, 1924. (A criticism of attempts to interpret Kant in terms of modern relativity theory.)

Siegel, Carl, "Kants Antinomienlehre im Lichte der Inauguraldissertation," in Kant-Studien, Bd. XXX, Heft 1–2, Berlin, 1925. (An interesting, but incorrect account of Kant's thinking in 1769.)

Vaihinger, Hans, Kommentar zu Kants Kritik der reinen Vernunft. Stuttgart, Bd. I, 1881; Bd. II, 1892. (The standard German commentary on Kant. Encyclopedic, genial, giving Kant the benefit of every doubt. Inaccurate as regards Kant's thinking in 1769.)

Vleeschauwer, Herman J. de, La Déduction transcendentale dans l'œuvre de Kant. 3 vols., Paris, 1936. (More valuable with reference to Kant's later views.)

——— "Les Antinomies Kantiennes et la Clavis universalis d'Arthur Collier," in Mind, Vol. XLVII (July, 1938), No. 187. (Follows Cassirer.)

Whitehead, Alfred North, The Concept of Nature. Cambridge, 1930. (A major study of the philosophy of space. Bears somewhat the same relation to his later views that Leibniz's theories of phenomena bear to his doctrine of monads.)

——— The Principle of Relativity with Application to Physical Science. Cambridge, 1922.

——— Process and Reality, an Essay in Cosmology. New York, 1936.

INDEX